The Secret Wars
of Judi Bari

The Secret Wars
of Judi Bari

A Car Bomb,
the Fight for the Redwoods,
and the End of Earth First!

KATE COLEMAN

First edition published in 2005 by Encounter Books, an activity of Encounter for Culture and Education, Inc., a nonprofit corporation.

Encounter Books website address: www.encounterbooks.com

Manufactured in the United States and printed on acid-free paper.

The paper used in this publication meets the minimum requirements of ANSI/NISO Z39.48-1992 (R 1997)(*Permanence of Paper*).

FIRST EDITION

Library of Congress Cataloging-in-Publication Data

Coleman, Kate.
    The secret wars of Judi Bari : a car bomb, the fight for the redwoods, and the end of Earth First! / Kate Coleman.
      p. cm.
    Includes bibliographical references and index.
    ISBN 1-893554-74-0 (alk. paper)
Bari, Judi. 2. Earth First! (Organization). 3. Environmentalists—California—Biography. 4. Green movement—California—Citizen participation. 5. Forest conservation—California, Northern—Citizen participation. I. Title.
GE56.B37 C65 2004
333.72'092—B22
2004059146

10 9 8 7 6 5 4 3 2 1

For Larry Lee,
whose memory still
inspires me.

CONTENTS

ONE

TOWARD THE END OF 1989, an idea began percolating in the brain of one of those bushy-chinned visionaries who populate the North Coast of California: to raise a People's Army to save the noble redwoods from the lumber companies' rapacious logging.

This visionary's name—like most names of those in his tribe who had escaped the urban jungles for the redwood forests—conjured up the sacred earth. He was "Fred, the Walking Rainbow," although he had started out his life as merely Fred Moore. Walking Rainbow, a physicist by training, had invented a well-balanced cart that he used to schlep around his goods and necessities. He had plans to walk the circumference of the earth. (Eventually he would bicycle to South America with all he owned or needed on the bike.) He did his cooking in one pot over an ingenious stove that he built from a thin sheet of lightweight steel formed into a secure cone, at the center of which he burned twigs and other wood fuel, with his single pot resting on top. His inventions—his whole being—embodied the ethos of "voluntary simplicity" and its complementary slogans: "living off the grid" (using alternative and more ecological power sources, like wind or sun) and "deep ecology" (a philosophy that gives no more value to humans than to any other creature or plant).

By 1989, Fred the Walking Rainbow was just one among thousands of eccentrics, hippies, former radicals, lesbians, communards and Vietnam veterans who colonized the rugged coastline and northern rainforests that stretch from San Francisco through Mendocino and Humboldt Counties to the Oregon border. This territory—encompassing hundreds of miles of semiwilderness dotted with small towns and hamlets—was California's last frontier, and it had always attracted such dreamers. Long before these recent seekers of alternative community, other radicals and freethinkers had migrated into Mendocino County. Finnish Communists, for example, settled in and around Fort Bragg after 1905. They started the co-op movement of cooperatively owned and run grocery stores and businesses that eventually spread to Berkeley and other Bay Area cities, creating the chain of Co-op food marts and credit unions that flourished there in the Fifties and Sixties. There was also a steady trickle of arty types—artisans and bohemians and the occasional writer—mixed in with the loggers and fishermen in the years before and after the Second World War.

After the Sixties, the back-to-the-land movement began to attract greater numbers. These were lifestyle immigrants, seeking self-sufficiency outside the commercial rat race they perceived in the rest of America, and bringing their dope-smoking, funky radicalism along with them. They created a loose fabric of tiny communities in the redwoods, a virtual world outside time that endured after the demise of the urban counterculture they had left behind.

The newer rural refugees plunked themselves down on the land side by side with the older generations of fishermen, loggers and bohos along the jagged coast. They lived in collectives, in lean-tos, in geodesic domes, in trailers and yurts, near small towns with names like Elk, Little River and Albion Ridge. When coastal property values inflated, they moved inland in a constant pilgrimage to find cheaper land, settling among farmers and more loggers in the area stretching from Boonville in the Anderson Valley, north along the Highway 101 corridor through Ukiah, Willits and Laytonville.

As the numbers of tie-dyed immigrants swelled, the established citizenry of these towns viewed them with dismay and suspicion. The more industrious of the new arrivals tried organic farming and raising goats. Many lived by planting and harvesting marijuana crops secreted deep in heavy forests on federal land. And soon, too, sprinkled among the crops of pot there were clandestine labs turning out methamphetamine, which some of the younger loggers found to their liking.

Jim Jones and the People's Temple came to Redwood Valley in

Mendocino after cutting adrift from their first congregational moorings in the Midwest. At one time Charles Manson hung out in "Mendo-land," whose chief attraction for him was that it was a place so big it was nearly impossible to police.

These newcomers all believed they'd found the open space that assured personal freedom. And even if they didn't exactly know the names of the local fauna and flora, they quickly developed a mystical passion for the ancient redwood forests, streams, fish and wildlife—a pristine environment against which they measured the decadent America they had escaped. They imbued the trees and other living things with the pagan spiritualism that passes for religion in the hippie outback of America.

As their movement reached critical mass in the mid-1980s, the pace of logging in Mendocino and Humboldt Counties—as well as the whole Northwest, including Canada—also increased dramatically, stirring up alarm among environmentalists. This was especially true in Mendocino, where the last of the forests not secured on federal or state holdings was being cut by lumber combines anxious to cash in before it was too late.

In the earliest North Coast fights to preserve the redwoods, individuals and small groups taught themselves the tools of investigation and litigation. They hectored county clerks or strode into court to block the harvesting of trees on large tracts that they and other new environmentalists claimed were vital to the health of huge ecosystems. In mastering the particular skirmishing skills that bedeviled the logging companies, this first handful of clear-cutting opponents became disciplined paralegal professionals.

David and Ellen Drell, for example, after inheriting a small fortune from her grandfather, devoted themselves full-time to the fight to keep Yolla Bolly Wilderness away from the mining and timber interests. Roanne Withers, a former bartender, made herself an expert at lobbying local supervisors and state agencies, and became adept at litigation and filings.

Withers and the Drells were later joined by transplanted Colorado activists Betty and Gary Ball, who started what would become the influential Mendocino Environmental Center, the MEC, in Ukiah. Further up Highway 101 in Laytonville, a team of gay lovers, Michael Huddleston and Stephen Day, put almost a decade of scrupulous investigation into an effort to preserve the Cahto Wilderness near their home.

They were all like indefatigable Kafkaesque clerks, filing sheaves of dense technical and legalistic documents in the plodding courts. They had mastered the arcana of environmental impact studies, restraining orders and threatened-species arguments that had the legal power to forestall the axes, saws and bulldozers under federal statutes, some of which were first enacted by President Richard Nixon.

Early filings concerned federal and state forest holdings. After a first generation had achieved success in this arena, newly arrived and more radical enviros began audaciously to concentrate on forests standing on private property, challenging lumber companies' right to profit off their vast holdings. But the federal government remained the archenemy, because it conferred cheap leases on timber and mining companies to harvest on public land.

The logging companies had reason to want to harvest their oldest trees—those that were considered sacred by the environmentalists not only for providing habitat for threatened species but intrinsically for their age and beauty. These so-called virgin redwoods, which can be first or second growth of 500 to 1,000 years of age, not only are taller, but have denser and heavier wood than trees grown on previously logged land, and therefore they bring the highest dollar. If timber industry profits were as marginal as some environmentalists suggest—a bare 3 percent—it was no surprise that the logging interests should go after the choicest trees to support their bottom line.

Greg King, a young, passionate environmentalist then writing for the *Sonoma County Free Press,* made it his business to find those old threatened groves that were invisible and unknowable to the outside world without trespassing on company land. He pored over the logging companies' timber harvest plans, required by state law to be publicly posted, and he hiked the forest floors with charts and documents in hand, mapping out the potential impact of the harvest. He often found that the plans he examined were harmful to the surrounding watersheds and to the general health of the forest. The erosion caused by timber company clear-cuts led to the buildup of sediment in streams, the dying-off of fish and the loss of habitat for threatened species. The bushwhacking expeditions of King and others like him turned up the details that put teeth into court filings.

DARRYL CHERNEY, A RUN-OF-THE-MILL New York advertising copywriter, had come west in the fall of 1985 on his own private quest: to find again the majesty of the redwoods he remembered from a childhood family vacation. When his funky van reached the town of Garberville in Humboldt County, he stopped at the ramshackle environmental center and was struck by a leaflet with a huge cartoon depicting a meaty clenched fist over a background of redwood trees, along with the legend of the group Earth First! and its motto: "No compromise in defense of Mother Earth!"[*]

Intrigued by the logo and the slogan, Cherney wanted to know more about the group. The locals wouldn't tell him anything. But he kept on pestering them until he finally met a few of the publicity-shy forest "monkey-wrenchers," as the environmental saboteurs called themselves, and at that moment Earth First acquired not only a convert, but an unofficial press officer.

When Greg King and Darryl Cherney met and joined forces, their combined efforts drew the first public attention to a famous grove of ancient virgin redwoods that became known as Headwaters. This stand of old growth was owned by the Pacific Lumber Company and was scheduled to fall, until Humboldt Earth First—publicly, Cherney and King—launched a struggle to save it. Continuing well into the new millennium, the fight would eventually involve Wall Street barons, the U.S. Senate and thousands of protesters. But a real mass movement to save the redwoods all over the North Coast didn't start until 1987, when Cherney began romancing Judi Bari, an East Coast veteran of Vietnam War protests who was still living with her estranged husband and their two small girls in Mendocino County.

In the years ahead, Bari would become the single most important face and personality in the timber wars. Her charisma and

---

[*]The exclamation point that the group uses as part of its name will generally be omitted here.

political savvy, along with her zeal and organizational talents, quickly inspired a legion of young followers from among the hippie dropouts of Mendocino and Humboldt, and galvanized older back-to-the-landers as well. She also became a feminist icon to large numbers of females-only collectives in Mendocino and to militant feminists in Berkeley, Santa Cruz and other cities in and beyond California.

Bari started out helping Cherney in Humboldt County, and riding on his coattails; but her fame and notoriety soon eclipsed his. Part of her reputation came from the articles on timber issues that she wrote for the *Anderson Valley Advertiser,* a counterculture newspaper. The AVA's tall, country-squirish publisher and editor, Bruce Anderson, and Bari, the mini-powerhouse environmentalist, would be an odd yet effective team during the timber wars to come.

In 1988, Bari joined the Cahto Wilderness struggle and more or less took it over, inspiring cadre to sit down in the road and block bulldozers with branches and boulders. Out of that early success, Bari started her own chapter of Earth First in Mendocino County in 1989. She named it "Ecotopia," a nod to a 1975 cult novel by Berkeley author Ernest Callenbach that postulated an environmentally conscious utopia covering Northern California, Oregon and Washington—a place where the food is all organic, with no sugar to be had; where loosely fitting clothes are of purely natural fibers; and where the work week is a leisurely twenty hours, because the population has been weaned from automobiles and other material objects.

Bari was at least a decade older than most of the soldiers in her prospective army, and she brought to the organizing table an oratorical and political style developed from decades of activism in the various causes of the left. She moved into Earth First like a modern CEO trying to remake a nineteenth-century family business into a modern corporation. She helped to broaden Earth First with her political organizing skills and her jealous grip on the instruments of power—she held onto all the private phone lists of donors and followers—in a group that had previously been suspicious of leadership and hierarchy.

And so, when Fred the Walking Rainbow was looking for a leader to convey his ideas about how to save the redwoods toward the end of 1989, it was natural that the Mendocino Environmental

Center would direct him to Judi Bari. He was also seeking a base camp for his peripatetic journeying around the countryside and found himself steered to the home of Pam Davis, a rising star in the local environmental movement and a lieutenant to Bari. Davis put Walking Rainbow up in her home in Sonoma (the county south of Mendocino) and granted a patient hearing to what others might have dismissed as a harebrained scheme.

Camped out at the home of Pam Davis and her kids, Fred the Walking Rainbow told her of his plan to build a mass movement to save the ancient redwoods. Davis got excited. She felt that Judi should hear what Fred had to say. But she also knew that her friend was impatient with the county's eccentrics and tree-huggers, and regarded a good percentage of them as stoned-out idiots.

When the Walking Rainbow showed up, Bari happened to be staying at the county hospital, watching over her younger daughter, Jessica, who was sick with bronchitis. Pam Davis drove him to the hospital, where he unburdened himself to Bari in the waiting room. As a veteran politico of an earlier age, he invoked the successful strategy of hard-pressed civil rights activists of the South in the early 1960s. The Mississippi Summer Project in 1964 had successfully imported a stream of northern white sympathizers—college students, for the most part—to register the disenfranchised blacks of rural Mississippi. Why not bring a new generation of idealistic young people in to Mendocino and Humboldt Counties to stand between the chainsaws and the targeted redwood trees? Wouldn't the same media attention that had watched the roughing-up of northern whites in Mississippi in 1964 likewise follow these activists to the North Coast and spotlight the rape of the environment?

Bari was impatient with what she regarded as the New Age blather that infected most environmental cheerleading. In another setting she might have blown off Walking Rainbow. But stuck with him in the hospital waiting room, she listened to the bearded ascetic and realized almost immediately that he was on to something.

Bari quickly embraced the idea of mass public civil disobedience, but expanded it into an even greater scheme including marches and rallies, and communal living centers that would become bases for political organizing. She phoned her Earth First co-leader and lover, Darryl Cherney, and breathlessly communicated this idea. By

March 1, 1990, they were spreading the word about the summer of demonstrations they dubbed "Mississippi Summer in the California Redwoods" to evoke the civil rights movement and the film *Mississippi Burning* (later shortened to "Redwood Summer"). It would galvanize the rest of the country and would also put the North Coast's tiny chapters of Earth First on the map.

In the following months, Bari was a dervish of activity and organizing. She threw herself into fundraising among the small political groups that dotted the countercultural radical landscape, and she went on "road shows," as Earth First called the dog-and-pony recruitment drives where she and Cherney mapped out their "Freedom Riders for the Forest" rendezvous for the summer of 1990.

A TINY CARAVAN HEADED SOUTH from Mendocino on one of those road shows on May 23, 1990. Bari was in her white Subaru with Utah Phillips, the graying Pete Seeger knockoff who sometimes shared billing with her and Cherney at political folkfests. "Dakota Sid" Clifford, another folkie, and Phillips' wife, Joanna Robinson, rode behind in Phillips' van. Greg King drove down separately. Cherney took his own van and rode with banjo player George Shook, who had lately been performing with him and Bari.

Bari and Cherney were scheduled to do a Redwood Summer recruitment event on the Santa Cruz campus of the University of California the following night. The advance work done by students in the local Earth First chapter on the UCSC campus promised to make this the biggest event in a tour planned for campuses and hippie enclaves. But they had one stopover before Santa Cruz, in Berkeley at the Seeds of Peace House, a ramshackle commune in a pocket ghetto next to North Oakland, where they would meet with representatives of the small political groups whose help they needed to bring off Redwood Summer. Working on the cheap, the Seeds communards provided latrines, soup kitchens, tents and sound systems —even a few computers and the skills to operate them—to public events and demonstrations put on by Bay Area political outsider groups. This planning session would be crucial to getting people, money and strategy organized in order to make the Redwood Summer happen.

Some thirty participants from different organizations attended the meeting at the Seeds House. In addition to Berkeley Earth First and the Seeds kids, there were official reps from Rainbow Action and Earth Island Institute, among others. Earth Island Institute bore the full imprimatur of its founder, the wily environmental contrarian David Brower, who had taken over the venerable Sierra Club in 1952 and turned it into a modern force to fight for the environment—and then, after losing a bitter leadership struggle, walked out in 1969 to found Friends of the Earth and built it to over fifty chapters worldwide. But once again, an unhappy Brower walked, founding Earth Island Institute.

The Archdruid, as Brower was known, was viewed by many in the ecology movement as a kind of living link to John Muir. Inspired by the Scotsman who brought Americans their first inklings of the value of wilderness, Brower completed first ascents of twenty peaks over 13,000 feet in the High Sierra during the 1930s when he was an unemployed student. He was the first white man to climb Yosemite's El Capitan.

Brower had fought with many comrades in the environmental movement, mostly within his own organizations, and he regarded many as sellouts. But in meeting the feisty Bari, he adopted her as one of his own. She was the answer, he believed, to the ossification and corruption of mainstream environmentalism and was closer than his discarded environmental partners to the credo that Brower himself had expressed in *For Earth's Sake:* "Every time I compromise I lose."

The meeting nailed down the logistics and responsibilities for the participants in the months to come. It was also decided that Bari, Cherney and Shannon Marr, a young spiky-haired blonde from Seeds, would collaborate on trying to write a convincing grant proposal to the Grateful Dead Foundation the next morning.

During the course of the evening, Bari expressed her horror at the household's sleeping arrangements to Seeds elder statesman David Kemnitzer when the two stepped out to share a joint. Kemnitzer was an Oakland substitute teacher and veteran radical activist.

He had first met Bari back in February on the campus of Humboldt State University in Arcata, during one of the periodic rendezvous of far-flung radical affinity groups known to insiders as "The Anarchist Coffee House." Kemnitzer later recalled Bari's discomfort at the prospect of crashing in a sleeping bag at the Seeds House because she was, after all, forty years old and past sleeping in a sty with a bunch of twenty-somethings. So Kemnitzer offered her the spare bedroom in the old Oakland Arts and Crafts–style cottage he shared with his wife and his teenage foster son. She seemed pleased with the cute house and stayed up half the night talking with Kemnitzer and smoking the endless shared joints—a custom common to the Seeds kids and the Earth Firsters.

At some point that evening, according to Kemnitzer, Bari mentioned the death threats she had recently received in connection with her announcement of the Redwood Summer of protest. She had two daughters to think of, she told him, and she confessed to being frightened. It was something of a shock for Kemnitzer to hear her voice these fears in the wee hours of the night. Before, he had seen her public bravado; now he saw her as vulnerable.

Early the next morning, Kemnitzer drove his foster son to school, and then picked up croissants to bring back to the house. He and Shannon Marr went upstairs to work on the grant proposal, while down below, Bari and Cherney tuned up their instruments to practice for the Santa Cruz gig.

Suddenly, Bari and Cherney were arguing, their voices rising so high in acrimony that Kemnitzer and Marr heard it all. Bari was critical of the slide show that Cherney had put together. She told him it was too macho because it didn't show women, and she didn't know why women should have to "put up with all that dick-waving." It was especially egregious, she pointed out, since the greater number of Earth First supporters in Santa Cruz were women. Kemnitzer later quoted her as saying, "You know, Darryl, this just won't fly. There are a lot of dykes in the audience."

Although it was true that there was a strong feminist and lesbian presence on the Santa Cruz campus, Cherney answered grudgingly, "Not all women are dykes."

"No, Darryl," she sneered, "just the lucky ones." Her zinger, vintage Bari sarcasm, silenced him.

CHAPTER ONE

Kemnitzer and Marr finished the grant proposal before noon. Cherney and Bari had to return to the Seeds House for a rehearsal with George Shook, the banjo-playing third member of their touring musical group. Cherney was to pick up his van before the three of them headed south for Santa Cruz. Just before leaving the house, Bari suddenly asked Cherney to ride with her on the trip back to the Seeds House, instead of with Shannon Marr, who was leading them because Bari didn't know her way back and felt a little lost in the East Bay.

It was a sunny and breezy Thursday, the kind of May day that promised to be clear, smogless and Bay Area perfect. Bari pointed her Subaru down 24th Street, behind Marr's white Datsun with its "Feed the People, Not the Pentagon" and "Peace and Freedom through Non-Violent Action" bumper stickers. Both cars came out fast on Park Boulevard and headed toward the freeway entrance that led back to Berkeley. The Datsun in front went past the large campus of Oakland High School on the left and then crossed MacArthur Boulevard, just before the freeway underpass.

"BOOM!"

There was an ear-splitting metallic scream as an explosion ripped through the Subaru. The noise was heard in the schoolyard and across the street and inside the AM/PM Mini-Mart and gas station on the corner of Park and MacArthur.

The blast tented up the roof of Bari's car. Glass and metal debris spewed out onto the street. The Subaru conked out immediately, but continued forward as if floating on a dark puff of air before it veered left, a crippled thing, rolling across the path of oncoming traffic and finally colliding with the corner guardrails that prohibited pedestrians from crossing there.

Oakland High students quickly gathered at the corner, gawking. This sunny day smelled of gunpowder, and fragments of the blast littered the whole corner. They kids could see the injured pair inside the wrecked car: the driver with her long, thick brown hair and doleful eyes, in shock, and the passenger with black curly hair and a bloody face, bent over the tiny woman.

It was deadly silent inside the car. Broken glass had cut Cherney's face and blood trickled down off his chin. Bari was ashen and motionless. Blood seeped into her seat cushion and pooled inside her from internal injuries. The blast from the pipe bomb had ripped through her seat, driving shrapnel, including a coiled seat spring, up into her body.

The force of the explosion had punched a hole out the driver's side of the car. Yet with all the damage it had done to Bari and to her car, the bomb had only partially exploded. Had it functioned fully as designed, she would have been killed instantly and Cherney along with her.

And she knew instantly what had happened, as she would later tell Beth Robinson Bosk in her interview monthly, New Settler: "I knew it was a bomb immediately. I never experienced a bomb in my life, but there wasn't any question in my mind what it was. It was the loudest noise I'd ever heard. The noise of the explosion was so loud that the sound had a physical force of its own, it was that loud."

Cherney leaned over her, breaking the silence. He tried to comfort her in his scared voice, telling her repeatedly that he loved her and that she would not die.

Up ahead, Shannon Marr had been startled by the noise, and then had smelled the foul air of the explosion. Looking into her rearview mirror, she saw an ominous black cloud. She pulled over and ran back to Bari and Cherney.

Just then, Kemnitzer—following along the same route, the way all the locals would go to get on the freeway—came upon the tableau of the wrecked car, the smoke, and Marr crying loudly as she also tried to comfort Bari. He noted that Bari was awake but uttering no sound. She was pinned down by the seat spring; and her car was wedged up under the pedestrian barrier in such a way that the "Jaws of Life" emergency equipment was soon summoned to cut her out.

While the medics were trying to stabilize her, one of them asked the still conscious Bari who had done this to her.

"Timber," she said.

Meanwhile, Cherney told the driver of a second ambulance, "They threw a bomb at us!" Later, under police interrogation, he would name neo-Nazis from Fort Bragg, members of the "Sahara Club" who had threatened the activists over the pending summer of demonstrations, as some of the likely perpetrators.

When Bari lay afterward at Highland Hospital in a reverie of untreated pain (the supervising emergency doctors needed her that way in part so they could determine the extent of her injuries), the police interrogated her outside the operating room before the order-lies wheeled her in for surgery. They would be removing the seat spring and other fragments lodged inside her and would try to patch up her shattered pelvis. Bari was able to utter only three staccato words: "Timber," "Nazis," "Fort Bragg."

Just before her surgery, after the police had finished prelimi-nary questioning, she moaned again that she wished she were dead. An angel of mercy finally stood over her with a big needle. "We're going to put you out, Honey," the nurse said, hugging her gently. She also warned Bari that she'd probably wake up with a colon bag to remove her bodily waste, a treatment that might be permanent. She wanted to prepare her for the worst.

TWO

IN A WAY, JUDI BARI HAD BEEN PREPARING for the worst most of her life.

She was born Judith Beatrice, on November 7, 1949, in Baltimore, the second daughter of Ruth and Arthur Bari. Her sister Gina was a year and a few months older. Martha, the youngest in the family, was born over a decade later. An episode that occurred in the first year of Judi's life marked the way Ruth and Arthur would choose to raise their girls.

In the late summer of 1950, the FBI suddenly descended on the Bari family home one morning shortly after Arthur had left for work. For Ruth it was a harrowing visit. The agents threatened and badgered her even with her two baby girls in arms. They were interested in a recent houseguest—Morton Sobell, a Soviet spy in flight from the federal government.

Sobell had become a fugitive that June upon learning of the FBI questioning and subsequent arrest of Julius and Ethel Rosenberg. Both the Rosenbergs and Sobell were now accused of running an atomic spy ring for the Soviet Union. All were Communist Party members.

As good Communists, Arthur and Ruth had given Sobell refuge at the party's request. Sobell had then moved to another "safe house" on his escape to Mexico, where he and his family were finally caught and turned over to U.S. agents at the border. He was convicted of espionage and sentenced to thirty years.

The FBI never arrested Arthur or Ruth for harboring a wanted man, but the fear that this drama generated in Judi's home left a scar. The G-men's visit instantly changed the couple's ideas on how they wanted to live, prompting them to hide the radical political heritage they had inherited from their own parents and grandparents.

According to Judi's daughter Lisa, Ruth's family, the Aaronsons, were Bolsheviks who fought against the czar in Russia. (Ruth was born in 1917, the year of the Russian Revolution.) Arthur was born to older parents, also Communists, shortly after they had immigrated to America from Italy. His parents never learned English. Their family name, Castalaneta, was discarded when Arthur was three years old; at the bidding of a much older uncle, they took the name di Barisciano, apparently to avoid a blacklist. Ruth and Arthur married as di Barisciano. Later they shortened this to Bari, the surname that appeared on Judi's birth certificate.

Despite the fact that Ruth and Arthur were both from radical, secular households, their marriage was apparently frowned upon by both sets of parents: the divide of ethnicity and culture was still huge. In particular, Ruth's Jewish family, aspiring to culture and class, believed that Arthur Bari's Italian working-class status would be a millstone for a daughter who eventually got her master's degree in mathematics at Johns Hopkins University in 1943. Ruth dropped out of the Ph.D. program to be with her young children at home, but later returned, completing her studies in 1966, becoming the university's first female Ph.D. in math. After receiving her degree, she was offered a teaching position at George Washington University in D.C., where she won tenure and then taught until her retirement in 1987 at the age of seventy.

Arthur Bari proudly told journalist Fred Gardner, who interviewed him outside Judi's hospital room after the car bombing in May 1990, that he had willingly sacrificed his own education and career in order to help his brilliant wife. Arthur was a craftsman, a gem cutter, and also an inventor of gem-cutting tools. Lisa Bari attributed her mother's drawing skill to Arthur's gifted hands.

Probably after the FBI visit and certainly after the execution of the Rosenbergs in 1953, Arthur and Ruth not only quit the Communist Party, but buried their past political history and never brought it up again until Judi was in college. They moved to Silver Springs, Maryland, an upscale bedroom community outside the nation's capital, and gave their daughters a perfectly normal bourgeois upbringing. During their growing-up, there was no indication that the Bari girls would ever return to the Communist ghetto of their parents' past or that they would pursue a trade. They were pushed to excel academically, like their mother; Judi only half jokingly called her forced practice for her violin lessons "fascist."

Ruth and Arthur were both short and all the Bari girls took after them in this respect, but Judi was the shortest, at barely five feet. She had her mother's strong features, with a prominent jaw line and a large nose. Eastern European Jewish dark circles under her eyes made them look bigger and almost mournful, even when she was clowning. In high school, Judi had Gina iron her thick, nearly blond hair flat, and she wore long bangs that covered her eyebrows. In later years, she let her mane grow long, parted in the middle and flowing in natural waves, hippie style. As she matured, her tiny tomboy figure filled into curves. She had ample breasts for her petite size, broad shoulders and a large head.

One female journalist later said that Judi was odd-looking because "she had big bones in her face and you'd expect to see them on a much larger, taller person." Mitch Clogg, a Mendocino resident who became a supporter of Judi's organizing for the forests, described her looks as "gnomish"; he said she had a "masculine face."

Her older sister, Gina, with dark hair and delicate features resembling her father's, was pretty in a gamine kind of way. She was also more popular in high school than Judi, and she always excelled academically (although, according to a hometown Princeton article published in January 1998, she once had to take a remedial course "because she talked too fast"). Gina's better grades and wider social acceptance aggravated the often acrimonious sibling rivalry that developed between the two sisters. Her accomplishments were always just beyond Judi's reach, and those who knew Judi well thought it was an abrasion on her soul that she, only a year younger than Gina, had to be measured against her.

Although Judi stood in Gina's shadow when they were growing up, she had her own accomplishments. She was a National Merit finalist and was on the prom committee during her senior year. Judi's daughter Lisa later described her mother as "one of those rah-rah spirit girls" for her high school's athletic teams. But she also mowed the lawn and worked on cars. She was proud of her grease-monkey status and for the rest of her life would take satisfaction in mastering practical and traditionally male skills.

Sports had been big at Judi's school. Despite her feminist inclinations, she was eager for male approval and later boasted that she had football hunks as boyfriends. She laughed about it even as she admitted that she "spent [her] time trying to get dates with…all of these just wonderful jocks, most of whom it was important to make sure to appear not to be smarter than." Among friends, the self-mocking memories of her high school days were even raunchier. Bruce Anderson, publisher of the *Anderson Valley Advertiser*, remembered that when narrating her early life, Bari "called herself a 'jock sniffer' and half complained, half bragged that she couldn't cross the high school cafeteria without guys yelling out to her—because of her boobs."

All three Bari girls, according to Judi's daughter Lisa, were big dieters. In high school, Judi began a habit of drinking Diet Cokes that she kept up even in motherhood.

In 1965, Gina went off to college at the nearby University of Maryland to major in microbiology. After graduating in 1969, she studied molecular biology in the Ph.D. program at MIT, but decided that she didn't particularly enjoy lab work. So she returned to Maryland to get a master's degree in applied mathematics in 1973, and then pursued a writing career, working as a senior writer at *Science* magazine and also freelancing and writing books. She began writing for the *New York Times* in 1987 under her married name, Gina Kolata, and eventually became the paper's chief science correspondent. Today, Gina—petite, well groomed and still very pretty—lives in Princeton with her husband, William, a physicist, and their two children in what Judi scathingly labeled a "bourgeois" home. "She'd sneer at her sister's big house, called Gina a 'yuppie' and dismissed her as living a 'stupid life,'" Bruce Anderson recalled.

Adding fuel to Judi's contempt for her sister was Gina's conversion to Catholicism, which brought with it opposition to abortion. That alone would have made for rancorous fights between the siblings, considering Judi's participation years later in a nasty and militant confrontation between pro- and anti-abortion demonstrators in Ukiah. Her sister's middle-class ways would always be a target for Judi and a way for her to define herself by opposition.

In Maryland, the two girls fought—sometimes literally—all through high school and even college. Gossip about fisticuffs between the sisters even circulated later among newsies because of Gina's *New York Times* connection. Their fights were rumored to have continued into young adulthood.

What good family times there were when the Bari girls were growing up revolved around food. After Gina and Judi were in college, there were still Sunday night family dinners. But even on these occasions—according to what Walter Penny, Judi's fiancé at the time, later told muckraking journalist Mark Dowie—the two sisters quarreled so bitterly that one or the other would finally have to leave the house. Penny recalled Judi's typical rejoinder to statements that Gina made during these conflicts: "I spit on that!"

Their fighting was the subtext of the Bari household all through the years that the sisters were in proximity, and it continued long-distance even to the end of Judi's life. As she told several friends, Judi's resentment was stoked by the fact that Gina never acknowledged their relationship publicly once Judi was well known as an environmentalist—as if Gina were ashamed of her sister's radicalism and scornful of her accomplishments.[*]

Judi got along with her younger sister, Martha, the mildest of the Bari sisters and adept at playing the last child's role of mediator. A little taller than Judi, with brown hair and features that look like an exact cross of her parents, Martha remained at home long after her elder sisters had departed. At the time of the car bombing, she was still there, a graduate student studying art history with a specialty in nineteenth-century European art. Martha had come to California for visits, and was with Judi when she gave birth to her second child. Judi later would tell her friend Bruce Anderson, "You would love my sister. All she loves to do is read books."

Judi had no inkling of her parents' former Communist Party membership until she was in college, when her own growing political activism drew out a confession from them. (When she came home waving Mao's Red Book, her mother admonished her, "Don't make the same mistake we did: socialism in America has to be American.")

---

[*]In connection with a new book she had written on exercise, Gina Kolata began using "Bari" as a middle name in 2003, it was omitted in earlier books and articles.

Judi resented her parents for having kept their political past a secret; she felt that she had been denied her birthright as a red-diaper baby. She could have learned the hard lessons of Marxism directly from her parents instead of having to do it all for herself. She felt it would all have been easier for her if her parents hadn't allowed themselves to be forced into a middle-class masquerade.

If the protests against the war in Vietnam had not been at full throttle when Judi hit the University of Maryland in 1967, perhaps she would have chosen a path similar to Gina's. But from the very beginning of her academic career, Judi's major preoccupation, she would later write, was plumbing "the cultural side of the revolution." ("In other words," she elaborated, "I spent a lot of time hanging out in the dorms smoking pot and trying out all the new exciting psychedelic drugs that had suddenly appeared on campus.") She became interested in politics soon enough, although her interest in drugs did not decline. She later confessed to one interviewer that she was "a needle freak," meaning she mainlined methamphetamine and possibly heroin as well.

In a 1990 hospital interview, Bari told Catherine Bishop, then working for the *New York Times*, that she had been truly radicalized— like so many other college youngsters—during an antiwar demonstration. "It was a profound experience," she said. "I got tear-gassed. Up until then, I was a sweet innocent hippie."

Soon she began attending political meetings and demonstrating in the streets. "We had outrageous riots," she enthused years later about the street fighting against the Vietnam War. And she found the group of people she would join. They referred to themselves as "Mad Dogs," and were something akin to the "affinity groups" she would join in the 1980s during protests against American involvement in Central America and against nuclear power plants.

Later on, she bragged about throwing rocks at the cops during the antiwar demonstrations. With great bravado she told of withstanding the police bearing down on her and her comrades, swinging their clubs. She and others lobbed tear gas canisters right back at the cops when the University of Maryland protesters did battle, shutting down the main artery of Route 1 that linked Baltimore with Washington, D.C.

The following year, the going was not so easy. According to

Judi's UM friend David Katz, when the activists yelled "'Mad Dogs assemble!'...the [cops] came back with armored personnel carriers and better tear gas and pepper gas. And, by the third year, there would be a riot, and you wouldn't even get to Route 1. The police would be there with tanks, and people would be arrested very quickly, and they had it under control."

As she became more deeply involved with the Movement, Judi cut classes, quizzes, exams and theses, and finally quit altogether, without any consideration for her parents' expectations. (She told Catherine Bishop: "I quit before I was thrown out.") Turning her back on academia was a stab at her own mother's accomplishments, and her mother's proxy—her sister Gina, the star student. But as she later said—along with thousands of other New Leftists—she felt that formal schooling was corrupt and irrelevant: "I got the best education in the streets."

After her first two years at the University of Maryland, Judi was in solid with the most prominent and interesting campus agitators. One of them was a Vietnam veteran named Madison Jones, a poised older engineering student who was the campus leader of antiwar politics. He made a successful bid for student body president, running as a representative from the engineering school, and then appointed Judi and David Katz, who was two years behind her, to the student committee that held the purse strings of student funds— which in a student body of thirty thousand were considerable.

The appointment of two Mad Dog street fighters signaled a revolutionary moment in Maryland. "Historically, it was the conservatives—the fraternity people—who allocated the money," Judi later reminisced. It's true that the lefty charities she voted for in her new office were not exceptionable—rock concerts, the "student homophile association"; what was more telling is which groups she and the others on the committee *neglected.* "We gave zero to the cheerleaders," she said triumphantly. "We told the sports department to raise its own money. For the first time in the history of the university, the regents vetoed the budget."

Full of sophomoric radical pronouncements, Bari spouted the same sentiments as thousands of other awakened would-be radical students. She thought she'd had a revelation during the street battles on Route 1 and on campus when the police finally roughed up one antiwar demonstrator, bouncing him down the stairs and apparently causing permanent brain damage. At this moment, she later told the *New Settler* monthly, she saw "how shallow the veneer of civility this society has. That the rule of the corporations is enforced by the military."

The rhetoric was not particularly original. But in her later radical career, Judi always referred back to the violence she learned at the hands of law enforcement. "Some of my earliest political experiences were of 20-year-old national guardsmen beating my 18-year-old nonviolent friends senseless and bloody," she wrote over twenty years later.

Still, however somber she made it seem in retrospect, Judi and those like her found that protesting the war was the most fun you could have with your clothes on. "We had a sense of joyousness, that very joy of living that these corporations suppress," she later remarked. She and the other Mad Dogs used to say, "We are the life culture; they are the death culture." She would still see the world in these Manichean terms two decades afterward when she fought the timber wars.

One of the radicals she met at an antiwar demonstration at the university in 1971 became her lover and best buddy—Walt Penny. He had been a pretty good jock, a competition swimmer, who became radicalized along with the rest of them. Judi spent time with him when she was still a student living in the dorms. David Katz was Penny's roommate until Judi moved in.

At this time, Judi and a friend got busted for pot possession. The charge was ultimately dropped. When she later talked about the episode, Judi attacked "the system" in radical boilerplate: "We were fortunate that the arrest took place in Maryland, a state whose government is so openly corrupt that if you are white, all you have to do is hire the right lawyer and you can get things taken care of. We got off with probation without a finding of guilt." She neglected to mention who it was who'd hired the right lawyer for her—her white, "privileged middle-class parents."

JUDI DROPPED OUT OF THE University of Maryland without a B.A. in

1971, after five years of enrollment; but she stayed in town, working as a uniformed cashier in the cafeteria. She later told friends she had felt humiliated in this role because privileged students looked down on her as a "working person." Judi moved into Penny's commune in the slum neighborhood of Chillum Heights, the tackier part of Takoma Park. The place was called "Buffalo House," and Judi remained there for the better part of a decade. Her lifestyle had become a way of showing her parents what she thought of them for having sold out their left-wing ideals in their youth. Every week, as she later told Bruce Anderson, she'd riot, go home, shoot up "crank" (methamphetamine) and then have sex.

When Buffalo House members decided to learn self-defense, Judi joined them in karate classes. She earned a brown belt and was invited as a guest to several summers of karate camp. It was a skill she employed over and over again as she got older, confidently decking people even though she was barely five feet tall.

After the cafeteria job, Judi was hired as a bakery clerk at the Grand Union grocery store—number 629 in Hillandale, Maryland—in 1972. The following year, she was made shop steward in her union, the Retail Clerks Union, a position she had sought. To hear her talk about it later, the clerk job was the cutting edge of the labor struggle. She would remain proud of the fact that she'd been fired four times.

In their search for political authenticity, Bari and Penny sat together at Buffalo House in the evenings, reading aloud to one another from Marxist tomes: *The Communist Manifesto, Strike!,* and Philip Foner's four-volume *A History of the Labor Movement in the United States,* where she first learned of the International Workers of the World (the IWW or "Wobblies"), which would later play a role in the fight for the redwoods.

Bari was quickly able to translate the theoretical into practice at the most basic level, according to Katz. But she never rose to the forefront of the Movement. "She was a good debater," he recalled, "but she wasn't such a good public speaker."

Her first "labor action" was prompted by her abrupt dismissal from her grocery store job. She protested her firing, which earned a visit from the local retailer's union representative. He was an inferior person, she instantly decided, a judgment based on his attire: "a sleazy coat" with "white shoes and white belt." But she admitted to being "fascinated, by the way that the union rep and members called each other 'brother.'"

Bari won her job back with the help of her "brothers," and began attending meetings of the Retail Clerks Union. She later claimed that she led a walkout of the rank and file with her spirited rebelliousness. In her version of events, she had argued with the white union president from the floor, boldly yelled "bullshit!" to his face, and in the process inspired the black workers to tear up their union contracts and riot.

Eventually she soured on the union; in her assessment, it was too closely identified with management. The walkout wildcat strike of seventeen thousand workers she claimed to have sparked was soon crushed, and she and her fellow wildcatters all lost their jobs. But she had acquired a taste for battle.

Judi's next working-class job, in what she would later claim as a seven-year history of unionism, was at the huge U.S. Postal Service Bulk Mail Center in Largo, Maryland. She even managed to pass the physical requiring the applicant to hoist and shoulder a seventy-pound mail sack! There her emerging working-class ethos was more successfully wedded to her student activism. She helped publish an underground workers' newsletter called *Postal Strife*, in mockery of the official in-house organ, *Postal Life*. Instead of the latter's United States bald eagle on its logo, Judi wittily posted a buzzard. Instead of the eagle's olive branch clutched in its talons, Judi's postal buzzard held a marijuana joint. *Postal Strife* ran sardonic mottoes like "You mail them, we maul them." Apparently she and some of her coworkers did just that—"maul them"—because she later claimed that "people started sneaking in cameras and taking pictures of this messed up mail."

Postal Strife frequently satirized the post office manager, a woman named Julie. Just as Judi had judged her last union rep as lacking in taste for his polyester clothes and white accessories, she took aim at Julie for wearing designer dresses and driving a Porsche. One of her cronies from those days, John Wood, a union leader, commented that "to Judi, that was just distasteful." Her campaign against the manager sometimes got personal, as when she published photos of "Miz Julie" entering her car wearing big, unattractive curlers. Another time, after the manager tried to cut a secret deal with the union, Judi ferreted out the facts and published them.

Judi related all this much later to journalist Jonathan Littman for a 1990 *California* magazine piece. But others told Littman a different story—one about a disabled supervisor at the plant who was so terrorized at the prospect of being lampooned in *Postal Strife* that he agreed to "expedite her grievances" if Judi promised never to depict him in her publication. After that, coworkers gave her the nickname "Mafia Mamma."

Judi was also poised to do battle against men who bugged her in a sexist way. In his magazine piece, Littman quoted Joe Cuppy, a fellow worker who watched her cold-cock a fellow employee who made a pass at her in the company lunchroom. Cuppy said she'd first warned the flirt to take his hands off her. Then she knocked him to the floor with a karate punch. The vanquished man pulled himself up off the floor and said with menace, "I'm going to get you for this!" But by then, Judi had nonchalantly resumed her conversation with Cuppy and others.

In her own telling, Judi was a labor firebrand who tore up the Maryland Bulk Mail Center with her union activism just as she had torn up the grocery store. Once again, she led a group that bucked management. Rather than just walk out and be fired—it was illegal to strike against the United States government—they had slowdowns and sick-outs. They even had "walk-ins," when the two shifts during changeover would literally walk into the manager's office.

"Now you have to realize the fear of this," Judi later explained. "The workers are mostly black and the management is all white, so we had that little Mau Mau-ing aspect that scared them to death. We had a trash-in one time. We caused wrecks of the machinery. We sabbed [sabotaged] the machinery—exactly the Earth First! tactics." In her version, the workers always won: "We broke their power."

Her life in Maryland assumed a routine. She worked hard all day and then returned to her boyfriend and the communal rituals of shared drugs, food and politics. But the camaraderie of her fellow radical workers and her growing ideological fervor made her restless. The ardor of her relationship with Penny cooled. The couple had actually split up at the end of her retail clerk job, before she went to work for the U.S. Postal Service, but she continued to live in the same house with him as a fellow communard, not as a lover.

Already there was a new romantic interest in her life. Judi had been corresponding with a San Diego man named Mike Sweeney, who was also in the Retail Clerks Union. Their early courtship was based on the fact that both were radicals in the union, doing parallel political work by putting out non-mainstream union newsletters and organizing wildcat walkouts. They began corresponding in 1974 after hearing about one another's deeds. And after Judi left her bakery job for the Bulk Mail Center position, she began sending Sweeney her *Postal Strife*.

When she encountered union difficulties, as on one occasion when the union tried to expel her, she turned to Sweeney, whom she described as being "really good at legal things." He express-mailed her court precedents that she could use to fight her bosses. His worldly political radicalism impressed her as being far more sophisticated than what she'd so far encountered in her union activism or at Buffalo House. In particular, she pointed to an article that Sweeney had published in the irregular union newsletter *Checkout* accusing the Retail Clerks Union of having been involved in the 1973 overthrow of leftist Chilean president Salvador Allende. She was so taken with Sweeney's article, by the way he marshaled his evidence and how he "named names, and printed a photograph of the CIA agent on the International Retail Clerks staff," that she reprinted the piece in her own renegade newsletter.

In January 1979, Sweeney, recently divorced from his wife, decided to come and visit this kindred soul with whom he'd been corresponding for five years. "When we met each other, we decided that we wanted to have kids for eugenic purposes," she joked later on. "I was breeding for intelligence and hair color." After corresponding with growing urgency through the spring, Judi visited Sweeney in the summer. And that seems to have clinched it: she made plans to go west, although she took a six-month leave of absence just in case it didn't work out.

THREE

MICHAEL SWEENEY, LIKE JUDI BARI, wanted to be a working-class hero. But unlike her, he had managed to graduate from college—Stanford class of 1973. By the time Bari met him, Sweeney had gone to adult-education school and become certified as a heating, refrigeration and air conditioning engineer. He was also a radical labor organizer and the editor of the militant Retail Clerks' newsletters, *Checkout* and *Wildcat*.

Sweeney kept his past political activities very much hidden to almost everyone; but he must have shared something with Bari in their first encounter, because afterward she conceived an image of him as a "political heavy." She would later tell one interviewer that Sweeney "was good in those days," meaning politically.

Born in Hollywood on October 4, 1947, Sweeney was a middle child: he had an older and a younger brother, an echo of the birth order in Judi Bari's family. But otherwise their respective upbringings were dissimilar. Sweeney had many more battles to fight with his conservative father than Bari had with her Communist parents—at least about politics.

His father, Don Sweeney, had been born and raised in Los Angeles, leaving when World War II broke out to become a war reporter. While stationed in London, he met an Irish woman named Anna, whom he married and brought back home. As his fortunes rose, the Sweeneys moved to Santa Barbara, where they raised their three sons. It was a privileged upbringing, even though the Sweeneys were not overly indulgent parents.

Santa Barbara in the Fifties and Sixties was a town as solidly conservative as it was wealthy. Don Sweeney was an oil man who rose to become a Mobil executive. A loyal Republican, he later earned a minor post in the Nixon administration.

Mike Sweeney was not quite eighteen when he entered Stanford in the fall of 1965, a typical white suburban upper-middle-class freshman who gave no indication of the radicalism to come. His first notable foray into politics occurred when he was elected editor-in-chief of the *Stanford Daily*, the campus newspaper, in 1968. Classmates remember that he ran on an antiwar platform and increasingly devoted the paper's pages to resistance against the Vietnam War. One newspaper colleague accused him of having a hidden radical agenda, claiming that Sweeney "didn't reveal his intentions" until after he was secure in his new post.

Steve Talbot, a PBS documentary filmmaker who produced *Who Bombed Judi Bari?* a year after the bombing, looked into Mike Sweeney's background at Stanford, interviewing nearly a dozen classmates, many of whom had worked with Sweeney on the *Stanford Daily*. Talbot learned that after his first year as a square freshman, Sweeney had "a virtual overnight metamorphosis to a committed revolutionary." Talbot said that former classmates remembered Sweeney as focused and intense, a quality that would be noted by others later on when he worked as a recycling official in Mendocino County.

But there were also memories of Sweeney's bad temper. Talbot read to me from the notes he had taken during his interviews with former Stanford students who had known Sweeney. One described him as a "rich guy" who was "hot-tempered." Another said he was "a touch arrogant," with "a lot of anger." A third recalled his "steely quality of hate."

As Sweeney's radicalization and his growing sympathy for the working class became evident to his classmates, his interest in the mainstream *Stanford Daily*—and indeed in academic life altogether—appeared to wane. By 1970, both he and his girlfriend, Stanford coed Cynthia Denenholz, were committed radicals who found student life at the university too constrictive for their burgeoning revolutionary zeal.

Sweeney had come under the sway of the briefly notorious Stanford professor H. Bruce Franklin, a Melville scholar who had formed an ultra-radical group called Venceremos.[*] Under the charismatic Franklin, Venceremos was one of the radical groups in the Bay Area advocating armed struggle in the overthrow of "Amerikkka" (always with three "k's"); but unlike other New Left groups, Franklin embraced communism and tried to reinvent it with such revolutionary pronouncements as: "Every day, Joseph Stalin means more and more to American youth."

The often violent rhetoric of Venceremos was more than matched by its actions. Venceremos members were widely believed to have been the architects of the 1970 attack on the Bank of America at Isla Vista, in the environs of the University of California at Santa Barbara. After student demonstrations, a daylight attempt to burn down the bank was followed that night by an act of firebombing that became legendary in New Left lore, and by the shooting death of a night watchman who attempted to put out the fire.

That fall, Sweeney wrote a hit piece on the Bank of America and its founder in the radical monthly *Ramparts*. In it, he quoted someone he identified as one of the arsonists, without any explanation of how he had access to the source: "Said a 17-year-old bank burner: 'Well it was there…the biggest capitalist establishment thing around.'"

Starting out as a cultural liaison outreach group recognized by the California State Prison bureaucracy, Venceremos organized among the state's tough felons; and it offered military training to its members, stockpiling explosives (some of which were provided to the Black Panthers) and teaching the art of constructing bombs. During their approved visits to prisons, the radicals managed to recruit a convicted robber, Ronald Beaty, who was serving time in Chino. In October 1972, Venceremos members—in an act that would ultimately destroy the organization and put all its members in jeopardy—ambushed the prison van that was transporting Beaty to San Bernardino to testify in a hearing. The "liberators," in two separate vehicles, pulled alongside the prison vehicle on a deserted highway and ran it off the road. They opened fire, killing a young unarmed

---

[*]Not to be confused with the similarly named Venceremos Brigades, which traveled to Cuba in the early 1970s to cut sugarcane in Castro's Cuba and foster sympathies between American radical youth and revolutionary Cuba.

Hispanic guard and seriously injuring his unarmed fellow officer before fleeing with Beaty.

For several months after the break, Beaty lay low in safe houses. Then, acting on a tip-off, the police captured the fugitive along with a female Venceremos member after a shootout on the San Francisco Bay Bridge. Beaty immediately began to talk, fingering not only the Venceremos members who shot the prison van guards, but eleven others as well, including Bruce Franklin himself. Beaty named Franklin as a participant in the planning of the ambush and the escape, who afterward harbored him, providing him with cash and a car.

Franklin was indicted as a co-conspirator. His attorney was Charles Garry, the leftist lawyer who was father figure and counselor to Huey Newton and other Black Panthers. Ultimately, the charges against Franklin were dropped for insufficient evidence; but his arrest and trial factored into Stanford's decision to fire him for inappropriate conduct that included posing for a poster holding a gun. Subsequently, Franklin sued unsuccessfully to get his job back.

Venceremos's Bay Area membership, estimated at five hundred, reached out to prisoners and would eventually include virtually all the central figures of the Symbionese Liberation Army—the revolutionary group that burst into the news in 1973 with the kidnapping of heiress Patricia Hearst. SLA members Emily and Bill Harris were initially members of Venceremos. Nancy Ling Perry, who died with other SLA members in a Los Angeles house during a shootout with police in May 1974, had also been in Venceremos. So were Joe Remiro and Russell Little, both later convicted of "executing" Oakland school superintendent Marcus Foster, an African American whose sin was instituting student identity cards as a means of excluding the nonstudent drug traffickers who plied their trade on Oakland school property.

Although Sweeney was remembered by close friends to have been involved in Venceremos, he was never named publicly in any government or criminal investigation into the organization or into the SLA. Nor is there evidence that he ever participated in any of the above activities.

On November 26, 1971, Sweeney married Cynthia Anne Denenholz, also of Stanford and Venceremos, in South San Francisco. They moved to San Diego, where he learned the refrigerator and air conditioning business, becoming sufficiently competent to get a contractor's license. Given Sweeney's association with Venceremos and H. Bruce Franklin, some Bay Area radical insiders regarded the choice and timing of his new profession as suspicious. Bombing requires technical know-how, and Sweeney's new practical skills could have wide potential. But Sweeney's decision to become a contractor was also very much in keeping with the Maoist rhetoric of the day, which made blue-collar "organizing" a highly regarded "vanguard" activity.

When Sweeney decided to move to San Diego, the city was becoming a hotbed of radical politics. (Judi Bari later told Steve Talbot that Sweeney had gone there specifically in anticipation of the Republican Party's decision selecting the city as the site for its 1972 nominating convention.) The usual leftist groups began drifting into town for the expected protests. A number of radical enclaves were already flourishing at San Diego State and on the University of California campus, which is sandwiched between the Marine Training Center and a Navy installation downtown.

David Helvarg, an investigator who years later worked with Talbot on his PBS documentary about Bari, was a young antiwar demonstrator in the city when he first met Sweeney: "I encountered him in '72. And his role then was to condemn the hippies in Ocean Beach who were organizing against the convention. He was disdainful because they were hippies, not workers." Helvarg today is fairly skeptical of the politics that Sweeney then seemed to represent: "You ended up in those days with young militants with nowhere to go. They were privileged kids pretending to be Maoist."

As plans for massive demonstrations escalated throughout the city, the Republicans rethought San Diego and moved their convention to Miami.

In May 1972, Cindy Sweeney gave birth to her first child, Zack; a daughter, Heather, was born three years later. Perhaps it was the birth of their children that prompted both parents to return to Stanford to finish their undergraduate study. Cindy went on to graduate from law school, eventually passing the bar. After getting his degree in economics, Sweeney stuck with his work as a heating and air conditioning mechanic. His day job paid the bills.

The couple moved to Santa Rosa and, with a loan from Mike's parents, they bought a modest house. But the marriage was filled with tension, and the couple separated in June 1978. Cindy and the children stayed in the new home, while Mike had to live elsewhere with a roommate.

According to later court filings, Mike resented this. Angrily and persistently, he took Cindy to court a total of five times over a three-year period after the divorce, seeking reduced support payments as well as increased visitation rights. Cindy later wrote in court filings that immediately after the divorce became final on October 29, 1979, "he purchased a new house for over $60,000 ...about 200 yards away from where I live, primarily I think to make matters more difficult for me."

In response to Mike's fourth filing against her, in 1982, Cindy wrote, "My ex-husband is belligerent, tenacious and self-righteous .... He rejoices in imposing his will on me.... He has filed all of these motions to disrupt my life as much as possible. He timed this motion, for example, so that I would be served with these papers on the first day of my California Bar Examination—and then told our youngest child, Heather, to wish me good luck on the exam."

FOUR

JUDI BARI LIKED MIKE SWEENEY well enough in person when they first met in January 1979 to think of him as a prospective father for the children she desired to have. He was about five-foot-nine with a solid build, a round face with a large forehead and a small, chiseled nose. He had thinning dark hair, a beard and uneven teeth. His gaze could be cold, penetrating and unsettling. Yet he could also be charming and he had a nice smile. Bari was much taken by him.

After their first meeting, they kept in close touch. The distance appears to have deepened the connection. Sweeney's Stanford degree commanded Bari's respect, but his commitment to the left-revolutionary politics of the day was the big attraction.

Her friend David Katz observed later on, "She fell in love with him because here was a guy just like her." The coincidence that they were both middle children among same-sex siblings reinforced the sense of being made for each other.

For Bari, the move west to live with her new lover would be a big break from her parents, to say nothing of her comfortable niche at Buffalo House. No doubt Arthur and Ruth were chagrined at the course that Judi was charting for her life. Had they sacrificed for respectability and success so that their daughter would opt to do physical, blue-collar labor and take such risks with her radical, sometimes violent politics?

Until now, despite her impatience with her parents, Bari had never really left the family nest. For all her bravado in the streets, she hadn't been brave enough to travel far from Maryland. But now, with a prospective lover who was, like her, a serious lefty, she had met her Cinderella moment. After their trial visit in the summer of 1979, she made up her mind to cast her lot with Sweeney.

IN NOVEMBER, BARI DROVE BY herself across the country to California and moved into Sweeney's new house on the bucolic-sounding Primrose Lane, in a dirt-road community southwest of Santa Rosa and a scant 150 yards from the house where his former wife lived with their kids. The area was once unincorporated farmland, but it had been absorbed as a suburb of the fast-growing Sonoma County hub town an hour north from San Francisco on Highway 101. Their one-story house on Primrose had three bedrooms with low, oppressive ceilings. Sweeney said in papers filed in his divorce from Cynthia Denenholz that he chose the place because it was close to his children's school, making it easier for them to visit him.

Bari planted a vegetable garden in the small enclosed yard. But the end of Primrose abutted large swaths of fallow lowlands, and the garden couldn't quite overcome the mood of that flat, dreary countryside. Still, Bari blossomed away from the manicured life of her parents. She got pregnant, and she and Sweeney married in 1981, just one week before their first child, Lisa, was born in January. David Katz remembers their wedding picture: a shotgun aimed at the bridegroom, a sardonic joke about bourgeois marriage by a pair of irreverent lefties.

Later that year, Judi went home to her parents in Silver Springs to show off Lisa and pick up wedding and baby gifts. Her parents then drove their daughter and granddaughter three thousand miles across the country back to their Sonoma County home. The reason had more to do with left-wing family values than with concern for the new mother and baby: apparently none of them wanted to cross the picket lines of the striking air traffic controllers whose PATCO union was soon to be broken by President Ronald Reagan.

Although this trip seemed to indicate a new closeness with her parents, it actually marked Judi's final declaration of independence from them. Friends that Judi made over the next decade frequently remarked upon the evident coolness of her relationship with Arthur and Ruth. Anna Marie Stenberg, who worked with Bari on Mendocino County labor issues and became one of her closest friends, later noted, "She'd talk to her parents only once in a rare while." Another friend, Pam Davis, who had done carpentry in the Primrose Lane house, observed, "When she did reminisce, it was only about her political involvement in the past—her work with the post office and her joke newsletters during a strike." The family was part of that other, bourgeois life which Sweeney had helped her escape once and for all.

Nor did she find any consolation with her new in-laws. She later told publisher Bruce Anderson that the elder Sweeneys "hated" her, and she complained to filmmaker Steve Talbot that they treated her "like dirt." And Bari joined her husband in his antipathy toward his former wife.

Cynthia Denenholz's written testament in response to Sweeney's fourth court filing seeking joint custody included a depiction of Judi as the stereotypical wicked stepmother. Complaining about the court-imposed five days of uninterrupted visits her children had with Sweeney and the hardships it imposed on them, Denenholz wrote: "The arrangement has proven to be very difficult for both of the children. Zachary and Heather...have frequently complained about...their long time away from 'home.' They also tell me that when they are over at their father's house during such long visits, they are frequently left alone with their step-mother, who often yells at them. Zachary has told me that she has hit and kicked him."

Denenholz also bitterly complained that Sweeney paid support money only when he was about to take her to court. In addition to serving her with papers on the eve of her bar exam, she wrote, he filed his first "bad faith litigation two days before Christmas when my family was visiting me and when I had the children. He takes a perverse pleasure in timing his motions to cause me as much grief as possible." Denenholz even quoted Bari's words as confirmation of her view of Sweeney's litigiousness as diabolical and mischievous: "His present wife, Judi, once told me that he times his legal motions against me so as to have the maximum disruptive effect on my life. What he actually wants is power and control over our children and over me. I am pleading that this court do something to get him to leave me alone."

Some time during these divorce and custody battles, Sweeney and Bari sneaked onto Denenholz's nearby property and sabotaged her water system. Bari herself admitted to Talbot years later that she had accompanied Sweeney on the venture. So she knew early on what her new husband was capable of when he was angry.

Soon Denenholz moved away from the neighborhood. Sweeney seethed because she'd moved in with her lover, a local attorney who, Sweeney charged, "directly subsidizes her household expenses." He attacked the couple's standard of living: "They eat out frequently. They vacationed most recently in Hawaii." He, on the other hand, was suffering from the "prolonged depression in the construction industry" that adversely affected his own income.

AROUND THE TIME SWEENEY WAS splitting up with Denenholz, he had become acquainted with Mary Moore in connection with their political work in SONOMore Atomics, an anti-nuke affinity group begun in 1978. It was part of the Abalone Alliance, the statewide organization attempting to block the building of the controversial Diablo Canyon nuclear plant in San Luis Obispo, or, more precisely, in the little town of Avila.

Moore was a proud native daughter of this community, having been crowned Avila's Fiesta Queen in 1953. She liked to say during demonstrations that she didn't like them "putting a nuke in my home town." She participated in two Alliance mass demonstrations at Diablo Canyon—the first, in 1977, resulting in some 430 arrests. Moore also gained some notoriety for the demonstrations she mounted outside the sylvan Bohemian Grove, where captains of industry and government communed together each year in the woods. The Grove was only a few miles down the road from Moore's own digs in the tangled wilds of Camp Meeker in West Sonoma County.

During their shared affinity-group days—before Judi came on the scene—Moore regarded Sweeney as quiet and serious: "He sat back and took things in. He didn't say much." She approved his "overall political analysis" and regarded it as infinitely more sophisticated than that of the others in the group. She also embraced him as a fellow political veteran like herself, although she knew nothing of his prior involvement with Venceremos.

On several occasions, Sweeney brought his children, Zack and Heather, to the group. Moore liked him for that: "We all looked at him as a good father." But as she saw more of him with the children, she was unsettled by his habit of staring at them so intently it bordered on the obsessive. At the time, she explained it to herself as a father showing obvious love for his children. But she observed that for all his staring, he wasn't that affectionate.

At this point in his life, Sweeney was making a go of things in his refrigerator business and had a new girlfriend, a country hippie known as "Whisper." She had earned the affinity group's respect by getting arrested at the Diablo Canyon nuclear protests. So when Moore found out that Sweeney had abruptly dumped the youngster and taken up with a new woman from back East, she and the rest of the group, she said, "were all prepared to hate her."

As it turned out, the opposite happened. "I just fell in love with Judi Bari," Moore later said. Bari won over the group immediately "because she was smart and she was funny." Moore would always remember her excitement at the start of their friendship: "We hit it off and went out a couple of times by ourselves. There was a women's coffee house in Roseland on Sebastopol Road in Santa Rosa. We spent a few evenings just talking about it all. So we got close. We became really good friends."

Moore liked Bari for her hard edges, which contrasted with the touchy-feely activism that dominated the affinity-style politics of the rural activists in the anti-nuke movement: "Judi had a wicked sense of humor. She was just fun to be around." Moore was a little disturbed by the way her new friend would cut people down behind their backs, but she loved Bari's first witticism at the expense of Sweeney's now ex-girlfriend: "If she's Whisper," Judi quipped, "I'm Shout!"

"Judi was very good at *dissing* everybody," Moore recalled years later. "She would put down anyone she thought was ignorant. She had a cruel streak in her, all right." But unlike Sweeney, whom Moore would come to see as an obstructionist, Bari dutifully showed up for Moore's Bohemian Grove demonstrations. She was dependable on key issues, even when Sweeney opposed her. Moore remembered one such incident in 1979.

After the Three Mile Island nuclear plant meltdown in March 1979—and shortly after Bari had come to California to live with Sweeney—a contingent of anti-nuke activists, including Moore, went to Sacramento and took over Governor Jerry Brown's office in a sit-in. The group was demanding the shutdown of the nearby Rancho Seco nuclear plant, an exact replica of Three Mile Island.

Slyly undercutting the activists, Brown refused to expel them, so they continued to sit in for the better part of three months. "Jerry still came and went to his office," Moore remembered with amusement years later, "and he met with us a couple of times."

The long sit-in began to wreak havoc on Moore's business life. She had to give up the vintage clothes shop she ran. Without income, she requested funds to support herself from other members of the group back in Sonoma.

Most of the group agreed to send money to keep Moore going. Sweeney balked. Worse, he insisted that she meet with Citizens for Safe Energy, a Sacramento group that Moore felt was far too moderate. "But Judi supported me," Moore recalled. "Mike was back there saying no money until you do this. Judi was mad at him for that. She took my side."

Moore points to his stand during the nuke plant demonstration as just one of the signs she saw of Sweeney's "chameleon-like politics." Later on, she realized that Sweeney was undergoing a transformation. It would be years before the change was complete, but he seemed to be putting his militant political activism behind him, just while Judi seemed to be arcing toward hers.

IN LATER YEARS, BARI SOMETIMES said she'd been a "worker" during the time she lived in Sonoma County and that bottling wine in Sonoma wineries had been one of her jobs. She still liked to cast herself as a labor organizer, fighting the bosses. But the seasonal nature of the wine bottling business cast a shadow on this claim.

She related a more authentic version of her life in Sonoma

County to two older leftist Mendocino archivists and oral historians, Russell and Sylvia Bartley, in 1990. "I wasn't real active when I came out here," she told them. "I didn't know anybody and I was kind of too harsh for the Californians. They were all kind of offended by me.... I had a baby fairly shortly after.... I was also helping take care of [my husband's] young children...which kinda took me up for a while." To *New York Times* writer Catherine Bishop, she identified herself back then as a "housewife—the whole suburban trip."

Bari later claimed she was an experienced carpenter, but she nonetheless hired a young carpenter named Pam Davis to work on the Primrose Lane house. From the very first time she met Bari, Davis recalled, "we totally hit it off." Bari just made friends quickly when she liked someone. And although Davis was almost ten years younger than Bari, she had a political history that earned Bari's respect. While still a high school student in Mill Valley in Marin County, she had been a force in the Tamalpais High Women's Union. As a teenager she had organized to defeat the 1978 Briggs Amendment that sought to ban gays from teaching in the classroom.

Beyond shared politics, both women had young children about the same age. Davis later commented on Bari's devotion as a mother and how her behavior with her girls contrasted so clearly with the short shrift she often gave people in the Movement whom she found tiresome or stupid: "She could be offensive and abrupt. She wasn't particularly patient with anyone who wasn't smart. You know there are a lot of airheads out there. She tended to be tough and she was impatient with what she viewed as softness. But she was very tender with her children. They were the most important thing to her."

EVEN BEFORE THEY GOT MARRIED, in 1981, Sweeney and Bari were operating as a political team. They had become involved in several community issues, one of which impinged directly on their life together in their tract home on Primrose Lane. It concerned a nearby airfield that had been a naval facility, built during World War II.

At the time, the facility had multiple commercial uses—as a small airport for private planes, as a pilot training school and as a staging area for crop dusting and banner hauling. The airfield's enormous size—over 700 acres and two runways, one over 7,000 feet long—gave it the potential to generate a small-city-sized boom-let in development. The owners had bought the property from the government after the war. They'd been content to sit on it for years while it appreciated in value as part of the growing Santa Rosa sprawl. But by the end of the 1970s, they decided to seek expansion of the airport itself to be able to handle more flights, including larger planes and jets.

This expansion was just part of a proposed development of commercial and residential facilities on the vacant piece of prime real estate. Santa Rosa had grown exponentially by 1980 to become the biggest city north of San Francisco and change the character of the whole area. (Alfred Hitchcock set his own favorite movie, *Shadow of a Doubt*, in Santa Rosa, using it as a metaphor for small-town decency—echoed pointedly in the Coen brothers' 2001 film, *The Man Who Wasn't There*, set in the Santa Rosa of 1942.)

Sweeney and Bari spearheaded local opposition to the airfield's expansion. Bari told the archivists Russell and Sylvia Bartley:

> [Mike] got obsessed with this little airport...it was right near us....
> [The pilots] used to do their "touch and goes" and they'd go round and round. They'd circle over our house really low. It was annoying, but it wasn't a major political struggle to me.... I really wanted to work with him politically, and he wouldn't work on anything that I was interested in, so I said, "well, okay, I'll work on this."

Bari made it clear, however, that this work was beneath both her and Sweeney's talents as radical organizers, and that they were "way too good for this scenario.... We quickly got a ruling that they could not do that in a residential area." But ultimately, they failed to halt the expansion.

At a 1980 meeting of Sonoma County Board of Supervisors, Sweeney complained that their house was under the flight path and pointed out sarcastically that already the small planes were inter-rupting the neighborhood's afternoon martinis and barbecues. But then an event occurred that made all discussion of the airfield expan-sion moot. In the dark early morning hours of October 30, 1980, flames leaped skyward and engulfed the airport hangar that stood on the huge tract. It was a firebomb that consumed three planes and two businesses operating out of the hangar, and nearly killed the flight instructor for the airport, who was asleep in his camper next to the blazing structure.

According to Bob Williams, whose business was one of those incinerated, the instructor was lucky to escape at all. Williams never forgot the incident and years later his suspicions were rekindled by the car-bombing. He tried to convince journalists, county officials and filmmaker Steve Talbot (in a long correspondence) to reopen the investigation. But clearly Williams didn't have any real evidence involving Sweeney, and Sonoma County law enforcement declined to act on his urgings.

The investigation showed that whoever rigged the firebomb had wired the underground fuel dump containing thousands of gallons of gasoline. A second fuel dump nearby was also wired to blow up, but the device failed to go off. The fire had been set off with bombs, triggered by a Kmart timer device. Bob Williams described the construction: "Now we're talking about hundreds and hundreds of feet of wiring with electronic fuses, surrounded by volatile materials—in some cases just soaked gasoline rags—but stretching throughout both hangars and right into the underground fuel dump."

Sweeney always emphatically denied any involvement in the airport inferno. But Bari would later tell several people—including Talbot and Anna Marie Stenberg—that Sweeney had, indeed, set off the conflagration. She told Talbot that her husband used to "rage at the planes" flying overhead, piloted by student pilots, and that he vowed to "protect his own space." As she explained it to Talbot's investigator, David Helvarg, Sweeney had firebombed the airfield because "if he burns it, he doesn't have to organize." To some confidants, Bari had seemed to be bragging about her husband's radical resourcefulness; to others, she emphasized her disapproval of her husband's role.

EVEN BEFORE THEIR MARRIAGE began to come apart at the seams, Bari was ambivalent about Sweeney. She took pride in her husband for having been, as she told several friends, a "heavy" in the Movement.

But she also resented his machismo and his pulling rank on her in their shared political endeavors.

Soon she began telling a select few of her friends that her husband had smacked her around. These stories of domestic abuse did not surface until after the car-bombing. At that point, people around Bari quickly divided into two camps: those who had been told by Bari of her husband's abuse (and were willing to talk about it), and those who had not.

Mary Moore recalled the incident that tipped her off to the dark side of her friend's marriage. It was in 1982, when Moore had enlisted Bari to apply her creative efforts to a leaflet Moore had in mind for use in protests over the Diablo Canyon nuclear power plant. When Moore arrived to pick up the completed work, Bari answered the door in tears. Moore recalled: "She's got the graphic already done, but instead of just grabbing it and going to the printer, I felt I had to spend some time with her because she was so very upset. And that's when she told me that Mike had just hit her. And once she'd told me that, then she told me of the other times. I think that if I hadn't stumbled on it like that, she might never have told me. She let me know she didn't want that going around. I kept it pretty quiet." But Moore acknowledges that she didn't see any wounds or bruises or other signs of the beating that Judi claimed she had just suffered. In any case, whatever trouble was brewing in the marriage, Bari gave birth to her second child, Jessica, in 1986; and Moore assumed that the couple had gotten their relationship back on course.

But others too were aware of problems in the Sweeney-Bari marriage around this time. One of them was Toni Novak, a long-time political activist then involved with the leftist Peace and Freedom Party, who had met Bari during the Bohemian Grove demonstrations. In 1984, as Novak recalls it, Bari didn't actually block the way and risk arrest, but she did support work for those who did and she attended a big party for them. The house where the party took place was bustling, but Novak said that she and her partner Eldon stood right next to Judi as she engaged in an "intense conversation" in which she told Robin Latham and others that she was "looking for a way out of her marriage." Novak recalled, "She said the marriage was very violent and she wanted to get out. She talked about her options and leaving."

42

Novak occasionally saw Bari and Sweeney socially after that. "There was always tension between them," she recalls. But on the other hand, Bari never described any specific acts of violence. Novak admits that she interpreted Bari's characterization of her marriage based on patterns she recognized from her experience in social work.

One person who recalled a specific story about abuse was David Helvarg. He said that Bari told him of an incident when the couple lived on Primrose Lane. In the middle of an increasingly heated exchange over his first wife, Sweeney became so enraged that he turned on Judi, grabbed her by the throat and slammed her against the wall.

Although Judi told others of her husband's alleged abuse, she never filed a complaint or called authorities or even cited domestic abuse in her divorce proceedings.

For his part, Sweeney consistently and vigorously denied that he had ever physically abused his wife. In a letter challenging a *Los Angeles Times* story that raised the issue of domestic abuse, Sweeney wrote:

> The claim that Bari was a silent, secret victim of domestic abuse is absurd in the context of everything that is known about her. She was a brown belt in karate, famously tough in all her disputes with people, and a militant feminist. To suggest that she would suffer beatings without calling the police or getting a restraining order, or even just moving away, is ridiculous. There is no documentation of any kind to substantiate domestic violence against Bari—not a medical report, photograph, eyewitness statement, or any comment in Bari's voluminous writings or interviews. A deputy sheriff who kept [a] close eye on his neighbors lived next door to Bari and Sweeney from 1987 to 1990, and never reported any sign of domestic strife.

Was Bari lying when she talked of being a victim of abuse? She told a half-dozen friends and acquaintances about suffering at the hands of her husband during their marriage and after their divorce, when they were still residing on the same property. But the fact remains that she was not always truthful in other areas of her life.

DESPITE THE MARITAL TENSIONS, Bari and Sweeney continued to work as a political team on occasion. Both were involved in efforts to block Hewlett-Packard from building a big facility in Rohnert Park, a fast-growing suburb just south of Santa Rosa. The proposed HP facility would be enormous. Once again, Bari said she had joined her husband reluctantly. "It was very well done, but not a good target.... But we ran a good campaign," she said of the 1982 neighborhood canvassing waged by a handful of people under Sweeney's direction. "I was certainly [equal to] Mike—actually probably more—but Mike wanted to be the General and me to be the First Lieutenant, and I wasn't willing to do that either."

Already a presence in the community, HP relied on its workers, who proved big boosters of the company. The new facility, estimated to cost $345 million, would be able to employ some 8,000 workers, and eventually put as many as 12,000 to work.

Sweeney and Bari argued against the plant on environmental grounds, accusing HP of polluting ground water and other environmental crimes, and citing some cancer clusters in the area to bolster their claims. They filed a lawsuit against HP. They were represented by Susan Brandt, then a rookie attorney, who went on to become a well-known environmental attorney in California.

Apparently Sweeney and Bari didn't understand that they would be personally liable if they should lose the case. They did, and were assessed $12,000 in court costs. Though there had been twelve others involved as plaintiffs, most of them didn't own property like Sweeney. The court ruled that Hewlett-Packard could assess the plaintiffs individually. Sweeney's response to this turn of events won grudging praise from Bari. When one of the HP executives called their home looking for financial information, Sweeney told the man that he and his wife wanted to drop the suit but others in their group wanted to appeal, and that the rift was causing the group unity to disintegrate. Sweeney then told the man that in order to drop out, he needed to "get out from under this $12,000." HP agreed to let the plaintiffs, who until this time had been held jointly responsible for the judgment, withdraw from the legal action individually. "So everybody with property dropped out," Bari laughed in retelling the story in 1990.

Subsequently Bari and Sweeney filed another suit, this time against Caltrans, the state highway agency, and collected on this one by signing off on a contested overpass for the widening of Highway 12 from a two-lane to a four-lane artery. The couple was learning that there was gold in bringing nuisance suits under the moral authority of the environmental movement against deep pockets like the State of California or Hewlett-Packard. It was win-win: good politics and good money.

But while Bari bragged about her husband's tactical "brilliance," she was bothered by his withdrawal from radicalism. "He became very parochial and small-minded," she said later on. "I mean, I thought I had married my comrade-lover and I thought it was a breach of contract that he didn't want to go to the meetings and stuff." Her sharp-tongued criticism of his "moderation" increased the tension between them. She later quoted Sweeney as saying he had sworn off radicalism because "it didn't work." Bari said she responded with a declaration of her own: "So I said, 'Well, fuck you, I'm still going to be politically active.'" Bari became involved in Central American politics and at one point even enlisted Sweeney to help her raise money to buy tractors to send to the Sandinistas.

The couple decided that with a new baby, they should try to patch up their crumbling relationship. They planned to leave Sonoma and began house-hunting in rural Mendocino County to make a new start. They purchased a partially developed site in Redwood Valley, moving there in November of 1986.

Bari and Sweeney hosted a goodbye party in the back yard of their Santa Rosa house. Judi's friend Mary Moore showed up with the affinity group SONOMore Atomics, including her other pals Tanya Brannan and Darlene Comingore. Bari's intention to move forward into radical politics, even if this meant doing it without her mate, seemed to be confirmed by a gag photo taken at the party showing her, Moore and Brannan holding up Mao's Little Red Book. Bari also waved the red flag of revolution.

FIVE

NINETY MILES NORTH OF SAN FRANCISCO, Mendocino County is home to some of the most beautifully rugged coastline to be found anywhere in the world. The wild Pacific sends its waves crashing against house-sized boulders. Strewn just offshore, these stone outcrops look as if an angry Colossus standing on the edge of a continent had hurled them into the sea. Much of the year, for all its beauty, the North Coast is fogged in. But on a fine late-summer day, the Mediterranean pales by comparison.

Highway 1, the scenic coastal route to Mendocino, is arduous—all hairpin turns; so most visitors from the Bay Area prefer to come by freeway to the town of Cloverdale and then take the rambling Highway 128 through the rolling golden hills of the Anderson Valley, before dropping down again into the apple orchards and sweet-smelling wooded banks along the Navarro River and through the town of Boonville. Boonville is the home of the Mendocino County Fair under a harvest-hot September sun, with its famous pig races and sheepdog trials, and fruits and vegetables that are judged on appearance, not taste.

Boonville is also the seat of Bruce Anderson's quirky muck-raking and community-minded *Anderson Valley Advertiser* (AVA). It has hip subscribers all over the country, and also sells well in Berkeley and San Francisco kiosks. Its motto of "Peace to the cottages! War on the palaces!" invokes a revolutionary fervor that is more whimsical than incendiary, but is still a reminder that there are yet Trotskyites and Stalinists to be found amid the touchy-feelies and rednecks scattered through the hinterlands of Mendocino.

Boonville's downtown is only seven blocks long, but its cultural heritage is strong. The town has (or had) its own language, "Boontling," an insider's way of talking, described in the colorful novel *Boonville* (by Robert Mailer Anderson, nephew of Bruce) as "the town's odd lingo...which had sprouted around the turn of the century at 'hop-pickin' campaigns,' a mish-mash of slang that used English as its base." The novelist describes the longtime residents of the old Boonville as men in "dirty work shirts, rifles in the gun racks of their pickup trucks, a half-mouth of teeth between them." They said "wee heese" for small house. "Horn of Zeese" is Boontling for "cup of coffee," because that was the name of the town coffee shop. (It is still there.) Boonville is called "Boont" in Boontling, good food is "bahl gorms" and tasty wine to wash it down is "bahl seep." For the devotees of Boont, words were a means of keeping people out.

Thomas Pynchon's *Vineland* is a testament to the oddball behavior in the county, including the beefs between and among its citizenry. The notoriously reclusive author lived in the county for a spell, and the mythological place of the book's title is clearly Mendocino County. At one point, Bruce Anderson fully believed that the extensive and very literary correspondence addressed over several years to the AVA from a "Wanda Tinaski" was actually written by Pynchon, but then Wanda turned out to be a literate older hippie drunk who eventually murdered his wife and then killed himself.

LEAVING TOWN, HEADING WEST, Highway 128 continues through the tiny hamlet of Philo ("Poleeko" in Boontling), home to radio station KZYX—full of half-baked revolution, composting tips and country recipes, and also at one point a venue for Judi Bari's own show.

Across the road from Philo is Hendy National Forest with its stately groves of virgin redwoods, which are among the most beautiful in the county. The forest floor beneath them is soft as a down pillow and seasonally dotted with the single-blossomed trillium, providing a retinal shock of pointillist white petals.

There in Philo too is the Navarro Vineyard, whose beauty looks deceptively as if it had been passed down through the centuries and whose Gewürztraminers are unequalled, particularly when sipped under the pergola in back, along with artisan cheeses that rival some of the best in southern France. During harvest season, large swarms of black starlings blot out the sun as they wheel in arcs above the staked vines. The Navarro is one of many vineyards that have sprung up in Anderson Valley to take advantage of a hot summer climate cooled nightly with Pacific breezes, ideal for Pinot Noirs, Pinot Gris, Chardonnays and sprightly Rieslings.

The Navarro River eventually winds out to the coast and descends to the ocean, while the Coastal Range above the river rises sharply to 1,300 feet before dropping abruptly to the Pacific. Dozens of waterways emerge from the forests up and down the Mendocino coast and come out at Highway 1 to meet little towns and communities perched over the sea, like Gualala and Elk. Albion Ridge rises above a fishing hamlet on the Albion River, lifting off steeply up a spine of hillside and stretching inland, away from the Pacific, then broadening to high grassy land that was settled and subdivided during the 1970s by pioneering feminists—most of them lesbian and quite a few of them self-identified poets. They built barns and raised Nubian goats and gardens, and for a while discussed the banishment of male sons (but not the billy goats) so as to preserve harmony with their vision of a militant Sapphic polis—a kind of country Amazonia wedded to organic Mother Nature.

In 1975 they published *Country Women: A Handbook for the New Farmer,* which encouraged women to get out there and hoe, while handing down the how-to's of farming, building, land purchasing and everything else a gal needed to know in order to be independent on the land. In contrast to the pragmatic good sense of this book, these women also dosed their following with the pagan spirituality and woman/goddess worship that persists throughout the county and is manifest in their soft-sell poetry:

> Thru [sic] many moons the mountain was waiting:
>> For a dancer to float above its fog.
>> For a spirit to soar high as its hawks.
>> For a body to roll thru [sic] its flowers.
>> For a laughter [sic] to echo its joy.
>> For a soul to drink of its secrets.
>> And for a smile to soothe its storms.
> Now, in this thirsty year of the big snow

the mountain found
a woman Diane
who calls it home.

On another bend on Highway 1, near the hamlet of Little River, there are wondrous pygmy forests set in sandy soil and then, further on, the shacks and humble structures with their country debris outside, the telltale detritus of back-to-the-landers. North from Little River is the perfect little seaside town of Mendocino proper, one of only two nationally registered village heritage preserves. It is a village of kitschy Victorian bed-and-breakfasts transformed from manses and old-fashioned stores of the rural past.

Steven Spielberg shot the townie scenes from the movie *Jaws* here, shamelessly masquerading Mendocino as a faux New England village. (Ditto the 1965 satire *The Russians Are Coming, the Russians Are Coming.*)

North from Mendocino along twisting roads lined with gnarled cypress, the coastline continues past Fort Bragg, a town founded on lumber and fishing, although the catch is dwindling year by year. Once it was a company town for the timber corporation Georgia-Pacific, but the company has recently closed its doors: the big trees are gone for the most part in Mendocino except for those on federal and state preserves.

Up from the coast to the ridges and spilling down the eastern side is the coastal range of redwoods, among them virgin stands—groves that have never been logged—whose enormous trees date back to the time of Christ. The magnificent trees and the coastal bluffs as well are draped with cloud cover much of the year. Along with the heavy rain for almost four months during the winter, this climate is perfect for the mighty redwoods. (In adjacent Humboldt County, which is also home to virgin redwoods, the rainfall is some 200 inches a year!) In the few groves of ancient redwoods remaining in Humboldt and Mendocino, there are primordial ferns, some taller than a man, that suck their nutrients out of the decay of dead trees and their foliage, which thickens the forest floor up to twelve feet deep.

As recently as forty years ago there were 30 mills in the little hamlet of Branscomb alone, between the coast above Fort Bragg and

Laytonville on Highway 101. There were 30 in Laytonville and 30 more in Willits. Today there is only one independent concern left in the area, Harwood Lumber in Branscomb, a small company with 270 workers producing 140 million board feet a year.

There is still forest primeval in Mendocino, according to Harwood's CEO, Art Harwood; and he believes that if you log selectively, the redwoods will always be there. But most of Mendocino's passionate environmentalists say it is already too late.

WITH SO MUCH UNINCORPORATED territory, social experiments in the form of communes and alternative communities began springing up in Mendocino County in a big way in the 1970s. Some exhibited a benign, back-to-nature silliness. Others achieved a niche commercial success. Wavy Gravy and Hog Farm members, originally memorialized by Ken Kesey for their psychedelic caravans around the country introducing LSD to the hinterlands, bought a huge chunk of land just north of Laytonville on Highway 101. The Hog Farm settled there as a commune for a while, then set up a counter-cultural camp where kids still come each summer, and an annual weekend music fest with admission in recent years pegged at forty or fifty bucks, including camping privileges on the ample grounds. Attendees can get stoned for the whole weekend, and rock out with plenty of good vegan food for sale at some of the hundreds of déjà vu hippie booths, which also sell crafts, tie-dye garments and leather fringes, along with bumper stickers and literature for causes updated from the Sixties and Seventies: legalization of marijuana initiatives, Earth First! and the Green Party.

Some communes have remained in Mendocino, but many more have come and gone. Mendocino County could boast of, or shudder with, the knowledge that Charles Manson hung out for a while in the tiny town of Albion. Jim Jones' People's Temple moved here in the late 1960s before it relocated to San Francisco and eventually mutated into a death cult in Guyana. The notorious child kidnapper "Tree Frog" Johnson also lived in Mendocino and, in the loose communal mores of the times, had access to the hippies' children to sexually molest as he desired.

The vast majority of criminality here in the backwoods—other than the usual drunken redneck fighting on the weekends—is in drugs. There was a "heroin cult" for a time, according to Fort Bragg writer and environmentalist Roanne Withers: "They'd shoot heroin for six months a year and then go back to fishing." But pot has always been the cash crop and money drug since the hippie invasion of the 1970s. Straight people grow it. Vets grow it. And, of course, all those un- or semi-employed folk who people the towns from Mendocino up to Humboldt grow it.

In Garberville, reputed to be the pot capital not only of Humboldt County but of the whole region, locals would note the sudden influx of folk from the hinterland right after harvest time. Everyone then was flush. And then after an orgy of spending and consumption those free-spenders would disappear for most of the rest of the year. There were also big growers who came to town in fancy pickups. With big money came lawlessness of a kind far more sinister than the hippies' casual libertarian misdemeanors. Roanne Withers and others rue the day the "criminal element" came to Mendocino and Humboldt in the 1980s because of the "guns and death" they brought with them.

For years, people had grown pot on public lands and camouflaged it—sometimes strung up in black plastic bags high up in the trees and watered by almost invisible plastic pipe. But increasingly, side by side with the new pot growers were the new methamphetamine manufacturers. The two types of criminality accounted for an increase in jailed drug offenders of 51 percent between 1983 to 1993. Nonviolent drug offenders increased 65 percent in just five years.

But no recitation of statistics can convey the sheer numbers of the population engaged in cultivation. Even back in Ronald Reagan's presidency, the Bureau of Land Management director, Robert Buford, estimated that the annual marijuana crop on federal land alone in California was in excess of $1.2 billion a year. In Mendocino and Humboldt Counties, most residents know full well that marijuana, not lumber or even tourism, is the primary source of income in the county; and this being the case, even that part of the population that opposes drugs in principle regards pot as a cash crop necessary for the survival of the whole North Coast economy.

With marijuana cultivation on the rise and logging on the wane, lumber still remained big business in Mendocino. It didn't matter that over 50 percent of the land ownership in Mendocino County was (and probably still is) in the hands of logging companies. The immigrants who began arriving in the 1960s couldn't help taking a proprietary attitude toward their new home's natural beauty. Many became expert so they could cite chapter and verse of watersheds, of sustainable yields, of how many acres a threatened spotted owl needed to survive in the forest. Many of them embraced the use of water and solar power sources (even as they burned vast quantities of wood in stoves and fireplaces to keep warm) and built composting outhouses to avoid having to sign up for any Mendocino County energy or sewer systems. Most put their deep ecology into practice, consuming little—except for dope—and eating low on the food chain. (One environmental attorney on North Coast timber issues, according to writer David Harris, claimed famously to have lived for a year on $65 worth of brown rice.)

In local towns they founded organic markets, recycled clothing boutiques and swap meets, solar power stores and hydroponic cultivation supply outlets; they sold indoor grow lights and everything else one needed for growing weed except the seed itself. These emporiums became marketplaces of social and political intercourse. If there was a contradiction in driving huge distances to get to such places, guzzling tanks-full of fossil fuel in the process, few pointed it out.

Given how many were engaged in illegal cultivation, and given the atmosphere of Wild West immigration, the land and the culture became a haven for subversive ideas and a distrust of government that rivaled the Appalachian moonshiners' hostility to federal agents. County government was virtually an absence of government, which meant there was a general laissez-faire toleration of illegal cultivation, until the DEA came in with choppers swooping down on public stashes and burning them, or landing on a remote back yard to arrest the natives and confiscate their crops. The *Anderson Valley Advertiser* is always filled with attorney ads promising help for drug arrests.

THIS WAS THE MILIEU THAT JUDI BARI and Mike Sweeney entered in 1986

when they arrived at their new homestead on Humphrey Lane in Redwood Valley. Immediately the pair went to work at making the garage into habitable quarters for the whole family so that their dream of converting the skeleton of the main house into a showcase to be sold at a good profit could be realized more quickly, and so they wouldn't meanwhile have to live amid the construction.

Once the garage was readied, they could gut most of the old house while retaining the walls to satisfy Redwood Valley's zoning laws and escape the need for a building permit. Irv Sutley, a friend and tenant of Judi's pal Pam Davis who shared lefty politics with both women, recalls the future upscale house as simply a shell on an early visit there. It was Sweeney's project, but Bari did much of the finish work on it.

In 1987, flashing a carpenter's union card, Bari landed a real job working for California Yurts in Hopland, just south of Ukiah, owned by David Raitt (brother of singer Bonnie Raitt) and his wife, Annie. When Raitt first met her, he said, Bari was financially needy, but wanting to strike out on her own. He had heard that she was a sheet-rocker. His company was looking for a subcontractor to sheet-rock the interior of a store called "Tin Man." Raitt first hired Judi to do only that job, but, satisfied with her subcontract work, he then hired her full-time to work for his yurts business.

David Raitt had come out to Ukiah in 1974 and started a yurt-making commune with friends from back East. Yurts are the native transportable nomadic domiciles of Mongolians on the Eastern steppes—the equivalent of the American Indian teepee, but roomier and more adaptable to modern life, especially with the improvements that latter-day hippie entrepreneurs like Raitt added to the original concept for back-to-the-land immigrants who wanted to live off the grid.

While yurts began as alternative housing in hippie enclaves, they later entered the mainstream as fast, cheap housing solutions for social agencies dealing with some dislocated populations, such as Central American guest workers during grape-picking season in Napa's many vineyards. The Raitts' yurts were multisided redwood structures and far more upscale. Instead of being made of animal skins as in Mongolia, they consisted of redwood panels running 36 to 48 inches wide and tall enough to be two stories high. These were put together in a circle. Raitt manufactured different sizes of yurts to suit the buyers' needs.

In the beginning, Bari didn't much care what material the yurts were made of; she was primarily concerned with money. She later told Catherine Bishop of the *New York Times* that she was a "self-taught carpenter," which in effect was an admission that the journeyman card she flashed at Raitt was a fraud. Nevertheless, she was one of the better workers he had, and based on the card and her demands, he made her foreman at his shop, a promotion that other employees resented. Raitt said that Bari looked good compared with his regular workers: "yahoo hicks, lesbian ironworkers and Indians, and one black guy." Years later he could still tick off from memory the houses Bari had labored on. She ran a crew of three or four men who "didn't want to take orders from a woman."

Will McAfee, for one, remembered Bari's investiture as foreman in a different light. McAfee, a fellow worker who first knew Bari from their Sonoma County days in Central American political demonstrations, saw her promotion in California Yurts as part of the political correctness of the times and also as a response to Bari's aggressive campaign to snooker her boss into making her management.

"Judi and I worked together in situations where she had no expertise, yet she insisted she be foreman on every other construction," McAfee recalled later. "She wanted to share duties with the regular foreman, who was very experienced. Raitt went along with it. He was willing to make concessions to her because he respected her politically."

It was during her last job for the Raitts that Bari went through what she would describe as an "apocalyptic experience." California Yurts had been hired by a veterinarian named Larry Chaulk who was intent on building a hip new structure with solar power and progressive architecture in the sweetly pastoral town of Boonville as a second home to complement his base in San Bruno. (He opened a second veterinarian office there as well.) Bari worked on both the manufacture and the installation of exterior redwood siding for the solar-powered home.

Years after her work there, Bari would still rail against Chaulk as "a rich man," and against his palatial digs—most notably in her interview with Beth Bosk in the *New Settler* before the car bombing early in 1990: "It was a 2500 square foot house, for one man—his country home which he would come to for weekends.... I was appalled. I thought the house we were building was disgusting anyway. It was a Playboy mansion, which offended me in the first place...and then to be using thousand year old trees on it."

Over the years, Bari would tell many listeners of the epiphany she experienced while installing the old virgin redwood on that job. In her recounting it would become the source of inspiration for her joining Earth First. Like all good storytellers, she told the tale repeatedly, imbuing it with the sin-to-righteousness narrative of the born-again.

This is the way the story went: One day she was at work in the Hopland headquarters of California Yurts. At the time she didn't know much of anything about redwoods. She just sawed it and hammered nails into it. She was looking at a twenty-foot-long slab of redwood, noticing the wood, admiring its tight grain. It was flawless, without any knots. Gary Ball was also working there at the company site in Hopland that day. He was the bookkeeper for Raitt, but also one of the prime movers behind the Mendocino Environmental Center—"the MEC"—in Ukiah. His wife, Betty, was then the MEC director.

Bari turned to him and asked, "Gary, is this old-growth redwood?" He told her that particular slab was a thousand years old and that it had come from the Salmon Creek clear-cut in Humboldt. She was savvy enough by that point to know that clear-cuts, where loggers stripped every living tree from a designated swath, turned the landscape into something resembling a war zone and had an adverse effect upon the whole ecology of the forest. The idea that she was hammering and sawing a thousand-year-old piece of nature changed her life.

But however dramatic this story was in the retelling, Gary Ball's revelation didn't stop Bari from working for the Raitts. She completed Chaulk's house, even after being profoundly affected by the old-growth redwood slab. Just as the job was wrapping up, though, she got herself a photocopy of the Salmon Creek clear-cut, framed it and put it up on Chaulk's wall as a parting shot.

It would gall her that a hunk of redwood so beautiful had been cut to satisfy a rich man's vulgar craving for luxury. For Bari there would always be the added rub that Chaulk was financially flush, and somehow the simple vows of country poverty taken by environmentalists and Maoists alike made the gap between the rich and the poor—even the voluntary poor—in such a setting more pronounced. For Bari that gap engendered more class hostility.

Judi Bari's version of her epiphany was recited verbatim with great pathos and emotion by her followers as if their heroine were Paul just returning from the Road to Damascus. Larry Chaulk's version conveyed a different truth. Chaulk always claimed he was innocent of environmental rape: he neither had the virgin redwood cut nor had it milled. As a matter of fact, he didn't order it at all and intended to use Douglas fir!

He had contracted out the work to California Yurts, but before Bari came on the job, Chaulk says, he and the Raitts got wind of a single old-growth virgin redwood tree that had already been taken and sold, and was slated to be shipped to Japan. The idea made Chaulk sick. A patriot who candidly admitted his hostility to all things Japanese as a holdover from World War II, he said that a good part of his motivation in getting that virgin redwood was "to keep it out of the hands of those maniac samurai."

Raitt agreed to help him. Chaulk thought the wood very beautiful and was glad to have it for the two yurts he put up on his forty-acre parcel, which included one of the largest stands of virgin redwoods held privately in the area. He insisted that he was no less reverent in his love of those rare trees than Bari, and no less suspicious of those who take out trees, having once worked for the forest service when he was nineteen years old. But Bari continued to freak out over the use of the redwood, complaining to the Raitts about it as well. After a while it got on Chaulk's nerves. He tried to tell her about the redwood being cut and milled for the Japanese before he ever got in on the deal. He asked her if she thought it should go there. She ignored the mitigation.

"I told her if she cared so much about the environment, she should be riding a donkey, not driving a car," Chaulk says. "At least a donkey fertilizes the earth. She'd be madder than hell when I'd pull that on her."

Years later, Chaulk sold off his property with the stipulation that the stand of virgin redwoods on it never be cut down. Bari never talked about that.

SIX

JUDI'S EMBRACE OF THE REDWOODS was less a matter of moving on to the next big thing than of filling the political emptiness she'd felt since marrying Sweeney. Soon after their arrival in Redwood Valley in 1986, her first entry into the political fray was not environmentalism, but "anti-imperialism." In Sonoma she had been involved in the Pledge for Peace in Central America. Now she anointed herself regional coordinator for the Pledge of Resistance, the militant direct-action group opposed to U.S. aid to the Contras in Nicaragua and to the U.S. intervention in El Salvador. It was a continuation of the same work she had taken on as part of her vow before she had even left Santa Rosa to break away from Sweeney's boring community work and return to the kind of militant politics she'd always preferred.

It was natural that Judi gravitated to Central America, then the front-burner issue for the left, although to hear Judi tell it later, she would have preferred union organizing, hoping to recreate the success she experienced back in Maryland. But Bari said she'd looked hard in both Sonoma and Mendocino Counties and found that capitalists had "exported capital, but also labor." In truth, she did find the proletariat she sought in the wine industry, but lamented to Russell and Sylvia Bartley that she couldn't "speak Spanish" and therefore could not organize the predominantly Mexican laborers. She then reasoned, "ergo, imperialism is the primary contradiction. 'I will work on Central America.' And that is how I got into the Central American Movement."

In Northern California, the Pledge of Resistance demonstrations were held regularly at the Concord Naval Weapons Station at the edge of Livermore, the sleepy valley town about an hour east of Berkeley and the Bay. Outside chain-link fences and barbed wire, the demonstrators assembled in ragtag groups with signs declaring their opposition to the Contras and U.S. aid. These demonstrators were peaceful and committed to civil disobedience, although Bari, according to her accounts and those of fellow activists, was always pushing for more militant actions, like tearing up the railroad tracks or ignoring guards and sheriffs to force their way onto government property.

The Pledge of Resistance was actually a loosely scattered group whose phone tree could round up hundreds of activists when a shipment of arms was about to depart from the Concord station. (In the days before e-mail, each person would call so many on his list; they, in turn, telephoned another list, and so on.) Most of the actions undertaken by the demonstrators were symbolic, such as sitting down on the tracks and then moving when the cops came. Bari wanted them to really stop the trains and trucks. (She was arrested in February 1988 for failure to disperse in a Pledge demonstration in front of the Federal Building in Santa Rosa.) But they weren't as radical as she was.

Will McAfee, Bari's California Yurts coworker who was involved with her in both the Sonoma and the Mendocino Pledge of Resistance, observed her souring on Central American politics. McAfee recalled one particular demonstration held at the Concord Naval Weapons Station. It was in the wake of activist Brian Willson's ill-fated decision to lie down on the tracks to stop a train transporting weapons from the depot to ships headed for Central America. Willson had failed to get off the tracks and the train could not stop. In a bloody horror, the train crushed his legs, both of which had to be amputated.

Neither Bari nor McAfee had been present that day, but Judi had quickly led the Mendocino Pledge contingent, including McAfee, in a caravan south to protest Willson's mutilation. Jessie Jackson, Joan Baez and Daniel Ellsberg were the headliners that day. When the speakers were through, the activists solemnly planted flowers around the railroad tracks, a gesture Bari regarded as pointless. "Judi was much more confrontational," McAfee said. "She was into pushing the limits: urging everyone to climb over the fence to stand on private land as she did later in the timber wars."

For all his criticism of Bari when the two of them worked for the Raitts—and his feeling that she had bamboozled David Raitt for the foreman job—McAfee, like many activists in those parts, ultimately admired her. He still cringed, however, when he recalled the demonstration they once joined at the El Rancho Tropicana—"a cheap, sleazy hotel," he called it (since torn down) at the southern end of Santa Rosa. The group was protesting the appearance of a Contra spokesman who was the brother of a major Nicaraguan Contra leader.

They had been sitting around chanting "Peace" and "We shall overcome." Then Bari appeared with her bullhorn—her way of making sure her voice prevailed—and took over. She began reading loudly from a list of graphically described atrocities attributed to the Contras. McAfee characterizes her and another woman, Susan Crane, as very "confrontational."

The manager of El Rancho Tropicana came out several times to warn them that if they didn't cease and desist, he would call the police. Crane wanted to stay and get arrested; but oddly, given her militant rhetoric, Bari did not. She had come to the demonstration with her daughter Lisa, who was then about six years old. She said she couldn't risk getting arrested when she had her daughter with her; so she took off, leaving the others to face the arrests that she had provoked.

One reason for Bari's caution may have been that a domestic war had been rekindled between her and Sweeney. She wanted to continue with her political activism, but according to one of her closest friends during this period, Sweeney "wanted her barefoot and pregnant."

Sweeney had grown more adamant in opposing her political activism—especially when she dragged along the couple's older daughter. In the troubled household, Lisa was increasingly her mother's runaround daughter, while Sweeney often took care of the younger Jessica, definitely daddy's favorite. (Bari told the archivists that after the couple's divorce came through in 1988, her ex-husband "stole custody of my younger daughter against the divorce agreement.")

The same close friend at the time characterizes Judi's relationship with Sweeney as a marriage of humiliation: "Mike definitely abused her on an emotional level—he didn't take her seriously—but there were also several incidents of physical conflicts. She'd come [to see me] extremely upset. I encouraged her to get away, but Judi was reluctant. She was still in the very emotional state of 'what the hell can I do?' She expressed fear of him."

And when it wasn't about politics and Bari's straining to get out into the world, it was about the house they were building in Redwood Valley. "The house became the record of the demise of the marriage," Bari's friend observes. She describes the house as having four bedrooms but only one bath for the four of them. She says Bari fought with Sweeney to get one room as an office for herself. Instead, he gave her a cubicle: "But there were no windows. It was very, very small. He called it a 'sewing room,' which was pretty derogatory. The whole house was pretty chopped up. It was a metaphor for the marriage."

For public consumption, Bari summed up her relationships, and particularly her marriage to Sweeney, this way to Beth Bosk in the *New Settler* interview that took place just before the car-bombing: "It's a real pattern in my life that men fall in love with me because of my activism and up-frontness, and then try to repress it as soon as they get into a relationship with me—like my daughters' father tried to get me to just stay home and take care of kids and not do anything else, which I was never willing to do."

She began hanging out more and more at the Mendocino Environmental Center in Ukiah. There she formed a friendship with Betty Ball, whose husband, Gary, she already knew from California Yurts. Betty was the resident mother hen of an odd brood of hippies and activists who used the MEC as a political clearing-house and communications center for Mendocino and even Humboldt political events, not only environmental but ecumenically leftist causes like the United Farm Workers (UFW) or pro-choice rallies. Betty Ball was also ready and willing to use the MEC network for people's housing or other needs, as she did when she got Fred the Walking Rainbow together with Pam Davis. The MEC's community posting board was a way for people to stay in touch before the advent of e-mail.

The MEC was in an old brick building, just across from the county courthouse. It was owned by John McCowen, who came from an old Ukiah family; his father had been a judge in the area. McCowen rented out the place for peanuts, even after surrounding property values climbed. In time, the MEC became a theater for Bari's politics. But initially it was the site where Bari first was introduced to the political aspects of the redwoods movement she had joined emotionally while working on Larry Chaulk's yurt. It was at the MEC that she began to hear about a group of radical environmentalists that sounded like the perfect antidote to the pallid politics of the groups protesting the war in Central America and nuclear power. The group was Earth First!—part of whose mystique involved the exclamation point at the end of its name.

EARTH FIRST, SO THE MYTHOLOGY GOES, was founded in 1980 by a bunch of environmentally inclined, college-educated, self-professed rednecks out in the Sonoran desert near Arizona, with environmental lobbyist Dave Foreman the natural leader. The group had gone camping and climbing in Pinacate, the Mexican National Park some twenty-two miles east of the Sea of Cortez. The stark landscape of sand desert and old lava encrustation was stunning, full of craters and cones. Fueled by generous rations of canned beer and marijuana—for the one pothead in the group—they decided the time had come for life to imitate art. In this case, the gang self-consciously chose to emulate the characters in Edward Abbey's best-selling novel, *The Monkey Wrench Gang*, and commit select acts of sabotage in the name of ecology.

The moment of revelation actually occurred just after the desert retreat while they were all driving home, spun out with retinal burn, booze and hiking fatigue.[*] They agreed that they had all lost faith in the Wilderness Society and other environmental nonprofits for which they had labored for long hours and low wages. They had been calculating the wilderness losses for months and years. They

---

[*] I am indebted to Susan Zakin's history of Earth First, *Coyotes and Town Dogs*, for the group's origins.

had watched the negotiating, the compromise that always meant a patchwork saved while ecosystems as a whole were lost.

The beginning of their collective disaffection could perhaps be dated back to 1968 and the ensuing years of struggle for the Black Mesa in high desert country, an area claimed by both Hopi and Navajo Indians as sacred. The plan for commercial exploitation began with a new coal mine to do stripping, a death knell for the mesa.

The Black Mesa Defense Fund (founded by Marc Gaede in 1970) managed in two short years to set off six lawsuits; but two years later, the mining proceeded. The efforts to save the land were a failure even though the environmentalists had extracted a weak promise by the Peabody Coal Company to restore some of the land after it was gouged. It was then that some of the disappointed enviros turned to "ecotage," according to writer Susan Zakin: "They also tried—and in true anarchist fashion, failed—to blow up a coal slurry line."

If Earth First's roots seemed to have sprung from that failure, there had been earlier glimmerings of the eco-radicalism to come. In Zakin's account, Marc Gaede and his childhood friend, *Cheers* actor Ted Danson, were already toppling billboards—five hundred of them, they claimed—in the desert along Route 66 or 180 near the Grand Canyon when they were teenagers in the Sixties. And there were other models for Earth First desert rats. One of them was a mysterious saboteur nicknamed "the Arizona Phantom," who for a while tore up Peabody's Black Mesa railroad tracks every night, as well as disabling heavy equipment by extracting vital parts of tractors, a grader and a scraper. The Phantom finally disappeared, but not before secretly distributing, as Zakin described it, gifts to neophyte eco-saboteurs: "hammers, tool belts, ten-penny nails in bulk—the tools and supplies for tree spiking."

Another anonymous character, "the Fox" (possibly so called after his locale in Fox River, Illinois), did his ecotage in the Midwest. In 1970 the Fox choked up the illegal (according to Zakin) drains of soap companies and "capped their smoking chimneys" as if acting out the mad chiaroscuro of outsider artist Heinrich Kley, who early in the twentieth century protested an industrial age by drawing giant, grinning genies straddling and derailing trains or stopping up belching smoke stacks with the palms of their oversized hands. The Fox also took credit for dumping a fifty-pound jar of sludge on the office carpet of a U.S. Steel executive.

Around Tucson, another fleeting ecotage group was born in the summer of 1971. Calling themselves the Tucson Eco-Raiders, these college kids tilted their lances at shopping centers, cheap housing developments and convenience stores that were rapidly supplanting the Sonoran desert landscape of saguaro and other native bloom. They slashed hundreds of billboards, pulled survey stakes of new housing tracts, ripped out electrical and plumbing fixtures of unfinished new houses, broke windows, sabotaged heavy equipment and, as one Eco-Raider confessed to the underground paper the *Berkeley Barb*, destroyed "any object representing the outer edges of urban sprawl." Finally targeted by law enforcement in 1973, the five Eco-Raiders were busted.

Dave Foreman had seen all this and more in the various jobs he held for the Wilderness Society. He, along with his western counterparts in the freewheeling organization, dubbed themselves "the Buckaroos" after a song by Jerry Jeff Walker, a country-and-western singer. While the rest of the country's youths were gyrating to rock-and-roll, Foreman and his fellow western ecology activists listened to Waylon Jennings and Willie Nelson; and they preferred copious amounts of beer to the psychedelics ingested by their contemporaries in protest movements. Foreman even disclosed years later that he'd once been a Goldwater Republican.

No one remembers exactly when Foreman had his revelation about the name of the new radical eco-organization—Earth First!— nor who coined the slogan "No compromise in defense of Mother Earth." But the organization was born on the group's way back from Arizona in 1980 with their mutual agreement on principles. It would be, above all, an organization unfettered by office hierarchies. There would be no official leaders or positions, and they wouldn't worry about fundraising. They would be happily anarchistic, "a nomadic action group" with no headquarters. They would spread the word in novel, imaginative ways and, as in the old Maoist mantra adopted by the New Left, "let a thousand flowers bloom." Not only could anyone join Earth First; anyone could *be* Earth First. Any and all were welcome to appropriate the name, to act locally and independently.

Earth First "members" were encouraged to take action in behalf of threatened wilderness in various ways. One was ecotage—the anonymous sabotage of development in the wild—and it ranged from the simple pulling up of surveyor's stakes, to taking out any big equipment by fouling fuel lines, planting explosives or whatever else worked. But while the tools of development were legitimate targets, the architects of development were not. "Do not harm human lives" was an explicit Earth First principle.

But later on, the seeming humanitarianism of Earth Firsters showed a callous side. One of them wrote anonymously in a 1987 *Earth First! Journal* essay that AIDS was nature's way of culling excess population: "If the AIDS epidemic didn't exist, radical environmentalists would have to invent one." And Foreman himself, referring to a devastating famine in Ethiopia, opined that "the best thing would be to let nature seek its own balance." In a similar vein, he expressed anti-immigration sentiments in an interview for an Australian publication about Mexicans and other South Americans seeking a better life in the United States, complaining about the use of this country as "an overflow valve for problems in Latin America." Another time he cavalierly said, "Send the Mexicans home with rifles."[*]

The apocalyptic fantasies underlying Earth First dogma were an homage to *The Monkey Wrench Gang*, where Abbey's hero, hirsute Vietnam vet George Washington Hayduke, obsesses over the Glen Canyon Dam. The construction of the 187-foot dam meant the drowning of an exquisite canyon, its side streams, its wildlife and the river that held magical beauty and Indian lore. Abbey had written about the naturally turreted canyon that he had paddled through before the dam in an essay included in *Desert Solitaire* (1968). And

[*]Bari scolded Earth First's founders for what she regarded as xenophobia, racism and homophobia—she called them "eco-dudes"—but she had misanthropic views that rivaled theirs. Asked in the June 1992 issue of *San Francisco Focus* (the magazine of PBS television station KQED), "If you had only one hour to spend in San Francisco, what hour would it be," she answered: "The hour that the city is flattened by a giant earthquake. I'd love to stand on Telegraph Hill and watch the whole thing collapse around me like a house of cards." Her apocalyptic vision of mass death and suffering is one she embraced wholeheartedly as being good for the earth and a just recompense for "Native Americans being forced off the land by land-grabbing white settlers."

he had written there, as he did in *The Monkey Wrench Gang*, of his unslaked yearnings to bring the dam down.[*]

Despite the rhetoric of desperation they would later embrace, the early Earth First crew from the Sonoran desert—Dave Foreman, Bart Koehler, Ron Kezar, Howie Wolke and Mike Roselle—and a few of their friends did not announce themselves to the world with an assault on Glen Canyon; instead, they chose to showcase their philosophy with a prank that was agitprop guerrilla theater at its best.

On March 21, 1981, Abbey was among the honored guests and friends who had been invited to what was billed as a rite of spring located at Lake Powell—or "Lake Foul," as the new Earth First crew called the body of water created by the Glen Canyon Dam. Abbey had not previously met Foreman and the others, but had quickly embraced the concept of Earth First. He was curious—everyone was—about the 300-foot rolled-up sheet of shiny black polyurethane brought to the dam by the activists. Law enforcement expected trouble, but assumed it would be directed at the dam's generator room. The Earth Firsters, however, slipped past guards and walked to the top of the dam, then climbed over a protective fence. One of the women, Louisa Willcox, fashioned climbing knots with which she fastened the black sheet to a running series of gates along the dam's walkway. From a nearby bridge across the canyon, the Earth First crowd of some seventy members and supporters began whooping it up as the pranksters unfurled the black plastic against the dam's face—a faux crack to suggest the demise of the structure they all hated.

"Earth First!" Abbey was reported to have yelled. "Free the Colorado!" Such antics soon became a regular part of Earth First's repertoire, although no other was as sensational as that first eye-catcher.

For the new recruits, another ritual would become institutionalized in the anarchistic and anti-authoritarian organization: the yearly rendezvous. The first site—Dubois, Wyoming—had served

---

[*]David Brower had signed off on the Glen Canyon Dam as head of the Sierra Club in the mid-1950s because he believed then that only by doing so could he save the Grand Canyon from a similar fate. Later on he said, "Ten years ago I was testifying in favor of a higher Glen Canyon Dam and I wish I had been struck dead at the time."

previously as a retreat for staffers of the Wilderness Society during the Bicentennial celebration. Foreman and the rest called it the first Round River Rendezvous, a campout where music, drinking, communing and talking philosophy and goals in an unstructured manner would set a pattern for subsequent Earth First confabs.

It was a chance, too, for members to discover who else was going about the work of liberating wilderness spots from development during the rest of the year. At that first rendezvous, most of the group were longtime environmental workers—many from the Wilderness Society, which was then in the process of culling staffers in a top-heavy organization that was losing touch with its grass roots—and friends of the founding EFers.

Then, in the newly formed *Earth First! Journal*, the founders hammered out what their new group was after. Susan Zakin summarized it in *Coyotes and Town Dogs:* "...a plan to preserve one major wilderness area in every ecosystem in the United States. To the Earth First Buckaroos it meant setting aside forty-four wilderness areas of a million acres or more. Slices of ecosystems had already been preserved, such as Maine's Baxter State Park, the Florida Everglades, and Big Bend National Park. This group proposed major, mind-blowing expansions of those parks."

And there was more: a million-acre preserve in Southern California to secure roaming space for the California condor, then nearly extinct; and similar areas in Texas for the ocelots and other critters. "It's time to be passionate. It's time to be tough," Foreman admonished potential recruits in a newsletter. Earth Firsters should be prepared to go to jail courageously as the civil rights workers did in the Sixties.

Their collective Rousseauan vision of America was one of a pre-Columbian pristine innocence. They wanted nothing less, they said. And their ambition to reclaim and preserve those vast tracts soon began trickling down into the imaginations of disaffected young people in counterculture enclaves across the country.

ONE SUCH PLACE WAS GARBERVILLE, where the self-styled hippie minstrel Darryl Cherney had landed after driving west over several months in 1985, crossing the country from New York City. He was drawn to the memory he still cherished of a summer vacation with his parents and sister when he was fourteen years old, visiting the West Coast and the redwoods. He was on the Oregon Coast, heading south in his funky Dodge van, when he saw a figure walking briskly along the shoulder of the road. The man appeared ghostlike out of the fog. Cherney—who never tired of telling interviewers this tale that seems lifted straight from the Arlo Guthrie canon of storytelling—somehow sensed that the man wanted a ride, although he was not hitchhiking. Cherney had noted the Indian rattle protruding from the man's rear pants pocket. He pulled over. The shaman hopped in. He told Cherney he was a "Cheyenne road man" traveling for the Native American Church to minister to his far-flung flock. His name was Kingfisher.

They drove in silence for a while. Then Kingfisher asked the 32-year-old bearded white vagabond what he wanted out of life. Cherney claims to have answered: "I'd like to learn how to live off the land and save the world." Kingfisher told him he should go to Garberville. They talked all night long. When the pair arrived in Garberville, they went straight to the Environmental Protection Information Center (EPIC), which, like the MEC in Ukiah, was a hangout as well as a clearing-house for environmental issues.

Cherney dropped into Garberville like someone from another planet, a fast-talking hustler with the soft white body and facial pallor of a self-absorbed New Yorker, full of manic energy. He'd been a precocious child who had worked as an actor/model beginning at age three, and appeared in some 35 commercials between the ages of five and thirteen, hawking everything from bologna to insurance. His interest in politics was equally precocious: when he was twelve years old he canvassed for Bobby Kennedy. And even as a teenager he was penning protest songs.

He had earned a Fordham University master's degree in education, taught English as a second language, done a bit of flacking for Capitol Records and Equitable Life. He'd even briefly run a moving business. None lasted very long. The moving company seems particularly improbable given Cherney's small, unathletic stature.

For a while he had worked as a record publicist for United

Artists, but this was after he'd taught typing and English for a cut-rate business school in Times Square. This was hardly the working-class résumé that Judi Bari bragged about, but Cherney's various hustles had given him a knack for selling whatever he was pushing at any given time—ideas and products. He knew ad copy, jingles and rhymes that he could harness in the service of the environmental movement after he had latched onto it.

When he landed at EPIC, the organization was in the middle of a lawsuit brought against Georgia-Pacific (GP) to save the Sally Bell Grove of old-growth redwood in the Sinkyone watershed on the Lost Coast, a rugged landscape skirting the furthermost end of the Coastal Range, where it dropped into the Pacific. It was another threatened area under private ownership by logging companies.

Julie Verran, who was working on the Sinkyone fight out of the EPIC office, remembers when Darryl Cherney first came around, telling his breathless tale of the Indian who'd led him to Garberville. "He used to sleep there in the EPIC office on the couch," she recalled.

Andy Caffrey, an early recruit to Earth First in Humboldt County, recalls a fellow activist's rendition of the Cherney arrival. "He told the story of this guy with a guitar coming in like a pushy know-it-all, and how everyone was reacting to him with a 'who are you' kind of thing. But then he would tell how Cherney got accepted because his songs were so funny and he was willing to be the butt of jokes—a real goofball. He was willing to play the fool."

Cherney dived in, bringing his adman media skills along with his innate hyperkinetic style. He began doing what he'd done in New York: seeking attention, feverishly contacting all media in the area and beyond to publicize his Yippie-like caper of trespassing on GP land to do a guerrilla planting of seedling redwoods. When Cherney was arrested, the small local media loved it and so did their audience. That action took place on the spring equinox in 1986 when he and a small group demonstrated over at the Sally Bell.

But just before the group was ready to go, Cherney discovered that his own van was inoperable. It was just at that moment that Greg King drove up in his clunker Toyota sedan and parked in the gravel lot outside the EPIC office. Cherney had seen the stranger coming, and when the car turned in, he knew it was the answer to his prayers. King, a young journalist covering forest issues for *The Paper* of rural Sonoma County had heard about the fight for the Sally Bell and wanted to see the turf for himself and write about it for his paper. He'd stopped at EPIC for directions to the Sinkyone.

Cherney more or less commandeered King and his auto. The group set off in a caravan. On the way, Cherney and King began a partnership that eventually moved the struggle for the ancient grove known as Headwaters to front pages all across the country.

On that day at the Sally Bell, however, King split off from Cherney's group, which was planting its little saplings with a journalist and a photographer for an audience. King went in another direction, exploring the forest alone. Hours later, he came upon a huge area of stumps and land that looked blasted atop a 300-foot incline. The slope dropped precipitously down to a narrow stream now silted over from the collapsed bank of taken trees. Overcome, King sat down and cried, while clouds of mosquitoes rose up from the stagnant pools around him.

King's similar tracking three months later, armed with a timber harvest plan and a geological map, led him to what he would later call "the world's last unprotected ancient redwood groves, Headwaters." King's discovery of the 3,000-acre threatened tract prompted his and Cherney's long campaign to save Headwaters.

The story of Headwaters is told in David Harris's *The Last Stand*. In 1985, the Maxxam Group was poised to take over the venerable Pacific Lumber Company from the Murphy family, who had operated it since their Detroit millionaire forebear purchased it in the first years of the twentieth century. As Harris says, it was "A. S. Murphy, the grandson of the Detroit millionaire, made president in 1931, who had instituted the moderate principal of 'sustained yield' that many environmentalists could almost live with. The old man had established a culture of sustainability and humane treatment of workers that lasted until the Hurwitz led take-over."

Sustained yield means taking old-growth trees at a reasonable rate, while planting second-growth redwoods that would reach maturity unmolested in time and assure continued profits and work for the loggers and employees.* Because of Pacific Lumber's past conservative logging policies over nearly a century, the company owned more stands of untouched redwood forest than any other company around. (In the mid-1980s, PL held some 200,000 acres of redwoods, much of it over a thousand years old.)

Maxxam chief Charles Hurwitz, working with junk-bond king Michael Milkin, had floated $750 million in junk bonds to buy Pacific Lumber. The deal, in turn, placed financial pressures on Maxxam that Hurwitz decreed could be met only by taking the ancient groves on PL holdings at a stepped-up rate that, according to writer David Harris, put an end to the sustained logging practices that had been PL's policy before Hurwitz bought the company. (Hurwitz also renegotiated the loggers' pension fund with a company controlled by his cronies, slashing the payouts that the loggers had always counted on.)

It was one of the nastiest deals of the 1980s, when junk-bond thieves Milkin and Ivan Boesky were in their heyday. Later, some of the manipulations of the pension fund would be overturned in a suit brought by Bill Bertain on behalf of PL retirees, but the cutting of old-growth virgin redwoods—meaty and dense and profitable—was proceeding at an alarming rate that no second-growth plantings could ever catch, because those trees too were slated for the axe.

Headwaters became the last-ditch battle on the North Coast between Pacific Lumber and the local Earth First environmentalists. It was Greg King who not only found the grove, but became the heart and soul of the struggle to save it. Cherney ran the publicity machine, but King was the silent forest athlete and sleuth.

In the short history of the campaign to save the redwoods in the United States, activists had adopted the tactics that had earned them the name "tree-huggers." The term originated in the so-called Chipko movement (*chipko* is roughly translated as "to hug") in the foothills of the Himalayas in northern India, where clear-cutting destroyed the peasantry who had eked out a subsistence from the

---

*Tim Hermach of the Forest Council Organization, however, says the margin of profit for timber today—about 3 percent—is so low that the industry is forced to take both the oldest trees (virgin timber) as the most lucrative, and also the new plantings; and "that makes sustainable yield in logging impossible."

forests. Chipko had been guided by two European female acolytes of Mahatma Gandhi who in the 1970s saw "tree-hugging" as a legitimate tool to fight the destruction of the local economy and ecology. *Time* described how the Chipko activists would run in front of the loggers and literally hold on to the trees, defiantly risking injuries as the sawing proceeded. Earth First had embraced tree-hugging, but advanced the concept of putting bodies on the line with the introduction of tree-sitting.

Andy Caffrey, one of the original Humboldt Earth Firsters along with Greg King and Cherney, describes King as "a wonderful guy, but kind of fragile." Caffrey credits King with teaching so many of them—himself and Cherney among them—how to do a tree-sit in a redwood grove, the tactic that brings logging to a halt.

First, the activists must sneak into the groves, usually at night to avoid detection. Once they select a tree, the challenge is getting a rope over a high bough. "They shoot a rock-anchored rope over the limb with a bow and arrow," says Caffrey. Early on, the tree-sitter would then simply climb up that rope and "hang out up there." Resupply people served the tree-sitter, bringing food, taking away bagged excrement and any garbage; but even so, no one could last more than a few days.

Then someone thought of constructing platforms and slinging them up into the trees. (A door was often used for the purpose.) O-rings were attached to the corners and two or three more were affixed along the edges. Each O-ring had a loop of climbing rope that went up to a teepee, a central point three or four feet high where a carabiner held it together. They ran the rope through the carabiner and to all the O-rings. The complicated mass of ropes, rings and loops was straight out of mountain-climbing technology. To get up, the tree-sitter would wear climbing spurs, unless it was a small tree and the climber was able to shimmy up and swing over onto a bough. The platform changed everything, providing the tree-sitter with a place to stay for a long period.

King studied timber harvest plans and then went to scout them out. "Greg did meticulous work," Caffrey recalls. "He'd get all the announcements of timber sales, of all the things being submitted and considered. He'd go to this area with his own copies of topographical maps. He'd copy their top maps with the cuts marked and put it on his. It was a manic thing. He showed incredible dedication, like he was trying to save his children's life."

King may have pioneered the cause; but without Cherney, the cause would never have made headlines. Cherney had spotted the Earth First sticker—the green ham fist modeled after the first one drawn by Mike Roselle, with the logo "Earth First!"—on a window-pane the very first day he arrived in Garberville. Cherney wanted to sign up right away, but after several months of asking questions, he had gotten no closer to EF. Given the tribal, spontaneous and lead-erless form of the organization—and the secrecy associated with ecotage—it was no wonder. Everyone around EPIC brushed him off. It took weeks before Cherney figured out how to subscribe to the group's journal. As David Harris writes, "When he then asked how he could attend an Earth First! meeting, he was told just to call one. Whoever came would be Earth First!"

Cherney and King discussed it endlessly, reviewing just what they thought it would take to mount a real and effective opposition to Hurwitz and Maxxam's plans to sell off Humboldt's last large tracts. And so Earth First!—the Humboldt County Earth First! Redwood Action Team—was born.

CHERNEY ORGANIZED A CONFERENCE in the fall of 1986 of some two dozen activists, firing them up with the saga of the PL takeover by Maxxam. Afterward, he headed for the regular Earth First national roundup in the redwood forests of Big Basin State Park. Some two hundred Earth First members would join him there in the Santa Cruz mountains, several hours south of San Francisco.

At first, Cherney was intimidated by the big macho dudes in Earth First, but one of them, the six-foot-six Mike Roselle, took an immediate shine to the funny little bushy-haired guy from Manhat-tan. Roselle was captivated by Cherney the performer, whose clever songs and manic energy he deemed an asset to their cowboy style. The others were too.

So Cherney was in. And, according to David Harris, he had inspired about one hundred Earth First members and their friends who'd attended the Big Basin conference to join him, along with others he recruited from among the Humboldt activists. Cherney staged an agitprop demonstration in San Francisco in front of the head-quarters of Pacific Lumber. They all howled—the Earth First wolf cry was a common ritual at the group's rendezvous and on demonstra-tions—and then Cherney led them in songs on his guitar, made speeches and did some guerrilla theater outside the company's locked doors.

He soon became the public face of Earth First on the North Coast, particularly because the organization had never sought the publicity that his inventiveness and compulsive hustling guaranteed. Julie Verran—who had moved into the Bridgewood Motel in 1988 at the suggestion of Betty Ball to function as the Sierra Club northern representative for Humboldt County—thought Cherney's operation at the Bridgewood was a marvel. Cherney managed the defunct motel—the place was not up to code—for the Hindu spiritualist who owned it. "It was a very nice little place with beautiful specimen trees on the bend of the Eel River," said Verran. "Darryl had an environ-mental office with a copier machine and he'd gotten a grant on condition that he'd let other environmentalists use the facility." Cherney charged her $200 a month for her room and access to the shared space. She admired his media operation: "Darryl was a genius at PR."

Other Earth Firsters had done their talking in their anonymous acts of ecotage, in the EF journal, and in the road shows of Foreman and Roselle. But Cherney's way was winning new admirers.

One of them was Judi Bari.

SEVEN

JUDI BARI GOT TO KNOW DARRYL CHERNEY through music. She had been studying the fiddle (and a little guitar) in a serious way over the preceding four years and was, by 1987, good enough to open a show that would feature Cherney, a much more accomplished musician, as the main event. "When I first saw him onstage, he had a lot of charisma," she later told the Associated Press. "I was really impressed." A few weeks later, she ran into him at the Mendocino Environmental Center in Ukiah.

At the time, Cherney was a protest candidate running on an anti-logging platform in the 1988 Democratic congressional primary against incumbent Doug Bosco, a shoe-in to win. One day at the MEC, he was bemoaning his own amateurish efforts to lay out his campaign brochure. Betty Ball listened sympathetically and suggested a possible solution to his problem: a friend of hers, Judi Bari, was a great graphic artist who used to put out a fantastic strike newsletter for the postal workers back in Maryland. And just as she said this, Bari walked in—"like a gust of wind," Cherney would recall almost a decade later. She agreed to help him, whereupon Cherney immediately invited himself over to her place, astonished by his own boldness. She told him she was happy to have him come over and she would do his graphics for him, but only if he promised to entertain her two-year-old daughter, Jessica. (Lisa would be in school.) So Cherney quickly improvised a little song for baby Jessica and, at the appointed hour, arrived, sang his ditty and charmed the mother.

In Cherney's account, the two of them settled down to work on the brochure, but not without Bari lighting into him. "She was ridiculing my run for Congress——telling me that the system didn't work, and that I was a fool for thinking I could change anything by running for office. She razzed me with such incredible humor and gusto that I fell in love with her."

All that teasing banter in such a tiny body engaged Cherney immediately. Bari was hardly in the mold of the pretty, much younger hippie women he took up with later on, after the pair's relationship failed. She was older by six years and showed from the beginning that she could dominate him with her quick brain and sharp tongue. As for Bari, her friend Pam Davis later observed, "Darryl melted a soft spot in her heart. He gave Judi some comfort." But the two of them were clearly opposites: "Judi was a loner, very tough," Davis said, while describing Cherney as "mushy—a wimp."

There were other factors that explained the mutual attraction. One was the shared patina of East Coast Jewishness. Notwithstanding Bari's Italian legacy on her father's side, she was an honorary New York Jew just by dint of her parents' Communist past and her tough-girl way of talking. And just as Judi's mother became a college professor, Cherney's father was an adjunct professor of English at New York University. His mother was an office manager.

The pair were also physically compatible: Bari was barely five feet tall; Cherney under five-five. He had dark curly hair and wore a full, dark beard. In his own mind, he was very much like his hero, Youth International Party (Yippies) cofounder Abbie Hoffman, who was also short of stature with wiry black hair and Jewish features. Cherney tried to copy Hoffman's wild and improbable political antics—the old guerrilla-theater school of activism—although he had a long way to go to match his hero's inspired gesture of throwing dollar bills onto the floor of the New York Stock Exchange so as to watch the brokers dive for them. Still, Cherney's public trespassing on the Sally Bell Grove to plant a guerrilla sapling on a clear-cut was definitely in the Yippie tradition.

Cherney and Bari became knows as the "Dynamic Duo" or the "Dynamite Duo" over the next few years. (Cherney, however, still held on to his "Feral Darryl" nickname). The two of them became lovers as well as partners in agitprop.

Although Bari and Sweeney had agreed by that point to see

others outside their marriage, there was plenty of rancor left between the officially separated couple. Judi and the girls then occupied the made-over garage; the spec house was empty and Sweeney lived in a funky green trailer he'd bought and hooked up barely fifteen feet from the garage. He was close enough to hear Bari's lovemaking with Cherney and with other lovers who followed once she and Darryl had split up.

The sounds of his wife's trysts enraged Sweeney. One person who caught a brief, early glimpse of his anger at his wife's lover Cherney was Irv Sutley. A friend of Judi's pal Pam Davis, Sutley would soon become Davis's tenant in Sonoma County. But in the spring of 1988 he was working on the congressional primary campaign of Eric Fried, the Peace and Freedom candidate who, along with Cherney and others, was vying for Democrat Doug Bosco's seat. Although ostensibly rivals with different party affiliations, Fried and Cherney hit the campaign trail together at times to deliver their similar "progressive" message. On one leg of their campaigning, Bari joined Cherney, and the four of them—Bari, Cherney, Fried and Sutley—toured together.

Like his friend Pam Davis, Sutley was a member of the Communist Party who had recently returned to California and immediately plunged into politics with the Peace and Freedom Party and the Pledge of Resistance demonstrations at the Concord Naval Weapons Station. While Sutley would later figure prominently in the Judi Bari story, that afternoon in 1988 he was simply acting as Fried's campaign manager—he and the candidate in one car, Bari and Cherney in the other, all headed to Bari's house to "crash" there overnight before resuming their campaign rounds the following day.

When Sweeney emerged from his trailer to check out the visitors, according to Sutley, his face was contorted with "a suppressed rage" at the mere sight of his wife's new lover. Fried, who had known Sweeney previously, greeted him; but Sweeney did not respond. He stormed off without a word and would not show himself again for the duration of the group's stay.

Bari ignored her estranged husband. Once again she was becoming involved with a man whose politics were an aphrodisiac.

That passion, according to Cherney, was cemented on their first "action" together—in 1988 at the Safeway food emporium on State Street in Ukiah, where they participated in a noisy event in support of a United Farm Workers' boycott of table grapes.[*]

It was a pathetically small group that showed up at the State Street Safeway. Sutley, who by now was friends with both Bari and Cherney, remembers no more than five of them. They positioned themselves outside the store as Cherney played his guitar and sang his improvised lyrics about scabs and picket lines, with Bari happily joining in. Sutley, perhaps because of his puritanical Communist Party sensibility, winced at Cherney's lyrics. "As a rule you don't screw with working people when they're shopping for their families' dinners," he later remarked.

Cherney was even more excited about the demonstration that he and his new lover planned together a few weeks later. Its purpose was to oppose the appearance of James G. Watt, the former secretary of the interior in the Reagan administration, at the Redwood Region Logging Conference in Ukiah. Watt was then the head of the anti-environmental Mountain States Legal Foundation and a declared enemy of even moderate wilderness groups.

"We thought he deserved a rousing welcome from Earth First," Cherney later recalled, "so we marched over to Ukiah's fairgrounds—the Redwood Empire fairgrounds—singing 'You can't clear-cut your way to heaven.' That was the first action that Judi and I really organized together."

Bari had reached out to form an alliance with the Mendocino County AIDS Network to challenge James Watt's stated homophobic views on the disease. It would not be the first time that Bari's politics would be more embracing and savvy than her lover's. But afterward, both were satisfied that they'd yanked the welcome mat from under James Watt in Ukiah; in fact Bari was overjoyed. Now she wanted more and would find it in the struggle over the Cahto Wilderness.

---

[*] Begun in 1984 as a reprise of the UFW's heyday in the 1960s, the boycott was languishing even though union founder Cesar Chavez began a fast to inject new life into his union in 1988.

THE BUREAU OF LAND MANAGEMENT (BLM) controlled this 17,000 acres of prime, publicly owned watershed land that encompassed the territory along the South Fork of the Eel River running from the coast to the redwood-surrounded hamlet of Branscomb, not far from Laytonville, the next big town north of Willits on the Highway 101 corridor. No one would have known about the impending commercial encroachment on the land were it not for the vigilance of two gay guys, Michael Huddleston and Steven Day. For ten years they had worked to save the land from being harvested for its timber.

Huddleston and Day had found a sense of belonging among the back-to-the-land folk who for the most part were decidedly heterosexual (excluding, notably, the Albion Ridge lesbians), but also, like them, looking for a simpler life. The two men felt a call to preserve the nearby threatened wilderness, especially the watershed area with its crown jewel, the 4,234-foot Cahto Peak. They walked its woods and steep hills. They researched timber harvest plans that laid out clear-cuts. In 1987 they discovered what they deemed an illegal sale of a ridge outside Laytonville.

They looked up dusty files in government offices and studied old treaties. They learned that the Native Americans in the region, the Cahto tribe, had been signatories to a treaty that barred the United States from cutting tribal forests except with the tribe's approval and for its benefit.

As things stood that summer in 1988, Huddleston and Day believed the major battle wouldn't take place until the following spring, when the BLM planned to sell large swaths of the Cahto Wilderness for commercial logging. The impending fight seemed to the two men to augur a last stand, but they thought they might postpone the inevitable by building a political movement to stop the cutting by private lumber companies.

Patricia Kovner was one of those who joined Huddleston and Day along with a handful of Laytonville-area activists. The Cahto watershed virtually abuts her back yard. The two men had impressed Kovner with their evidence proving the illegality of the sale. They showed that the proposed tract was, for example, within a quarter-mile of a wild river and thus protected from cutting. Equally damning, the site was on a steep hillside sloping down to the river and thus a potential cause of erosion and silting pollution. The clincher was the treaty with the Cahto tribe that the two men had uncovered. Kovner joined in the Ancient Forest Defense Fund (AFDF), newly formed with the objective of raising money, hiring an attorney and getting results.

Huddleston (who claimed to be half Nez Perce) and others did the delicate work of persuading the Cahto tribe to call California's liberal Democrat senator, Alan Cranston, for assistance in obtaining an emergency restraining order against the government sale. The AFDF helped the tribe with its arguments, principally that the land in question had never been surveyed for artifacts as required in federal regulations. The BLM ignored the Indians' protests, claiming that the $1 million sale to the Eel River Sawmill had already gone through. That was when Kovner and several other Laytonville residents decided to seek Earth First support.

Kovner headed into the MEC in Ukiah to attend an Earth First meeting. She remembers being shocked that Mendocino County's first EF chapter was composed of only three women and two men, with Bari in command. When Kovner arrived at the MEC, moreover, Bari happened to be in the middle of an "abusive" dressing-down of a woman called Sequoia, "an old biker chick," as Kovner described her, with a missing finger to complete her mystique. Watching the "surreal" scene, Kovner was at a loss to explain the furious verbal punishment that Bari was dishing out.

Kovner also chafed over Bari's rudeness. "She never introduced herself, never looked us in the eye. She said, 'Let's get started,' but she never even welcomed us." But the bad manners disturbed Kovner less than Bari's treatment of Sequoia. For many years Sequoia occupied a homestead on the collective Greenfield Ranch above the Parducci Vineyard in Ukiah. She had been the first visible face of Earth First in Mendocino County—at least a contact person, if not an organizer. Bari's humiliation of Sequoia that evening was preliminary to banishing her from any leadership role in the tiny Mendocino chapter. Bari would later damn Sequoia with faint praise in the New Settler: "There were many things that she does well, but bringing people into the movement wasn't one of them."

It was not only Bari's impatience with the others' soggy ineptitude that prompted her to assume leadership in the new Earth First chapter and the Cahto campaign, but the cycles in her own life. She explained to Beth Bosk after the car bomb, "I used to organize for a couple of years, and get into these intense public situations—like I did in the unions—and then I'd drop out for a couple of years, and I'd go get a job and I'd be a mom, I'd just live my life as a normal person. And then when I had recovered enough from the glare of the public exposure, I would be ready to go out."

By the time of Cahto and Darryl Cherney, Bari had started separating her life from Sweeney's and was again immersing herself in the kind of movement politics that she'd been a part of back in her Maryland days—a period, she always said, that constituted the happiest days of her life.

WHILE HUDDLESTON AND DAY initially thought they had time to build a groundswell of support for preserving Cahto, their leisurely organizing pace abruptly shifted into a higher gear in the fall of 1988, when a road-building crew was spotted on its way up to the Cahto forest to open the territory to cutting. If they didn't go up there and do something right away, it would be too late.

It happened that at the same time, about two hundred eco-activists were scheduled to demonstrate up in Oregon for the preservation of Sanctuary Forest. Cherney was already involved there, but when the emergency loomed on the Cahto Wilderness area, he and Bari split off a contingent of the Sanctuary activists and came back to Mendocino County to join up with some twenty locals in a 24-hour-a-day blockade. The Cahto action ran for a total of three days, while Huddleston and Day frantically sought to push the Cahto tribe, whose nearby *rancheria* was home to nearly three hundred members, to get a restraining order barring any logging.

The first day, protesters sat down across the road, blocking the only vehicle access to the cutting site. Cherney performed his songs to lift the group's spirits; Bari played the fiddle alongside him. She had been practicing and learning his songs, playing her fiddle to his guitar and singing the former adman's simple lyrics. This day he sang his "Ballad of the BLM":

> Now the Bureau of Land Management
> is part of the U.S.

And they manage the earth much better
than anyone can, I guess.
. . . .
BLM, you ain't the friend
of the eagle and the bear;
But the corporations love you
'cause they get the lion's share.

At Bari's instigation, the protesters soon began erecting a series of spontaneous barricades. The logging crew had never encountered anything like it. Because the dirt road was newly cut, there was ample slash—branches, leaves and small downed trees. The demonstrators carried it onto the road. They dragged out boulders as additional impediments. Even without tools, they managed to scrape and carve out ruts in the road, making it rough going for the logging vehicles.

When the crews arrived that first day, they took one look at the seated activists and their barricades, and departed. Bari stayed that night with a skeleton crew of demonstrators. Spirits were high. Very early the next morning, demonstrators who had retreated for the night managed to sneak up to the road again. They reinforced their barricades, added more slash and awaited the day's skirmish.

When the sun rose, officials of the BLM arrived, bolstered by local police. They ordered the group to leave. But as Bari remembered later on, a plan suddenly inspired her. Instead of exiting the way they had come, walking down the hill to paved roads, the protesters would deliberately walk very slowly up the steep dirt road. They'd drag the whole process out, avoiding arrest but still managing to stall the cutting.

As they began their leisurely saunter, the authorities, joined by the logging crews, jumped into their cars—some fifteen of them—to follow. But they had to stop every few feet to remove debris from the road. There were twenty-two such informal barricades, and as Bari would later remember, "some of them were just a couple of rocks and some of them were a lot of brush and some of them were very elaborate."

The demonstrators got farther and farther ahead of the pursuing cars up the switchback road. When they were out of sight of the stalled posse behind them, the activists slipped one by one away into the woods, down to the river, to follow it back to where they could leave the area safely. It was a marvelous goof and it stoked Bari's sense of what was possible: "It took so long for them to remove these barricades, that the logging was essentially stopped. They only got a little bit in at the end of the day."

It was the same drill in the semidarkness of the next morning. Activists came and rebuilt the barricades. But several of them also managed to dig a trench in the road that was as large as three feet by four feet in places—too deep for a car to pass over. The police called it a "tank trench." Bari, who wasn't there because she was in her final days at California Yurts, exulted afterwards with the perpetrator. "God, how did you do it with no power equipment?" she asked. "I think I was a small burrowing animal in a former life," was the reply.

Meanwhile, the Cahto tribe with the help of Senator Cranston obtained the restraining order to prohibit tree-taking in the 17,000-acre area. An alliance had been formed among the tribe, Earth First and the Laytonville activists. Bari was its new voice even though Huddleston and Day had marshaled the struggle up to that point.[*]

Bari loved the militancy of the Cahto fight, but she also enjoyed the antic quality of an Earth First action in Sacramento, led by Cherney during the months of the Cahto struggle. Along with a handful of Earth Firsters and Laytonville activists, including Patricia Kovner, Bari and Cherney attended a meeting of the California State Board of Forestry in the state capitol. The forestry board has nine seats, most of them, in the environmentalists' view, industry hacks. This was an obligatory meeting. Bari and Cherney scheduled a press conference to be held during the board's recess; Cherney had worked around the clock to call every last media rep on his long list.

At the recess, nine of the activists rushed forward from their seats in the front and took the seats just previously occupied by the board. Then they donned various animal masks—squirrels, bears, fox and deer—declaring themselves the "true" forestry representatives while giving their spiel urging protection of the forests and its critters.

---

[*]In the end, four years later, the victory was secured: the BLM was ordered to return the money to the Eel River Sawmill, but at an inflated rate to compensate for lost business and for interest by several million dollars.

When the board members returned, there was a bizarre confrontation. The masked ones called for the "real board to come to order," meaning themselves. The forestry board told the group they'd have to leave or face arrest. No one was arrested. The masked forest critters got their pictures and their statements in the papers, and assumed that this raised the public consciousness. It was the lightness of Earth First, as well as its militancy, that won Bari's heart.

IN THE EARLY LAYTONVILLE MEETINGS on Cahto, Patricia Kovner noted that Bari had already taken control of contact lists, with names of the volunteers, phone numbers and so on. In a time before personal computers had made their way into the dens of North Coast counterculturists, this meant that she and only she knew how to get in touch with everyone else. Bari, according to Kovner, jealously guarded this resource. It was one basis of her growing power.

As the original Earth First "contact person" in Mendocino County, Sequoia had not done much more publicly than talking about EF on the community FM radio, or posting announcements from time to time at the MEC. Bari now sought to expand the public base and awareness of EF. She was willing to be a "media slut," as she jokingly called herself, to step up the demonstrations and recruit more members.

Bari was not only putting her stamp on the Ecotopia chapter of Earth First (as it came to be called) in Ukiah; she was also influencing the culture of the national organization as well. In one of the earliest Earth First national rendezvous she attended, she organized a seminar to teach the history of the International Workers of the World (IWW), or the Wobblies. They were really antiques from the earlier part of the twentieth century, the time of the legendary Big Bill Heywood and Joe Hill; but they had a history of involvement in the Mendocino area. Even Mickey Lima, a prominent Wobbly who went on to become the head of the Northern California Communist Party, had a summer retreat just inland from Fort Bragg that served as an adult camp and rendezvous site for regional Communists for many years.

There was something preposterous in the image of little Judi

Bari heading to an Earth First rendezvous and teaching all those wilderness eco-dudes and rednecks about the vanished IWW union anarchists, whose highpoint had come nearly a century earlier. And yet, such a gesture was totally in character for the self-described Maoist who, in her Baltimore days, had once sat up half the night with her then fiancé, Walt Penny, devouring texts of leftist dogma. But now, while trying to imbue Earth First with starchy Marxist class principles, she was not immune to influences from her potential recruits. With Cherney she'd become a hippie troubadour and bra-less adherent to the cultural ethos of the territory. That meant she could celebrate by lighting up a "hooter," a cheroot-sized marijuana joint, on any and all occasions, another sign that she had moved away from Maoist puritanism and toward the countercultural ways of Earth First.

She would later tell Beth Bosk that she liked the leveling process of Earth First and how, at the meetings, if some of the leaders were "getting a little full of themselves," they were mocked by the rank-and-filers who did a takeoff on an Indian ritual known as the "mudhead Kochina." "People did parodies of the leaders while they spoke.... There'd be naked people with mud all over them sitting near the stage imitating their gestures." It was a wonder that no one donned mud to mock Bari for holding a Wobbly seminar decades after the IWW had come and gone.

Bari's "seminar" must have been galling to Earth First old-timers. She even invited an IWW member as a "guest lecturer." Roanne Withers, who knew some of the original characters on whom *The Monkey Wrench Gang* was based, as well as some of the older EFers, recalls that the old guard "didn't take Judi very seriously."

But she was very serious about injecting class consciousness into her environmental activity. After teaching the seminar, in fact, she established closer ties to the remnants of the tiny IWW union on the West Coast. Together they would soon publish a joint edition of the IWW paper, *The Industrial Worker*—hardly more than a pamphlet—that called for common ground between workers and radical environmentalists. She had pointed out to her EF comrades that tree-spiking, for instance, was a tactic pioneered, along with various other kinds of machine sabotage, by the old Wobblies of the Pacific Northwest.

Bari was far more interested in the philosophy and political analysis of the Wobblies than in their tactics. As she saw it, they had worker legitimacy, and she was horrified by the anti-working-class sentiments she was hearing from Earth Firsters. "When I first joined Earth First, the first thing I noticed was the anti-worker, anti-logger attitude," she told Bosk. "I found a lot of people blaming the loggers. I felt this is so ironic because the loggers in the Pacific Northwest invented the style of protest that Earth First is now doing."

THERE HAD BEEN ENVIRONMENTAL fights over logging in Mendocino—with serious consequences for the workers in the industry—long before Judi Bari or Earth First came on the scene. Public-interest lawsuits over what and how the timber companies could cut had begun in the 1970s. According to land-use consultant Roanne Withers, who along with her live-in lover, Ron Guenther, had spearheaded some fifteen of these suits, virtually all of them were carried out by self-trained citizens. Although homemade, most of them were successful.

The big forest issue then was the monopoly holdings of Georgia-Pacific in Fort Bragg. The company had expanded from 1955 to 1965; then, during the 1960s, it had gobbled up forty-five companies to bring its timber holdings to some 2.4 million acres. It represented by far the largest commercial ownership of forest in Mendocino County—so large, in fact, that by 1972 the Federal Trade Commission ordered GP to divest itself of 20 percent of its assets to a new, independent corporation, and barred GP from future acquisitions in the timber industry for a period of five years. The FTC order allowed the new company, Louisiana-Pacific—lead by former Georgia-Pacific officers—to distribute stock of this "independent" corporation to Georgia-Pacific shareholders; the result was two companies owned by the same stockholders.[*]

But the companies were different in one important respect: GP was union; LP was not. Union members worried that the non-union

---

[*]These figures were compiled by George Draffan, Public Information Network, for "Profiles of Louisiana-Pacific," May 1999.

Louisiana-Pacific would exert downward pressure on Georgia-Pacific's wage rates, with union-busting the likely result.

Ron Guenther was a primary organizer who filed the first lawsuit challenging Georgia-Pacific timber harvest plans at the beginning of the 1980s—the first to be filed after the passage of the 1973 Forest Practice Act, which offered environmental grounds to halt or reduce logging. By the mid-1980s, environmentalists and loggers had forged an alliance to slow the stepped-up tree harvesting that resulted from the rivalry between the union and the non-union companies. Louisiana-Pacific (non-union) was filing timber harvest plans faster than the trees could be cut, simply to monopolize resources. But even Georgia-Pacific was increasing the pace of logging—both to compete with its new rival and to try to acquire resources while lumber prices were plummeting all over the Northwest. The International Woodworkers of America teamed up with environmentalists to track timber harvest plans; the woodworkers regarded the lumber companies' increased cutting as a threat, in the long run, to their wages and their very jobs. The IWA, according to Withers, were good guys then.

But the alliance didn't last. The collapse began with a wage cut that GP forced on the union in the mid-1980s in response to the free-fall in lumber prices. (In Oregon and Washington, where prices were at their lowest, fellow unionists had accepted the pay cuts, outvoting the Mendocino local membership.) Then within two years, in a move that would alter the whole labor picture of logging in Mendocino, Georgia-Pacific divested itself of its forest crews and trucking units altogether.

A new era of independent gypsy or gyppo loggers was ushered in. The gyppos bid on contracts with the lumber companies to cut designated forest tracts. They hired the workers, cutting out the unions and eroding their former power. Suddenly the loggers were doing piecework, not only at a lower wage, but minus their former benefits. To make a living under these new terms, explains Withers, loggers had to work faster, and only the owners of the gyppo companies—and, of course, the timber companies—now made good money. The displaced former GP loggers, who had been making $8 an hour in the union (plus benefits) even when cutting slash, clearing stumps and burning—the lowest-ranked forest work—now saw their salaries cut by half as the decade was ending.[*]

There was another cause for the collapse in logging wages: the importation of Mexican workers. They had first come to work in the seafood industry, processing the lucrative sea urchin export business, but the Mexicans quickly discovered that even at the reduced piece-meal wages of $4 an hour, they could make more in the woods. So they took over Georgia-Pacific jobs and became the new forest workers.

While Louisiana-Pacific was not unionized like Georgia-Pacific, the competition was still driving costs. In early 1989, LP closed down its Potter Valley mill, laying off 136 workers. They opened a chip mill nearby to make composite board, a material that requires a lot of glue and which Judi Bari would later denounce as toxic. (LP watched its profits soar 42 percent.) It was a continuing sad story for workers in the timber industry in Mendocino and parts north. The former coop-eration between the weakened woodworkers' union and the environmentalists disappeared. It was into this breach that Judi Bari inserted herself.

AT THIS BUSY MOMENT IN HER LIFE, not long after Cahto, Bari found a new collaborator in Anna Marie Stenberg, who became not only a crucial political ally on the labor front, but a confidante with whom she would share secrets. The two women became so close that they regularly talked by phone late into the night after Lisa and Jessica were asleep.

Stenberg was a Fort Bragg divorced mother of three who ran her Anna Banana's Day Care out of her house, a few blocks in from the coast and close by the Georgia-Pacific Company, which sprawled along the bluffs of downtown Fort Bragg overlooking the ocean

---

[*]In the mid-1980s, the minimum wage was not over $4 an hour and wages on the North Coast were generally depressed. Withers recalls working full-time in a book-keeping job in Northern California for $6 an hour; the same kind of work had paid her $15 an hour in Southern California ten years earlier. A Mendocino County teacher's salary started at $13,000. But as Withers acknowledges, the cost of living up there was also very low.

below. She was well rooted in the community: over the years some forty-six different families had sent their children to fill the twelve slots in her day care center; some of the kids were from timber industry families, but there were also children of doctors, lawyers and teachers, and Native American kids. Stenberg charged a sliding-scale fee. If people didn't have the money, she did work exchanges. Three employees helped her with the work. (She had started the day care so that her own three children wouldn't have to be put in another's care while she worked.)

Stenberg became a crucial, yet odd figure in the Bari saga. She describes herself as "Judi's best friend" and says that their friendship was forged out of the political alliance they organized with the mill workers of Georgia-Pacific. But it was also rooted in a kind of personal shadow play in which Bari's disintegrating marriage to Sweeney was reflected by Stenberg's own unraveling relationship with her second husband, Mike Koepf, and her ongoing fear that he would harm her as their marriage came apart. Stenberg eventually obtained a restraining order against Koepf, although she acknowledges that he never hit or hurt her.

Stenberg's interest in the loggers' plight began at the day care center when a Georgia-Pacific mill worker, Ron Atkinson, stormed into Anna Banana's to pick up his son. He was so upset that Stenberg wouldn't release the boy until he finally sat down and calmed himself.

There had been an oil spill over at Georgia-Pacific. It began with the discovery of oil leaking from a machine called a "hog." The hog breaks down redwood bark and other trash wood, which is mixed with oil and carried on a conveyor belt to be burned in the boiler. The combustion not only provided power for the GP plant's own needs, but also produced a surplus that was sold off to the large power plant down the coast.

Atkinson was the millwright called in to fix the oil leak by the woman who was acting as hog-tender. Another worker, Frank Murray, crawled under the hog to try to spot the source of the leak from below, while Atkinson climbed on top to search from above. Suddenly there was an explosion from the capacitor that dispenses the oil. The oil that spilled in the explosion contained PCBs, a fire-retardant that once lined connector wire boxes on telephone poles before it was banned as a health hazard. The PCB-laced oil—between five and seven gallons of it—gushed down through the hog and a big dose of it landed on Frank Murray's face. It covered his head and clothes; some got in his mouth. The poisonous liquid had also splashed Teeva, the hog-tender, and had pooled on the floor, where it was contaminating the workers' shoes and clothing.

This was the tale that Atkinson blurted out to Stenberg in her kitchen over a cup of tea. But the company, the safety inspector and even the union rep denied that there were PCBs in the capacitor, claiming they didn't use the fire retardant any more and that it was simply mineral oil. Initially none of them saw any reason to take Murray to the hospital, telling him simply to wash out his mouth. They later backed down and took him to a doctor.

Other mill workers were then ordered to clean the place up and burn any of the spill that remained. Because PCBs are a retardant, burning them in the boiler meant the heat had to be at its highest level, which would tend to make the PCBs even more toxic as they went up in smoke.

Stenberg's immediate fear was that Atkinson had walked through her house, contaminating her day care establishment and putting the kids at risk. But the larger health hazards were clear. Three shifts worked the GP mill; that was eighteen workers, all potentially exposed before the company shut down the operation as they cleaned up the mess and, on company orders, threw rags and spill material alike onto the conveyor belt to be burned in the boiler. Stenberg and other parents believed that the workers were exposing their families—indeed, the whole community—to toxins borne on their clothing and shoes.

The meeting between Stenberg and Atkinson was the beginning of a struggle over the PCB spills that lasted more than a year. The California Occupational Safety and Health Administration had signed off on any violations early on. Federal OSHA found eight violations, the worst one accusing GP of "willfully" exposing the workers to toxic PCBs. Stenberg, her teenage son Zack Stentz and all the activists meanwhile organized People for Clean Air Now and distributed petitions all over town. They had to sneak samples and documents out of the mill to get them analyzed and processed, because the local authorities were not competent to test properly. Finally, they forced the county to hire qualified testers.

For the big court hearing in San Francisco, Fort Bragg's angry citizen contingent hired several buses to bring them in so they could watch and testify. At the last minute, however, the hearing was called off when the various lawyers, including the federal government's, worked out an agreement that reduced the charges, making the offense one of negligence rather than willful intent.[*]

Stenberg phoned the one "good guy" who had come out to interview all of them from Fed OSHA. He had apologized profusely for the lawyers who'd sold them out, but as Stenberg remembered, "He said it was out of his hands and that that's the way it was with the lawyers. 'They work for us for five years and then it's a revolving door; they go to work for industry.'"

Despairing of turning the disaster around, a burned-out Stenberg turned on the local cable access channel one night to catch a debate between the IWA's union rep, Don Nelson, and someone named Judi Bari. The spill was scheduled to be discussed. Stenberg had never heard of Judi Bari, but what she saw thrilled her. "I heard her arguing with Nelson and she was brilliant! She knew it was a sweetheart union." This was something Stenberg herself had only begun to grasp during the PCB fight.

The day after the Nelson/Bari debate, she found Bari's phone number and called her in the middle of her day care work. "Judi," she said, "you don't know me, but my name is Anna Marie Stenberg."

"Oh I know about you! You're the one fighting with the workers on the PCB stuff," Bari replied.

Stenberg then poured out her story, telling Bari she had no idea what to do. Bari immediately suggested she call the federal judge and inform him that none of the workers had agreed to the settlement being reached in their name. Stenberg tracked down the judge in Colorado, where the actual jurisdiction for western Fed OSHA was headquartered. She made the case that although the union had signed off on the agreement, the rank and file wanted a hearing, not a settlement.

Stenberg was advised to submit a petition. The judge also told her that the workers' representation would have to be switched over

---

[*]When the case was finally settled, Georgia-Pacific was fined $114,000.

from their current union in order to sidestep the union-brokered agreement. Stenberg fretted over that one: "I couldn't be a day care worker and represent mill workers, after all." The kindly judge—in her characterization—had asked her, "Couldn't you start another union?"

Stenberg called Bari back. She needed her help to write the petition. Bari drove the narrow, winding road out to the coast, met Stenberg face to face and wrote the petition with Stenberg looking over her shoulder.

Bari also had the solution for the thorny problem of having Stenberg, the day care worker, acting as a union representative for a bunch of mill workers. The two of them could form a new International Workers of the World chapter, with themselves as the union officers and representatives. After all, Bari had already become acquainted with the tiny IWW group that was still holding on by its fingernails, with offices in San Francisco. This was very fitting, Bari explained, because of the IWW history of representing loggers in the Pacific Northwest in the first decades of the century.

Then Bari and Stenberg talked until the sun went down, about politics and everything else, and continued to talk in the months ahead. Their children—Stenberg's three sons and Bari's two daughters—were almost the same ages. Judi had left her husband; Anna Marie was about to leave hers. It was a friendship of unlimited possibilities. They were sisters emerging from troubled marriages, and they were both Wobbly union maids—now Local 1 of the IWW.

EIGHT

BRUCE ANDERSON CAN'T REMEMBER when in 1988 he actually met Judi Bari, but whenever it was, he'd already heard from her in a blistering letter. In it, she'd excoriated him for an article his paper had printed referring to her as Darryl Cherney's "sidekick." It wouldn't be the first time she would denounce him—and the *Anderson Valley Advertiser*—as sexist.

The first time they met, Bari—"sporting pigtails to her shoulders and looking like a skinny teenager," as Anderson remembers—walked through the door of his compound on Anderson Valley Way and, surveying his comfortable, book-lined living room, said, "Oh, this looks like a straight person's house!"

"It *is* a straight person's house," Anderson replied. "What did you expect?" It was the beginning of a bantering friendship both of them would savor—until it, like so many of Bari's relationships, soured.

Anderson was smitten, not so much by Bari the woman as by Bari the activist. He realized she had big ideas, and for years to come he put himself and his newspaper at her service. He fancied himself a crusader for the forests. When she asked for a reporting beat covering timber issues for the AVA, Anderson readily agreed.

His feeling for Bari was in sharp contrast to his relations with Cherney, who had been driving him crazy for several years: "He bombarded me with press releases. Called me damn near every day—the Eel River flood one time, the next something else. I thought he was just another show biz guy!" When Anderson, after he knew Bari better, complained about the steady stream of hype from

Cherney, she responded about her lover, "That fucking Darryl, he's so goddamned dumb. He's nonstop stupid!"

As with Mary Moore and other political veterans she wanted to flatter, she compared Anderson favorably with her young hippie followers. "Oh, Bruce, you're so smart. I'm surrounded by dummies. You always get it right away." Anderson would later admit ruefully that he was taken in by Bari's blandishments. But he never felt any ambivalence, even retrospectively, when it came to her writing. "She was a good, capable reporter. She had a good, clear prose style— she's certainly as good as her sister, Gina Kolata, as far as I'm concerned—even better. Judi was very smart and she did a good job covering timber issues."

She never asked for, nor did he offer, salary or pay. The AVA was the mouthpiece she was seeking. And Anderson was happy to have her write for him, as he was happy to offer a forum to others, like Nicholas Von Hoffman or Alex Cockburn, with a more national following. He liked the way Judi could hold her own in public venues, on radio or in open meetings: "She was terrific as an impromptu public speaker." He had heard her speak at the Mendocino County Board of Supervisors meeting and found her just as "well organized and articulate" as she was in her writing.

Anderson watched with amusement and fascination as Bari came into her own with the improbable advent of Local 1 of the International Workers of the World in Mendocino County. She attracted a handful of actual woodworkers into her small fold of labor recruits. As she cobbled together her new political vision of labor and enviros joining in a coalition against the timber companies, she saw the real possibility of organizing a broader group than just Earth First hippies.

Wanting to get Cherney back into the old Marxist labor box with her, Judi began lecturing him on the record of the IWW on the North Coast early in the twentieth century; she pressed a history of the Wobblies on him shortly after the pair got together. Ever the pedagogue, Bari actually made some headway with Cherney and others in Earth First, including some veterans like Mike Roselle and Karen Pickett.

But most of it was lost when Earth Firsters went head to head with the logging communities in Humboldt County. At a county supervisors' meeting on May 17, 1988, Cherney and Greg King and their friends thought they were going to be killed by the five hundred or so timber folk who showed up en masse. (Pacific Lumber boss John Campbell had actually given the day off to any employee who would join the show of power opposing Earth First at the Eureka meeting.) The logging community, incensed over the Department of Forestry's rejection of a PL timber harvest plan, was not hesitant about expressing its outrage at the role Earth First had played in squelching the cutting plans that represented their livelihood.

It seemed to the loggers that contrary to Charles Hurwitz's promise of good times and plenty of work after his Maxxam takeover of Pacific Lumber, every timber harvest plan was being held up by a bunch of sniveling tree-huggers, threatening their economic well-being. And at the supervisors' meeting, that's exactly what a Humboldt State College economics professor called as an expert witness told them was happening. The rejection of the particular THPs under discussion—which might have been regarded as run-of-the-mill before Earth First began its agitation—was potentially going to cost the community nearly two thousand jobs, half the number lost by local industry during the previous two decades.

Outgunned and outnumbered, Cherney and King were shaken and uncertain as they stood outside afterward being chewed out by the loggers and even their families, or just stared down with hostility. Cherney meekly protested that it was not Earth First's fault that their pensions had been ripped off; it was the fault of Hurwitz and the other bosses. And where would they be if they kept on cutting all the trees until there was nothing left to cut and no jobs to be had?

Bari was growing annoyed with Cherney's clumsiness, particularly because she was making progress in organizing the mill workers and even some of the Mendocino County gyppos who had signed up after the PCB spill. She began seeking other Wobbly recruits in a very different arena: the watering holes and honky-tonks throughout the sprawling county. She had begun traipsing to bars at night and tossing back beers with the "working class."

Bruce Anderson was somewhat incredulous when Bari bragged about holding her own and impressing gyppos in bars, especially the notorious Boonville Lodge in his own town.

Two of her newfound pals were the Pardini brothers, Ernie and Tony. She was rumored to have taken a sexual fancy to Ernie, and was bar-hopping with him in the Anderson Valley and out on the coast until the wee hours, when the bars closed. She also dropped in on Fort Bragg watering holes with various members of the Roach clan, whose family owned a large log-hauling firm.

At this time, methadrine—meth, "speed" or "crank"—was all over the county. Perhaps speed explains how Bari was able to do so much with so little sleep during those intense months. At night, after she had put her daughters to bed, she would go to bars looking for potential recruits to her movement. Add in the many late-night phone calls with Anna Marie Stenberg and others—Earth First cadre to whom she gave orders by phone, or just other friends—that went on from midnight or one in the morning until four, and it was a wonder that she didn't collapse from exhaustion. (Bari had bragged to Anderson about doing crank back in her Baltimore days.)

At the Boonville Lodge they held "breast contests": the female bartender was famous for flopping her breasts onto the bar in front of rummies and letting them bet on which one was bigger. The waitresses and the female customers were known to flip up their shirts and show their breasts in their own versions of "can you top this." Bari was reported by two different sources to have joined the fray on one occasion, lifting her own top to show her unfettered, pendulous breasts (as Patricia Kovner would later describe them).

Anderson and others thought Bari's organizing among what she claimed was the working class in the timber industry was bogus. Who exactly did she think was drinking with her in the bars? Anderson asked. The real Mendocino forest workers were home with their wives and kids. Most of the loggers hired as independents (as opposed to gyppos who had landed contracts with the industry) were Mexicans. They were certainly not out in gringo bars drinking with Bari. Some of the guys she was hanging out with were marginal figures who got in drunken scrapes and were known methadrine users. When Anderson challenged her on the subject of her "organizing," she blew him off.

But that was their relationship. He argued all the time with her—about things like Earth First showing up at the loggers' places of work instead of doing its demonstrating at corporate headquarters in San Francisco or wherever. He believed it was insulting to working people to confront them at their job, just as Irv Sutley, the ex-Communist and Peace and Freedom Party guy, had felt uncomfortable when Bari and Cherney confronted working families at Safeway.

And who was taking care of Lisa and Jessica when Bari took off for the Boonville Lodge or went to Fort Bragg for nightcaps? She often took her daughters, especially Lisa, to the daytime rallies and Earth First "shows" when they weren't in school. In the evenings it was her ex-husband who did the bulk of the baby-sitting, and he was understandably furious to see his daughters' mother gallivanting around the county, claiming to be organizing the working class.

Stenberg says she began doing baby-sitting for Bari to relieve her friend from Sweeney's hostility. Stenberg advised Bari *not* to ask Sweeney to baby-sit: it gave him too much control over her life. When Stenberg did watch over Judi's girls, she noted that Lisa hated to go home if it meant being under her father's care and that she refused to spend the night in his trailer. She identified with her mother. Younger daughter Jessica seemed much closer to Sweeney.

The argument between the parents had only partially to do with baby-sitting and what Sweeney viewed as Bari's lackluster domesticity. She was much more powerful now; she'd gone from being his wife to being Cherney's sidekick to being a writer for the *Anderson Valley Advertiser.* Now it was she who convened demonstrations and held the membership lists. She kept accounts of any donations. Bari would later gripe about the fact that she didn't get enough credit from the old-line Earth First men because she was a woman; but she would also brag about the fact that almost all the main players in North Coast Earth First *were* women, most of whom she claimed to have recruited herself.

Bari viewed herself as a multipurpose lefty organizer who believed, "whether it is in the factory, whether it is on Route 1 at the University of Maryland, or whether it is in the forest, it is the same struggle to me, it's the same movement, and it's the same joy." She placed herself on a continuum of radicalism. "I used to be a Red Book–waving Maoist—I'm not anymore," she told Beth Bosk. "There are some things that Mao said that are pretty appalling. Like, 'We've got to get rid of all these classes so we can get on with the business of exploiting the earth.' I totally disagree with that. But the man was brilliant—not only at analyzing the situation, but also in explaining it to uneducated peasants. So I want to credit him with this idea."

In the radical manner of the late 1960s, she went on to lecture about "the two kinds of contradictions we encounter," one between "the people and the enemy, or between the earth and the corporation, between the destroyers and the people who are trying to protect. That's the primary contradiction. This is the one we are fighting. Then there is another contradiction...and that is the contradictions among the people." Bari was referring to the battles between men and women or between workers and environmentalists, all of whom she believed should be fighting capitalism.

Bari tried to associate herself with the leftist icons of the day by citing them liberally in her talks. And if she could get two bona fide revolutionary citations into one piety, so much the better, no matter how pompous it sounded. In one anecdote, she said she'd mentioned her fear of personal danger to a Wobbly veteran, whose response put it all in perspective for her. "A revolution is not a dinner party," the Wobbly said, quoting the famous Mao aphorism, "and if you are effective, they are going to use whatever means they can to stop you."

She lectured and theorized constantly, belittling her political adversaries with pride in her own cleverness, as when she described urbanites as "the espresso-sucking pavement dwellers." Pam Davis thought her brilliant. Patricia Kovner thought her adorable and smart. Many of the old North Coast activists who encountered her were taken with her theorizing; she seemed to synthesize disparate strands of consciousness that before her arrival had drifted unconnected in what passed for the marketplace of ideas in Mendocino County.

Bari was as much about "raising consciousness" as she was about action. And she did raise the issue of the workers' plight—at least among her new camp followers in EF, most of whom had viewed the loggers and mill workers as the enemy before she came along. She made them more sympathetic, even if the timber workers as a whole felt threatened by EF and hated the organization and Bari herself.

The more frantically she worked at organizing, the less time Bari had to think about what was going on in her personal life. During the day, she could smother those anxieties with all her activities. But at night, her secret war with her ex-husband and all her tangled feelings would pour out to Stenberg, who was also a "night owl." With Stenberg in Fort Bragg and out of the loop of her Earth First group, Bari felt free to confide in her.

She told Stenberg about physical fights with Sweeney (Stenberg says she saw the black-and-blue bruises on Judi's arms and legs) and how, even after the marriage was over, he tried to prevent her from going out. He became angered when Bari began locking the door of the converted garage to bar him from walking in on one of her trysts. Bari told her friend that during one of the fights over the spec house, Sweeney had pushed a dryer off the porch in her direction.

What Bari feared most as their divorce was being finalized was that Sweeney would try to take her daughters from her and get exclusive custody. Their fights over her demand for half the value of the spec house—for him either to sell it and give her half the proceeds or to buy her out—were escalating almost daily. The couple's divorce was granted on May 1, 1988, the traditional workers' holiday, deliberately chosen by Bari (even though it fell on a Sunday) as a fitting day for her "liberation."

But even after their divorce was official, they both continued to live on the same property. Bari worried that her former husband was keeping a record of her derelictions for future use in court filings. She smoked pot liberally and admitted to filmmaker Steve Talbot that she had dealt it. Sweeney may have known about other drug use as well. She was running around with what authorities might view as a dangerously radical environmentalist group, and there was her arrest at the Santa Rosa Federal Building in 1988. It would all look bad to authorities in the simmering custody fight that continued after the divorce—as had likewise been the case after Sweeney's first divorce. While Bari wanted to get away from him, she could not afford to alienate him.

Bari also told Bruce Anderson (and later, Steve Talbot and Anna Marie Stenberg) that Sweeney had forced her to have sex and was beating her. Alarmed and seriously concerned, Anderson offered Bari and her daughters sanctuary at his home, but Bari turned it down. He then offered her a gun for self-protection, but again she refused. This seemed to call her claims about Sweeney into question, and at the time it didn't make sense to Anderson. Even so, Bari was taking steps to resolve her troubles by secretly renting a cabin on the remote String Creek outside Willits and surreptitiously moving her personal belongings and political files into these new quarters one small box at a time.

Judi Bari in her organizing uniform: EF T-shirt (sans bra). (AVA archives, courtesy Special Collections of the Shields Library, University of California, Davis.)

Mike Sweeney as recycling boss for Mendocino County. Judi joked to friends that she married him "for eugenic purposes," breeding for "intelligence and hair color." (Courtesy of Ukiah Daily Journal.)

The goodbye party for Judi on Primrose Lane. Holding Mao's Little Red Book aloft, left to right: Mary Moore, Tanya Brannan and Judi Bari. (Courtesy Mary Moore archives.)

Darryl and Judi, the "Dynamic Duo" of Earth First; they were no longer lovers, but she was not ready to sever the relationship. Darryl was still an asset whose help was essential for organizing Redwood Summer. (AVA archives, courtesy Special Collections of the Shields Library, University of California, Davis.)

Judi always resented her successful older sister, Gina Kolata, here greeting fans on her 2003 book tour. (John Storey for the San Francisco Chronicle.)

"Stop Redwood Slaughter": Part of the fight against Pacific Lumber to save the old-growth red-woods known as Headwaters. (AVA archives, courtesy Special Collections of the Shields Library, University of California, Davis.)

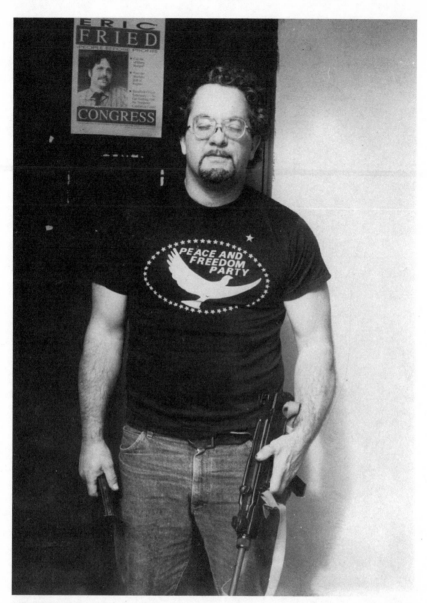

Irv Sutley, Peace and Freedom Party activist and gun enthusiast, willing to train people in their use, especially women friends. (AVA archives, courtesy Special Collections of the Shields Library, University of California, Davis.)

Flyer for Cherney's brainchild, "Day of the Living Dead Hurwitzes," a 1989 EF demonstration at Pacific Lumber headquarters in Scotia.

Bruce Anderson on the job as editor/publisher and chief gadfly of the Anderson Valley
Advertiser. (AVA archives, courtesy Special Collections of the Shields Library, University
of California, Davis.)

Judi Bari in her Highland Hospital bed, ready for her close-up. (Courtesy of photographer Katy Raddatz.)

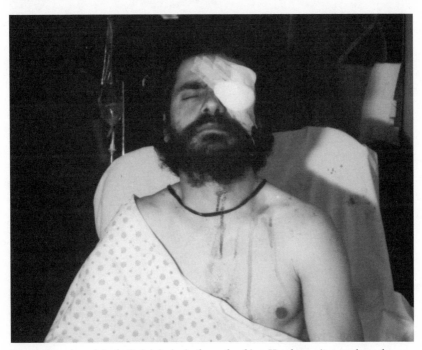

Darryl Cherney sustained minor injuries in the car-bombing. Here he awaits transfer to the Oakland City Jail. (Oakland Police photo.)

Judi Bari's bombed Subaru. (Oakland Police photo.)

NINE

THROUGHOUT THE SPRING OF 1989, Bari was consumed with meetings, with arguing before the Mendocino County Board of Supervisors in Ukiah, and with guest appearances on community FM stations—KZYX in Philo, Mendocino, and KMUD from Humboldt County. Her front-page articles on timber issues in the *Anderson Valley Advertiser* gave her heft as both a reporter and a commentator.

She hadn't felt this good about herself and her political involvement since the days she was running through the streets with her Buffalo House cohorts back in Maryland. On the domestic front, matters were far from easy: money remained tight. She made do with less of her bourgeois comforts (as she would call them)—partly as an outgrowth of her commitment to "deep ecology," but also because of her leftover Maoism. Her work as a carpenter faded away, although she still clung to her working-class credentials.

In June, Bari and Cherney organized a demonstration in the tiny mill town of Calpella in Mendocino County, where Louisiana-Pacific had set up their experimental chipboard mill. The chipboard, which bound leftover chips and scrap with epoxy and resins, was a salvage product that made sense where first- and second-growth redwoods were just about depleted and the loggers were downing third growth—skinny little eighteen-inchers that Bari called "peckerwood." The demonstration was to chastise the timber industry for having cut so rampantly that the peckerwood was all that was left. The regular mills had disappeared, Bari reminded the workers; the chipboard was actually a death knell for the timber industry and the workers' jobs in Mendocino, and for any forests that remained.

A dozen or so sheriff's deputies, joined by officers from the California Highway Patrol, kept Earth Firsters from the mill's gates. One logger was hanging around his pickup truck, periodically turning on his chainsaw in a noisy threat that he waved menacingly at the demonstrators.

As writer David Harris later described the scene, Greg King arrived late during one of these displays and approached the man with the chainsaw once he'd turned it off. He would hardly need it anymore in Mendocino County, King said, because the puny trees used for chipboard could be cut in a mere few months. Then he'd be out of work. The two jawed back and forth. The logger threatened King if he didn't leave. He wouldn't dare do anything, King replied, not with all the cops around. With that, the logger slammed his fist into King's jaw, knocking him down. King jumped up and grabbed a six-foot redwood branch from another EFer, pointed it toward his assailant and charged. There were more epithets, but no arrests were made.

After this outburst, there was a brief respite from heavy confrontations between Earth First and the logging community while the Earth First annual rendezvous convened in New Mexico. Bari and Cherney were among the hundred or so who attended. Kelpie Wilson, an engineer who now lives in Oregon, describes how every evening musicians performed in Earth First's ritual hootenanny. The men predominated, just as they did when it came to public speaking. Women were reticent to put themselves forward—except for Bari, of course, who was always comfortable in the spotlight. "Judi would step up and sing, undaunted by all the men. Then she'd say, 'Okay, it's time for the women now.' She'd walk around the circle of the audience and put her arms around a woman with a guitar and lead her up to the front."

THE TRENCH WARFARE OVER THE FORESTS resumed in August with an incident that the local press would describe as the "Whitehorn riot." Whitehorn was just a speck on the county map, but a locus for meth labs and repeated clashes between newcomers and earlier generations of settlers. One family, the Lancasters, owned a small logging company in the area. A confrontation ensued after a hippie environmentalist accused the Lancasters of cutting outside the boundaries of their timber harvest plan and called in Earth First.

On August 16, twenty EFers showed up outside the Lancasters' property. When a company logging truck finally appeared at the gate, the group—including Bari, Cherney and King—sat down and blocked the road, immobilizing the truck for the next five hours.

Most of the Lancaster clan had already gathered at the gate. It was mellow enough until one of the sons—"Logger Larry" was his moniker—drove down the dirt road with no sign of intending to stop. He scattered the crowd, which included the children of some local hippies. Then came shoving and shouting, and finally violence. When Earth Firsters began photographing Logger Larry, he stepped out of his truck, went for his axe and demolished the camera. The Lancaster matriarch threw a punch at Bari, who karate-punched her right back.

Another Lancaster son, enraged at the sight of his mother under siege, charged into the knot of Earth Firsters. Mem Hill, a fifty-year-old local hippie—who, according to witnesses, had been trying to cool down the exchange—happened to be in the way just then. The Lancaster son walloped her and she went down, unconscious, with blood spilling from her broken nose.

The crowd encircled Mem Hill's assailant, trying to prevent further damage, but soon it all escalated again. Cherney grabbed a guitar case to use as a club. A Lancaster seized a log. Greg King began taking pictures of a family member—clearly a provocation akin to waving the red flag before the bull—and found himself thrown onto the ground. Logger Larry hit a demonstrator with a log. Then an eighteen-year-old Lancaster fired his shotgun into the air and threatened to kill all the hippies.

Bari, Cherney, King and most of the others scattered. King drove down to a public phone and called the county sheriff. The California Highway Patrol and sheriffs' deputies from Humboldt and Mendocino all converged on the spot. There were no arrests. This rankled Bari and she talked about it for the rest of her life as proof that law enforcement was lax when it came to protecting the citizens in Earth First.

The very nature of what EFers were doing there—approaching

small companies like the Lancaster concern, blockading their vehicles in the middle of nowhere and then getting up close and taking photographs and the like—was a provocation to violence. Bari was likely justified, however, in thinking that the county's culture of law enforcement was probably on the side of the old logging families rather than the hippie element.

The situation bred paranoia among both the Earth Firsters and the old logging families. Greg King, for one, was getting so nervous that Cherney wrote a song about him at the Earth First rendezvous that year: "Paranoid Greg, Paranoid Greg, he'll steal your reefer hid behind your keg." In that climate, it was easy to suspect ill will from everyone in the timber industry—except the few loggers whom Bari and Stenberg were bringing into their little union local.

The night after the Whitehorn riot, they all went back to Bari's place in Redwood Valley to make banners and paint the undersides of the platforms they were using for the next day's tree-sit. Earth First was moving its show over to the Louisiana-Pacific logging operation near the Navarro River on Highway 128, west of Boonville. There they would orchestrate another blockade and hoist some demonstrators up into the trees. It was all part of National Tree-Sit Week.

The Navarro site tree-sit was meant to be symbolic, and by the end of the day, the sitters had climbed down. The following day there was to be a big rally over in Fort Bragg in front of the Georgia-Pacific mill, with Bari billed as the main speaker. It was to be the culmination of the whole protest week. On their way there, Bari, her two girls, Pam Davis and her two children, along with Cherney, were heading west on 128. Bari and Cherney were in the front seat of Bari's hatchback wagon; Davis, her son Ian, and Bari's daughter Jessica were in the back seat, while Davis's son Nicolas and Judi's Lisa were jammed in behind them in the hatchback's open trunk area.

As they were approaching the tiny town of Philo, five miles west of Boonville, Bari spotted a knot of pedestrians and slowed her car. She was looking at the pedestrians when, without warning, the car was forcefully hit by a logging truck. Fortunately, the truck wasn't carrying logs; when a truck is loaded, the added tonnage makes it plow through obstacles like a locomotive.

Recalling the incident later on, Bari said: "My car left the ground, sailed through air and hit another truck (which was twice the size of my car) and pushed that truck up two steps." The impact took out the post holding up the porch of the Philo Café, one of the few buildings in Philo's tiny center. (Ironically, the passengers of the vehicle that Bari's hatchback forced onto the café's porch were headed for a spotted owl count on Georgia-Pacific property.)

Her car was totaled. Bari claimed that her passengers all suffered concussions. "We were all out of commission for a month after that. So we didn't think real clearly about what to do about it." But when she saw the video of the Navarro site blockade and tree-sit of the previous day, she realized that the truck was from the same company they had blockaded. She later told Beth Bosk, "We got a description of the driver, and it matched exactly the driver we had blockaded the day before." Bari's conclusion—"that somebody tried to kill us"—was not shared by Pam Davis, who said "the guy just wasn't paying attention."

Bari pressured law enforcement to charge the driver with attempted murder, but officials ruled it an accident. Nonetheless, Bari collected on the accident in a generous settlement from the insurance company; and from that point on, the "attempted murder" became part of her regular spiel about timber industry enemies out to get her.

WHEN BARI WAS NOT BUSY organizing protests against logging, she made herself available for propaganda operations that included education issues involving her children or even kids in the next county. If the so-called timber wars were escalating by the end of 1988 and early 1989, so were the culture wars in the schools.

Earth First demonstrations over Elkhorn Ridge—part of the struggle to stop the logging of three hundred acres of old-growth Douglas fir in Cahto Wilderness—took place near the tiny hamlet of Branscomb where Harwood Lumber, a family-owned company dating back to 1950, was situated. Harwood was one of the last independent logging companies in the area.

It happened that the "Conservation Week" at the local school coincided with the climax of the Elkhorn/Cahto Wilderness demonstrations in the spring of 1989. Tensions spilled over into the classrooms.

Suddenly, timber industry parents were being accosted by their own children who had been "enlightened" by their teachers. Letters and phone calls flooded Harwood from employees and independent truckers complaining about this development. One of the letters read:

> In the middle school, an audio tape was brought to school by the daughter of one of our local Earth First Leaders. The tape was of an Earth First folk singer named Darryl Cherney (the person that sang at the protest on Elkhorn Ridge). While they played, the children were instructed that they could write a letter to the BLM [Bureau of Land Management] if they wished. Two children did so, and shared their letters with their classmates. To our knowledge the BLM has not been invited to the school to present their side of the issue.

As word of what was happening got out, parents complained about one particular book that was now required reading for second-graders in the Laytonville School District. It vilified workers in the timber industry—themselves—the parents said. They worried over how they would appear to their own children.

The book, *The Lorax* by Theodor Seuss Geisel, author of the popular Dr. Seuss stories, set off a tempest. To the logging community, in the words of Bill Bailey, a national logging equipment wholesaler, it appeared to "criminalize a very legitimate and needed industry, [and] implies lack of concern, ignores that we are planting trees, that we give a damn about the creeks and erosion." *The Lorax* contains lines like these:

> And at that very moment, we heard a loud whack!
> From outside in the field came a sickening smack
> of an ax on a tree.
> Then we heard the tree fall.
> The very last Truffula Tree of them all!

It's no wonder the families felt as they did, especially after the classroom discussions that had been so critical of logging.

Art Harwood would later remember that Judi Bari was not part of the original parents' group that got together at the end of May during Conservation Week. But as the *Lorax* controversy developed, she was in the middle of things: "Yeah, she called in all the major media on this one." Bari knew exactly how the story would play because she was spinning it: book-banners seeking to outlaw the book of a beloved children's author.

And so the timber families ended up being further vilified—in *People* magazine and in papers all over the state and country—as uptight, narrow-minded book-burners. Bari made the protesting families look like redneck, fundamentalist ignoramuses—something they didn't forget.

There was one other event that involved the children in the redwood wars, and this time Bari's own daughter would play a leading role. In December 1989, some thirty Santa Rosa school children, ages six to eight, put on an anti-logging demonstration in the city's Old Courthouse Square during the lunch hour. Along with Earth First members Pam Davis, Bari, Cherney and others, they marched and picketed. The kids were all enrolled in the alternative class at west Santa Rosa's public Olivet Elementary School. Chanting "Don't kill the trees!" and led by a bullhorn-wielding Lisa Bari, the children solicited donations for Earth First from passersby.

Their teacher, Jim Hamilton, claimed that all the kids' parents had approved the public display. But Jack Hansen, then superintendent of the tiny two-school Piner-Olivet Union School District, viewed the demonstration with alarm. It was a good thing for students to be exposed to a variety of ideas, Hansen argued to the *Santa Rosa Press Democrat*, but the real question, he said, was "the appropriateness of children, whom I consider to be a captive audience, taking someone's issue" and being pulled into a public protest.

It was Pam Davis who had brought Bari and Cherney into this action. (Davis's press release pointedly advised parents not to call the school secretary about the Earth First demonstration, but to call her instead.) Bari and Cherney sang songs, including one parodying Louisiana-Pacific. It must have been strange to see little eight-year-old Lisa Bari reading a statement criticizing Maxxam's plans to log Headwaters' virgin redwoods. But Judi saw no problem with exploiting her daughter to provide a "cuteness" factor to help the cause.

With all the demonstrating going on, however, Bari and Cherney still found time to attend the 46th IWW General Convention held in Chicago over September 2 and 3, when the Wobblies attempted to reorganize and Bari pushed the worker-and-environmentalist alliance.

JUST BEFORE THE END OF 1989, Cherney came up with the idea of doing an EF demonstration that would be a takeoff on the horror flick *Night of the Living Dead*, in which ghouls rise up and lay siege to the living. Cherney billed his brainchild as "Day of the Living Dead Hurwitzes." And so when Earth First gathered to march through the Pacific Lumber headquarters town of Scotia, the forty or so marchers, including Bari, showed up on Main Street decked out in masks made of Xeroxed copies of a mug shot of Maxxam chief Charles Hurwitz. The chosen photo, according to David Harris's *The Last Stand*, had caught Hurwitz in a particularly ghoulish light. Some of the demonstrators also donned Hurwitz's trademark black-suited attire. The group carried papier-mâché coffins labeled "Economy," "Ecology," "Community" and "Security." Inside one of the coffins was a little girl who was to jump out at the right moment—an attempt to dramatize the loss of jobs and future security. As they marched toward the PL office, they sang a Cherney song (to the tune of "God Rest Ye Merry, Gentlemen"):

> God rest ye merry, lumbermen,
> May nothing you dismay,
> Remember Charlie Hurwitz
> Has debts he has to pay.
> So watch him haul your redwood trees,
> And pension fund away.
> . . . .
> Oh tidings of hunger and fear.

It all seemed promising to Cherney as they first set off, according to David Harris, even though Cherney had actually consulted an astrologer prior to the march and the stargazer had warned him that the chosen day was not very propitious. But Cherney had already done his usual hustling, and the posters and leaflets had gone out with the unlucky date.

By this time, logging families and timber workers had taken their own page out of the Earth First playbook. They were out en masse in front of the Pacific Lumber office, just waiting to confront the demonstrators. They taunted the marchers and threw debris at them. Everyone was intimidated—except for Judi, of course.

When one of the counter-demonstrators singled her out as a "welfare cheat," Harris writes, "she shouted back that she was a full-time carpenter and pretty soon her wages were going to be paying for the taunters' welfare checks, once Hurwitz had mowed down all the old growth and there was nothing left for them to do."

As the two sides argued heatedly, the police arrived to separate them; they ordered the Earth Firsters to leave.

"How come they get to stay and we don't?" Bari fumed.

"Because they work here," the police answered.

Bari found out later (from a local newsie) that the heckling logger group had also included outsiders from the Eel River Sawmill and the Knowland Trucking Company. She was furious: the police had lied to her.

It was the first counter-demonstration, wrote Harris, organized by a new nemesis of Earth First named Candy Boak. She was a large woman who ran a day care center and was married to a gyppo logger. Once a hippie herself, Boak ran around questioning demonstrators on what they did for a living, then recorded their responses on the pages affixed to her clipboard. Based on her interviewing, she claimed that only one of the EFers had a real job, and that was for the Sierra Club. At that point, none of the EFers knew who she was and thus nobody was on guard when she spoke with them. They would not make that mistake again.

Flushed with the success of the counter-demonstration she'd organized, Candy Boak began to show up at Earth First venues around the county as a visible and active presence. She took to phoning Bari regularly, just to let her know she was out there. Soon timber industry workers and their wives would start showing up at EF rallies wearing yellow ribbons (a symbol from the movement to free American hostages held in Iran, which came to signify support for the North Coast loggers and their industry), as a counterpoint to the sassy guerrilla theatrics of Cherney, Bari and King.

Bari called Boak a neo-Nazi, but Boak was every bit as much a prankster as was Cherney. When the EF troubadour was ready to prove his mettle in his first tree-sit, Boak followed "Feral Darryl," as he called himself, in his every move by tracking the CB radio calls he made from his tree perch to the media throughout the state, or to Bari and others. After Bari gave tactical support by making calls to announce the advent of a "tree-sit village," Boak phoned the same media and, pretending to be Bari, called it off.

With Cherney perched high in the redwoods, Boak got a vial of skunk scent from her outdoorsman son, who used it for his trapping. Then she and her husband poured the foul-smelling liquid into a bucket and dumped it around Cherney's tree in the middle of the night. When the paranoid Cherney saw the dark figure of Boak's husband approaching his tree, he nearly flipped out. When the man poured something out around the base of the tree, Cherney was convinced that it was gasoline and he was about to be burned at his own redwood stake. Too high up in the branches to catch the skunk odor, he called everyone in a panic to come and get him down. Over on a nearby ridge, Candy Boak listened in to his plaintive CB cries and had a belly-laugh.

Boak organized among the wives of the gyppos, truckers and loggers. They began to make regular counter-demonstrations. Bari later complained, "Every place we went, they went."

Boak and her people were there in the town of Arcata in Humboldt County the following month when Cherney and Bari's small group of Ecotopia EFers did a "drum-in" at the offices of the Bureau of Land Management. Bari would later recount how she and her group had turned their tormenters' chants of "No Earth First" into "No Experts." She explained that this was a "Wobbly technique," although it might just as easily have come from the traded insults of the schoolyard.

AT THE SAME TIME THAT BOAK'S group was waging guerrilla war against her, Bari clashed with a group of fundamentalist Christians ready to demonstrate against abortion rights in Mendocino County. This demonstration, which occurred just after the November elections of 1988 in front of the new Planned Parenthood Clinic in Ukiah, would have repercussions later, after the car-bombing.

Responding to bomb threats and a reported threat of rape against the clinic's director, Bari called her own demonstration to counter the anti-abortion group's plan to block the clinic. She asked Earth First as an organization to join her. She said the men turned her down, saying it wasn't an Earth First issue. Bari was furious. She told Beth Bosk in her post-car-bombing interview that the harassment by Operation Rescue activists led by Bill Staley, a local Christian fundamentalist timber man, prompted her to mount a defense of the clinic he vowed would never open. Bari tried rounding up female support. She posted a signup sheet at the lesbian coffee shop in Ukiah and gained some recruits. ("Interestingly," she noted, "the lesbians didn't say 'It's not a lesbian issue.'") She also organized several health workers. Typically, she called her new ad hoc group the "Ukiah Anti-Fascist League." For all her efforts, however, she rounded up only about twenty-five people, around the same number as Staley had drummed up to demonstrate in front of the clinic.

Cherney, of course, was there with his guitar and four brand-new songs that he and Bari had composed for the occasion. Pam Davis, Bari's trustiest political sidekick, drove up with her tenant Irv Sutley. Bruce Anderson came. Anna Marie Stenberg's husband, Mike Koepf, and her son Zack also showed up, although Stenberg, conflicted over the abortion issue, did not. Mike Sweeney was there too, despite his divorce from Bari earlier in the year.

Cherney was depicted in a 1990 *California* magazine article as "dressed like a back-alley abortionist" that day, complete with jagged, unwound wire hanger. He did a soft-shoe dance with a cane. He and Bari also sang some unusually offensive songs, Cherney playing his very cheap, disposable guitar, anticipating that violence would ruin his good one.

Bari would later admit that the most outrageous of their songs was "Will the Fetus Be Aborted," with one stanza in particular that made the Christians gasp:

Bridget had two kids already
And an abortion is what she chose.
The Christians showed her a bloody fetus;
She said, "That's fine, I'll have one of those."

Bari said, "We did it with the intention of pushing their buttons to counter their—what we thought were—shocking tactics, by giving them a taste of their own medicine."

Bari and Cherney had intended to provoke the group to attack them, just as they had deliberately provoked the Lancasters by their antics at Whitehorn. But instead, the Christians formed little prayer circles.

In the recapitulation that followed the demonstration, Bari conceded, "I've always had a flippancy that has gotten me into trouble many times." Still, she couldn't keep from gloating: "But the song was too hilarious and I'm not sorry that I wrote it, at all. Jello Biafro and Mojo Nixon actually put out a punk version of it which is even funnier than ours."

Somewhere lurking in that crowd was the future author of what would come to be called the "Lord's Avenger letter." This letter would take credit for the bomb placed in Judi Bari's car and would refer back to that abortion demonstration as a touchstone event.

There were other troubling undercurrents in the air that day. Irv Sutley had filled his car trunk with guns: an Uzi 9mm carbine "Model B" semiautomatic, two Browning high-power 9mm semiautomatic pistols ("the standard sidearm of the Black Panther Party," Sutley dryly pointed out), a Smith & Wesson 547/9mm revolver, a Mossberg pump-action 12-gauge shotgun with an 8-round capacity, and a .22 caliber pistol. At the time, all of the guns were legal and required no permit.

Sutley had packed up his guns because he and Pam Davis were planning to go target-shooting after the abortion rally. They intended to caravan with Cherney and Bari up to the town of Piercy for the night—party, relax, then go shooting the next day. They were to stay at the Bridgewood Motel. Sutley remembered later on that "Judi was in on wanting to go gun-shooting. I had talked to her on the phone before the Ukiah abortion demonstration and I told her I was going to bring some guns to go shooting."

Once at Piercy, however, the group was just unwinding, drinking, smoking pot—all, that is, except for Sutley. He was a usually sober guy who had some strange ideas—about guns, for instance—and a wicked sense of political humor. He called himself the Dick Tuck of lefty politics after the Democratic Party operative whose antics had bedeviled Richard Nixon and other GOP candidates.

That weekend, when everyone was relaxing together, Sutley

spun a future possible prank after he told the group he'd tracked down the upscale home of Representative Doug Bosco, the congressman who had recently declared his commitment to "no drilling for offshore oil." Sutley only half-seriously suggested that should Bosco back off from his position in any way, or even if there were any kind of offshore oil spill, they should dump crankcase oil in his swimming pool, leaving a nasty ooze that would befoul the plumbing.

Then came an event that would have a Rashomon-like ambiguity in the retelling. Bari and Cherney swore it was Sutley who posed Bari holding the Uzi in a menacing Patty-Hearst-as-SLA-Tanya pose. Sutley insists it was the couple's idea, as a possible image for a prospective album of Cherney's songs: "They said, 'let's take photos with the guns.' They wanted to develop an album cover that would be outrageous."

It was Davis who took the photos of Bari holding the Uzi. Later, Sutley sent one of the photos Davis had offered him from that weekend to Bruce Anderson. Sutley had meant it to rib Anderson about the *Anderson Valley Advertiser*'s support of gun control—a position, obviously, that Sutley did not endorse.

Anderson wanted to print the photo with Bari as the new "pinup" poster on the front page, with the slug, "They don't make hippies like they used to." Pam Davis okayed the publication and asked for a photo credit. According to Anderson, Bari apparently liked the idea also.

Mysteriously, another photo of Bari in the Tanya pose from that same batch (Davis habitually ordered a double set of prints) was mailed to the Mendocino County Sheriff's Office in January 1989, with a letter accusing Earth First of taking gun training. The letter also offered to set Bari up on marijuana dealing charges, claiming she sold and sent pot through the mail. But the letter, which would become known as the "Argus letter" (because the writer named himself Argus after the all-watchful creature of Greek myth), didn't surface publicly until a year *after* the car-bombing—when filmmaker Steve Talbot was working on his documentary about the event and the Ukiah sheriff simply handed it over to him. By then the Argus letter had become part of the intricate conspiracy theories that marked Bari's last years.

TEN

IRV SUTLEY WAS BORN IN MARIN COUNTY "before it became Yuppieville." His parents were midwestern moderate Republicans. Sutley was not. His youthful radical inclinations, manifested in his grammar-school refusal to salute the flag (because of the newly inserted phrase "under God"), were confirmed in 1960 while he was attending Tamalpais High School when he heard the famous lawyer Vincent Hallinan, the left-wing Progressive Party's 1952 candidate for U.S. president, who had been invited to speak by the teacher of Sutley's oral English class.

At age seventeen, Sutley joined the Marine Reserves, signing on for eight years—a requirement then for any enlistee under eighteen. In boot camp in San Diego, he refused to attend mandatory church services. After that he was never promoted. Sutley served in a weapons platoon and became fairly proficient with an M-60 machine gun. He also trained in hand-to-hand combat. When instructed to "attack the instructors and hurt them," the burly Sutley offended his superiors by doing so "more proficiently than they expected." He was finally thrown out of the Marines for his opposition to the Vietnam War.

Sutley joined the newly formed Peace and Freedom Party in 1967 and soon began campaigning for its slate of candidates. Four years later he was recruited into the Communist Party, attracted by what he describes as their "political philosophy of atheism."

Sutley was a gun enthusiast and more than willing to train people in their use, especially women. In the late 1960s, he wore several guns through the passenger terminal of the San Francisco airport on the way to catch a flight. The police detained him before he got on the plane, but no charges were filed.

In 1988, Sutley was living in Santa Rosa and helping his friend Eric Fried, the Peace and Freedom candidate, in his run for Democrat Doug Bosco's congressional seat. Fried, Sutley and Pam Davis were friends and all members of the Communist Party Club in Santa Rosa. Fried was unopposed as a Peace and Freedom candidate; Cherney was one of three challengers to Bosco in the Democratic primary. At one point, Sutley tried to talk Cherney out of running so he wouldn't take "progressive" votes away from Fried. But Cherney stayed in the race and won seven hundred votes, losing to Bosco by a wide margin.

Some time that same year, Sutley was looking for a place to live. Pam Davis offered the garage at her grandmother's house in Forestville, a couple of miles west of Santa Rosa, where she had moved with her two boys after she had split up with their father. The garage needed work to be habitable. Davis agreed that Sutley could take the value of the improvements he offered to make—wiring for electricity and putting in drywall—off his rent. He had use of the bathrooms and kitchen in the main house through a breezeway that connected both structures. He often baby-sat for Davis's boys.

During his time at the Davis household, Sutley also got to know Judi Bari; he had an extension phone in his quarters and often answered her calls to Davis. Sometimes, he says, he and Bari had long talks about politics, and this led him to begin participating in demonstrations, such as the one at the Ukiah Safeway that Bari and Cherney put on in support of the United Farm Workers.

Not long after Sutley moved onto the grandmother's property, Davis began to have problems with a former boyfriend who suddenly moved into the rundown property next door. Davis felt threatened by his presence so close to her because she'd had trouble with him before—enough to obtain a restraining order against him, which had since lapsed.

The ex-boyfriend hung out with his lowlife friends in his front yard and worked on cars and motorcycles day and night, greeting both Sutley and Davis with baleful stares. Davis was truly frightened. Sutley offered to help her renew the restraining order. She retained a lawyer and Sutley accompanied her to court. In the meantime, whenever he entered or left the house, he prominently displayed one of his Uzis strapped across his shoulder to show that Davis was protected, and that, as he put it, "I'd kill him if he tried to harm her."

Davis successfully renewed the restraining order and the old boyfriend moved away. Not long afterward she spoke to Sutley in her living room about Bari's problems with her ex, Mike Sweeney. "It was Judi's knowing I was willing to use armed self-defense around Pam that led to Pam's approaching me with the solicitation to kill Mike Sweeney," he says. "I think it was in early '89 when the subject first came up." He set the scene: "I was in the room and standing by the front door when she started to talk about it. I can't remember her exact words, but she told me that Mike was hassling Judi and that he wouldn't do a property settlement with her.

"Judi wanted the property to be sold or Mike to buy her out. Pam said Judi had told her that the property was worth a hundred thousand and that if Mike died, Judi's share would be fifty thousand dollars and that I would get 10 percent of that or five thousand dollars. I wasn't even offered cash! I didn't know if I accepted it how they were going to pay. I was stunned. I'd never been asked to kill anyone."

Sutley told Davis he wouldn't do it, but he did offer to lend her one of his guns. He advised that Bari "ought to get out of there." At the end of the conversation, he says, he reiterated his position that a contract murder was "not the way to handle it."

"A little bit later," Sutley continued, "Pam talked to Judi and then Pam said to me that Judi had to have him taken care of." He was freaking out over the conversation. Should he alert Sweeney? Was he culpable if he didn't? Should he tell the authorities?

He sought the counsel of his ex-wife, Toni Novak. He felt good about one thing, he told her. At least, after his refusal "there was no way Judi could go ahead with it because the cat was out of the bag. Once she'd asked and been refused, I didn't see any way for her to do it. On the other hand, if you're solicited to commit a murder you commit a felony by not reporting it."

Toni Novak corroborates Sutley's story that he revealed the solicitation to her and her boyfriend at the time, although she wasn't sure how serious it was. After he related the offer, she told him what she'd overheard Bari say about her stormy marriage to Sweeney at the party that had followed the big Bohemian Grove civil disobedience in Sonoma County in 1984.

Years later, Bari's other good friend, Anna Marie Stenberg, confirmed that Judi had talked about finding someone who might help her problem with Sweeney, although at the time she didn't mention Sutley by name. Stenberg remembers the conversation as having taken place the winter before the car-bombing, when Bari was pushing her ex on the property split of the spec house. Without giving any new details, Bari said that Sweeney had become violent, Stenberg recalls. "Judi then told me that Pam Davis knew somebody who took care of Pam's abuse problems from an ex-boyfriend. And he was going to take care of her problem as well. I didn't know who she was talking about—only that he was a friend of Pam Davis."

In 1997, the last year of Bari's life, the *Santa Rosa Press Democrat* ran a story about the alleged solicitation to murder Mike Sweeney. The article focused on Irv Sutley's passing a lie detector test involving questions about it, administered by a retired Secret Service agent. A few days later, Annie Esposito interviewed Bari about the matter for her program on KZYX radio. Bari denied that any solicitation from or through her had occurred and she dismissed the whole affair as a "joke" by a "friend" of hers, insisting, moreover, that "everyone knew it was a joke."

Sutley believed it was real.

IN THE FALL OF 1989, BARI was souring on her relationship with Cherney, and he was not taking it too well. As *California* writer Jonathan Littman put it,

> Bari began receiving invitations to talk on the same Mendocino radio station that Cherney frequented, and soon people were listening to the sidekick more than to the showman. "As we kept interviewing them, Judi's star began to rise," says the show's then co-host, Andrée Connors. "She started eclipsing Darryl."

Cherney couldn't come out and say he was jealous, but he was always complaining or nitpicking. It didn't help matters that Bari was dismissive and often openly contemptuous of him. But it was also true that she had an outraged ex-husband, and so had less time and patience to deal with a sulking, high-maintenance boyfriend. Increasingly, the couple haggled over who would lead the Earth Firsters in Northern California and the Northwest. Cherney was still soliciting backing from the old redneck EFers who were increasingly alienated from Bari's Wobbly and Marxist-inspired environmentalism—but only behind her back. Around EF founder Dave Foreman and the rest of them, Littman wrote, Cherney "would rant militantly about tree spiking. Around Bari, he would wax eloquent about worker empowerment." This infuriated Bari. "He was an embarrassment," Bari said of Cherney. "Workers have built-in bullshit detectors."

So she dumped him. He was devastated, having been convinced they were a perfect merger of politics and love. KMUD radio host Andrée Connors was a witness to their bickering and recalled teasing Bari about her heartlessness. "I said to her, 'Judi, you broke up with him and within a week he's a madman.'"

Characterizing her affair with Cherney to Beth Bosk after the car bomb as a "somewhat loose romantic relationship," Bari went on to decry all her relationships with men, using feminist rhetoric as her justification:

> There is a barrier to how close I can get to a man. And that barrier is based on the fact that I have not met a man that in his very deepest gut can really see a woman as an equal. They can say all the words they want, they can mouth all the right phrases, but when it comes down to it, every one of them resorts to the lowest kind of sexism in an argument, in a moment of anger, and that reveals to me that way deep down inside of them, they don't think that women should be as pushy as I am, they don't think that women should be in the position that I am. It's a threat to a man to be with a woman like me who is assertive, who is vocal, and who is doing things that are traditionally reserved for men.

But she was not ready to sever the relationship with Cherney entirely. He was still an asset whose help was essential for organizing Redwood Summer. The manic minstrel could still delight the crowds.

ELEVEN

BARI HAD JUST BARELY SURFACED in Northern California Earth First when there was an event that raised the fear factor for the radical organization nationwide. In May 1989, the FBI busted Dave Foreman, Earth First's founder and most recognizable spokesman, in his Tuscon home while he lay in bed with his wife. He was charged with conspiracy to down the major power lines of a pumping station that served the Central Arizona Project (CAP), a huge $3.5 billion water system that took Colorado River water for the greening of Tucson and Phoenix.

Since CAP was federally funded, the FBI had jurisdiction. One of Foreman's alleged crimes was paying $500 to an undercover government agent to destroy the lines. Four others were also charged.

The conspiracy charges were a stretch. Moreover, the caper had been suggested by the FBI's own undercover agent, Mike Fain. The agent, who went by the name "Tait," had been a vocal proponent of sabotage, which raised the issue of entrapment. Indeed, "Tait" had even selected the target, the rest of the Earth First group maintained. As part of his infiltration, he had also turned one of the group, Ron Frazier, an ecoterrorist wannabe and druggie who'd used everything from heroin to LSD, into an informer. Frazier was reportedly paid a total of $54,000 for his collaboration.

The Earth Firsters were also accused of having even grander schemes for destruction. The FBI said it had interrupted Earth First plans to sabotage power supplies to three nuclear facilities: the Palo Verde power plant in Arizona, Diablo Canyon in Avila and a weapons grade plutonium facility at Rocky Flats, Colorado. The pumping station they'd tripped up on was merely preliminary to bigger ecotage to come.

Friends of Foreman quickly enlisted Wyoming defense attorney Gerry Spence, the buckskin-jacketed cowboy who had landed $1.8 million in damages (huge at the time) for the family of Karen Silkwood after she died under questionable circumstances while on her way to meet a *New York Times* reporter and blow the whistle on her employer, the Kerr-McGee plutonium processing plant. Spence took the Foreman case pro bono and immediately began the task of transforming his client into a bona fide Western hero, while casting the FBI in the familiar—for radicals—role of framer of the innocent.

Eventually Foreman pled guilty to a misdemeanor with five years' probation instead of a trial that many thought he'd win. In part, he wanted to spare some of his codefendants who had been pressured to testify against him. Also, the prospective trial was losing its media draw, fizzling into inertia. Once the plea-bargaining began, Gerry Spence bowed out. He was a courtroom showman, not a negotiator.

Spence and the attorneys for the other defendants had pointed to the two-and-a-half-year, $3-million investigation—part of the FBI's $35-million-a-year budget for domestic counterterrorism—in charging that the bureau was out to get Earth First. Bari and others immediately claimed that the FBI was on their trail too, naming Richard Held, then head of the San Francisco bureau, as the mastermind of spying on the North Coast EF. But one local FBI agent, speaking on condition of anonymity, later said that neither Earth First nor Judi Bari, nor any other activists in Mendocino, were targeted at all. It was the far right, not her group, that the bureau considered dangerous: "Judi Bari and the leftists posed no threat to this country at all!" It was a claim that Bari would have found particularly insulting.

This was the era of the Unabomber, however. Considering what was known of his anti-technology sentiments—to say nothing of the fact that one of his victims, Gilbert Murray, was a lobbyist for the timber industry—there might well have been detectives sniffing around Mendocino Earth First.

Julie Verran, the Sierra Club representative who once lived at the Bridgewood Motel when Cherney was staying there, believes that law enforcement scrutiny of the environmentalists grew out of that initial hunt for the Unabomber, whom many authorities—and, Verran said, the state police especially—believed was embedded in the North Coast of California. "They were harassing us in eighty-nine, looking for the Unabomber—looking real hard and for a while they thought Darryl or Judi was the one," she recalled. "The cops would come up behind me on the freeway—not to run license plate checks. They'd just be there for miles and miles. But people like Greg King and Bari and Cherney got the most pressure. I think Judi was genuinely being followed."

There was already a pandemic of paranoia in Mendocino County. With roughly half the population growing dope, with the large numbers of crazies who had fled their urban nightmares and were living on the dole, and with the overlay of radical hostility toward government agencies, paranoia was an ineradicable virus. Suspicion of neighbors, or of encroaching wineries, or of big corporations reinforced the garden-variety anti-law-and-order wariness.

Verran and others remember Bari herself as being out front in concocting scenarios of persecution and conspiracy. She denounced the ultraconservative Sahara Club in Fort Bragg and Candy Boak with her organization of loggers' wives and gyppos, and their counter-demonstrations of Earth First, as being officially sanctioned by the FBI and paid for by the timber industry. Bari refused to see the obvious—that Earth First's antics had spawned a small army of grassroots counteractivists determined to block the group's every step. Why would it take the FBI to get locals in the timber industry aroused? But over the years Bari had acquired a nasty habit of accusing anyone who opposed her of being an FBI or police agent—a way of delegitimizing their political views.

"Judi was convinced I was FBI," Verran says. She believes Bari's hostility towards her dated from an earlier encounter at the Mendocino Environmental Center in Ukiah. "I had scheduled the use of a room for a meeting of the Sierra Club, which I'd booked ahead of time. When I came in, she and her daughters had all the tables in use there for one of her art projects. I had to kick her out along with her kids. I think that's why she decided I was an agent."

If Bari's accusations seemed extravagant, they were in keeping with the paranoia that the people from Berkeley and elsewhere in the

Bay Area had brought with them when they moved to the North Coast in earnest during the 1970s. Bari was a later arrival, but more extreme than the others in the accusation department—just as she had been back in Baltimore when she accused a fellow student of being a police agent the time she and a housemate were arrested for drugs. She would become even more accusatory after the car-bombing, charging people who disagreed with her on political issues with being agents or even with *acting like agents* to sow dissension in Earth First, as a tactical ploy in an FBI conspiracy to destroy the organization from within.

EARLY IN 1990 BARI, CHERNEY and several volunteers from the Environmental Protection Information Center formed a convoy and headed across the country. They would be gone for nearly three weeks, spending almost two weeks at the Highlander Research and Education Center in Knoxville, Tennessee, to prepare for the summer of protest in the redwoods that Fred the Walking Rainbow had suggested as the Next Big Thing.

For Bari, setting foot on those hills must have been as emotionally charged as making his first *hadj* to Mecca is for a devout Muslim. Highlander was an authentic Communist landmark, having served as a retreat for battle-weary party members beginning in the 1930s. And during the civil rights movement it had played host to figures like Martin Luther King Jr. and Rosa Parks. With attractions like Pete Seeger, it still combined the appeal of nature with the esprit of the old Commie camps.

Bari and the others took seminars at Highlander. They studied "organizing" while sitting in with coal miners from Kentucky. They looked back over the history of the Tennessee Valley Authority project as a way of linking environmental and labor struggles, then traveled to West Virginia to see coal miners on their native turf. The group returned to California high on the experience and ready to go.

Highlander had preached a nonviolent model. Bari now emphasized nonviolence in her speeches, although she had not in any sense renounced the rhetoric of revolutionary violence, particularly with regard to international "liberation" struggles. She could talk her way around the contradictions. It may have been true, as Anna Marie Stenberg observed, that "Judi wasn't a Gandhian," but she saw that the planned summer of mass protest could create a potentially dangerous situation, and that the ideal of nonviolence would reassure the thousands of activists she expected to recruit (even if it wouldn't diffuse entrenched local hostility in the pro-logging camp).

But while she had spent time in the cradle of America's nonviolent protest movement, and indicated that she intended to call for nonviolence during Redwood Summer, Bari still would not condemn violence carried out by others. Speaking about the question to journalist Beth Bosk, she said, "We don't have a chance of saving the world ecologically...if we don't overthrow capitalism." (Socialism needed work, she said, but insisted it had a better chance than capitalism of redeeming itself on the ecological front.) Asked if she believed in "armed struggle," she showed only a shred of ambivalence: she would never, as she put it, "presume to tell the people of El Salvador [or elsewhere] not to pick up arms" in their "Third World liberation struggle." And where the environment was concerned, the situation was even more apocalyptic:

> I think that whatever we have to do to get rid of them [capitalists] before they destroy the earth is what we need to do, and I don't think it immoral to use violence if that's what needs to be done to save the earth, to save inhabitants of all species.... [W]e're talking about the death of the planet.... We can argue as long as we want whether it is moral or immoral to use violence or to defend yourself against violence, but when the planet is gone, it is gone, and we are very close to that. The ability of this planet to sustain life as we know it is very close to the end.

Within her tired, fatuous Marxist cant, Bari was expressing what almost all the citizens of enviroland in Mendocino and elsewhere passionately believed: Once the redwoods were gone, they would be gone forever.

Potential violence against Bari and Cherney was implied in the threats they were now receiving in letters and in flyers, about which they complained loudly, but without ever acknowledging that their provocative utterances and publications only intensified the climate of hostility. In fact, Cherney had put out his own not-so-veiled death warrant against Maxxam's Charles Hurwitz.

In January 1990, as the issue of the Headwaters Grove gained mounting publicity, Hurwitz, the head of Maxxam (which had become the new owner of Pacific Lumber), and Louisiana-Pacific's CEO, Harry Merlo, met with three leading North Coast politicians—Congressman Doug Bosco, Assemblyman Dan Hauser and State Senator Barry Keene—to hammer out a compromise on timber. It was an attempt to forestall, as Keene put it, "extreme results...dictated from outside." He was referring to the Forests Forever Initiative, which they feared would make it onto the state's fall ballot (and would have redefined management of California's forests to reflect a sustainable crop ideal that would curtail clear-cutting). The meeting was well publicized even though it took place behind closed doors.

Soon Greg King traveled to Sacramento with a small group to demand a meeting with Hurwitz. There they distributed flyers (designed by Cherney) announcing a $5,000 reward for Hurwitz under the heading, "Wanted." The flyer suggested the Old West's "Dead or Alive" posters, implicitly carrying the same threat.

Then one morning at the junction of Highways 36 and 101, a group of EFers captured a PL logging truck by chaining themselves to the vehicle. Cherney serenaded the group with his new song about Hurwitz, which went, in part:

> Now Earth First offers a reward:
> Five thousand we will pay
> Whoever captures Charles Hurwitz
> And puts that boy away.

And when, later that same year, Hurwitz showed up at his son's University of Texas business school to deliver a speech, EFers rushed the hall, distributing the "Wanted" flyers as one EF member shouted, "Hurwitz must die."

But there had been threats and dirty tricks on the other side. Anna Marie Stenberg's car was vandalized twice. Betty Ball received a death threat at the Mendocino Environmental Center. Cherney himself was sent a cartoon drawing of a hippie nailed to a redwood tree, with spikes through the hands and feet, Christlike—except for his Earth First T-shirt. Both he and Bari received copies of a leaflet announcing a "Nation Wide Tree *Shit*" with Earth First's clenched-fist logo and a drawing of two EFers up a tree on a platform, defecating over the edge onto the wildlife below. Across the bottom ran instructions to contact "Darrell [*sic*] Cherney." While the leaflet misspelled Cherney's name, it got his home phone correct.

Some of the threat letters were simply vulgar denunciations, such as one from the so-called "Committee for the Death of Earth First" that began with the juvenile opener, "It has come to our attention that you are an Earth First! fellatio expert and suck dicks in outhouses." Another letter from the same ostensible group conflated the names of Judi Bari and Betty Ball of the MEC, addressing someone named Judi Ball. It denounced this hybrid Earth First leader as a "lesbian whose favorite pastime is to eat box lunches in pajamas," and warned, "No longer can sleazy dikes like you operate with impunity through the guise of anonymity. We know who you are, where you live, and continue to home in on you...but you don't know who we are."

Bari was really frightened when a dead cat was left outside her door. Equally chilling was the photocopied image of herself caught in the crosshairs of an overlaid rifle scope, which was nailed to the front door of the MEC in the middle of the night. Bari told an interviewer that she had taken her girls and gone into hiding for a few days after this threat. And finally was the typewritten letter warning, "Get out and go back to where you come from. We know everything. YOU WON'T GET A SECOND WARNING." (This so-called "Second Warning letter" would later be linked to other letters in the Bari case and pored over for telltale signs of authorship.)

Such was the charged climate in early 1990 when Bari was debating whether to participate in a panel featuring both labor and environmentalists at the Environmental Law Conference in Oregon. Even this prospective appearance, she claimed, brought a threatening phone call from a self-identified union member of the Western Council of Industrial Workers, an American Federation of Labor union representing Oregon mill workers. The caller, according to Bari, warned her not to "set foot in Oregon" and said that if any of his workers spoke to her, "they'd be out of a job."

At one point, Bari decided against going to the conference. The reason was her worry about the death threats, according to Anna Marie Stenberg, with whom Bari consulted on her decision. It was a hard call: Bari loved the limelight. But Stenberg noted with alarm that her friend was developing a victim mentality: "When we were trying to decide whether she should go to the conference, she actually said to me, 'I am a martyr for the cause!'"

The two women then worked together to draft a statement that Bari and—insofar as she could speak for the organization—Earth First were calling for an end to tree-spiking as inconsistent with her attempt to build a coalition with timber workers. With the elimination of tree-spiking, there should be no further impediment to a united front of labor and environmentalists against corporate timber. (Tree-spiking had been made a federal offense in 1988.)

In March, Bari changed her mind and went to the Oregon Environmental Law Conference. When mill worker Gene Lawhorn, appearing with Bari on a labor and environmental panel, publicly challenged her to disavow tree spikes in the name of green and labor solidarity, she did exactly that.

It was only after having crossed this hurdle that Bari could make a public announcement about the "Mississippi Summer in the California Redwoods" they were planning. She and Cherney spoke about it at a student environmental rally in Sacramento and at an EF rally in Eureka. But the summer plans received wider publicity when she gave an interview about them to the *Santa Rosa Press Democrat*'s Mike Geniella, to whom she had been feeding articles on timber for long enough now that she had his ear. As Bari would exult in an article collected in her book *Timber Wars*, "It went national on the wire service.... Requests for info started coming in from all over, and we realized this thing was bigger than we thought."

She now went on KMUD-FM radio in Garberville and KZYX in Philo. She interviewed with the press and anyone else, talking a blue streak about how she hoped Earth First could forestall the cutting in the woods long enough for passage of the "Forests Forever" and "Big Green" initiatives that had qualified for the California state ballot in the fall. She traveled down to San Francisco and went before the city's board of supervisors to talk up the "Redwood Summer" (as it was now called because of resentment from veterans of the 1964 Mississippi Summer for civil rights, who were protective of the name).

There was one interesting demonstration in March at the Redwood Region Logging Conference in Ukiah. A half-million-dollar "fellerbuncher" owned by Okerstrom Logging was on display. This machine, one of three owned by Okerstrom, was capable of grabbing and chewing up dozens of trees at a time and would become a favorite target of local environmentalists. EFers, after creating a diversion, climbed the hated machine and strung a banner across it, proclaiming, "This Thing Kills Jobs & Forests." A few weeks later, the same machine burned up in the woods near Willits. Bari coyly celebrated her own smart-ass wit in her obituary for the fellerbuncher: "When asked if we were responsible, I told the press it wasn't me—I was home in bed with five witnesses."

But the threats of violence against her continued. She worried about herself and her girls, and she communicated those fears to Dave Foreman. She later credited Foreman with helping her psychologically. Bari told one interviewer that he had advised her, "Hang tough. You'll be remembered a hundred years from now."

When she finally contacted the county sheriff's office about the death threats, a move she made reluctantly because of her antipathy to police agencies, she was rebuffed. She later quoted Lieutenant Steve Satterwhite as telling her he "didn't have the manpower to investigate. If you turn up dead, then we'll investigate." This response showed how much Bari had angered the locals with her year of visibility as an Earth First rabble-rouser, and she never forgot the brush-off.

Things went no better when, a month prior to the bombing, she and Earth First managed to put Redwood Summer on the county board of supervisors' agenda for discussion. When Bari waved the written death threats she'd received in front of the board and complained of her treatment at the hands of Lieutenant Satterwhite, Supervisor Marilyn Butcher icily admonished her, "You brought it on yourself, Judi."

TWELVE

As Judi Bari planned for Redwood Summer, she left most of the recruitment road shows at California community and state colleges to Cherney. She wanted to be home as much as possible with her daughters and thought she could conduct her organizing activities by phone. Besides, Bari found Cherney increasingly difficult to work with and wanted to be away from him.

She was his opposite in her methodical and organized approach to politics. She carefully maintained the lists of names—the volunteers, the donors, the sympathetic or at least neutral logging folk—while he was all spontaneity and improvisational chaos. During that hectic spring of 1990, Cherney was getting in the way. In fact, to hear Bari's friends talk about it, he was having a breakdown. The ending of his affair with Bari had devastated him. He felt shunted aside. And as Bari saw it, he'd begun making some serious mistakes. So she called EFer Mike Roselle to take Cherney away to Arizona for three weeks to chill him out before the two were scheduled to appear in Santa Cruz on May 24.

One of Cherney's gaffes came during his appearance on the CBS show *60 Minutes*. It was a huge publicity victory to get on the show at all, but in Bari's view, Cherney blew it when he told Mike Wallace, "If I found I had a fatal disease, I would strap dynamite to myself and take out Glen Canyon Dam or the Maxxam building."

Bari was still cringing from this kamikaze statement when Cherney got himself into more hot water. And this time, he would drag Earth First in with him, just when Bari was attempting to make the group more widely acceptable.

The twentieth anniversary of Earth Day was being celebrated on Sunday, April 22, 1990. The *New York Times* estimated that 200 million people in 140 countries participated in what they billed as "the largest grass roots demonstration in history." There was a trash-pickup trek on Mt. Everest, a "lie-down" by 5,000 people to protest car pollution in Italy, 75,000 in Central Park, 125,000 on the National Mall. In San Francisco, the Grateful Dead headlined an Earth Day celebration.

To the annoyance of activists, Earth Day seemed to have gone mainstream as never before when the U.S. Environmental Protection Agency sponsored Earth Fest '90 at the Washington Monument, where some 2,000 people participated and John Denver sang a new song. Most galling of all to enviros was the rush by big corporations to wave their own green flags. Even big oil began producing nature-loving advertisements. Such attempts to paint corporations green were cleverly dubbed "eco-pornography" by San Francisco's maverick adman Jerry Mander.

The Monday after Earth Day, radical demonstrators made their dissatisfaction known. In San Francisco, 500 demonstrators rampaged at the Pacific Stock Exchange, throwing golf balls, rocks and eggs at police and shattering the windows of the nearby Bank of America. There were 49 arrests. In New York, in a demonstration of some 700 people, 204 of them were arrested, several for assault.

Another blow against the corporate embrace of Earth Day took place in the town of Watsonville, in Santa Cruz County, that same day. Eco-saboteurs unbolted a 100–foot-tall Pacific Gas and Electric wooden power transmission pole, toppling it. Three bolts had been unlocked; a fourth was cut off with a handsaw. The first power failure occurred at 1:37 A.M. Then, when PG&E crews transferred power to another line and caused a switching overload, a 3,000-foot, 115,000-volt transmission line in nearby Morgan Hill also crashed to the ground. A fire erupted in a substation during the switching process. The downed line sent up spectacular 25-foot arcs of electricity, visible from a mile away.

A second power transmission tower was sabotaged. Discovered only in the course of an aerial survey by PG&E over a remote area, it was repaired without incident, at an estimated cost of $300,000. Officials said the complete repair would take at least three weeks. Nearly 100,000 people lost power in communities from Watsonville north to Scotts Valley, including area hospitals. Some didn't have power restored for nearly eight hours. Dominican Hospital's emergency generators failed for about thirty minutes, necessitating the delivery of twin baby boys by flashlight.

A group calling itself "Earth Night Action Group" or ENAG claimed responsibility for the two acts of sabotage in a letter delivered to the *San Francisco Examiner*, the Bay City News Service and the Associated Press. In it the group said it had targeted PG&E as punishment for its horning in on Earth Day:

> Corporate absolvement [*sic*] through support of Earth Day is a farce. E.N.A.G. apologizes for any inconvenience, but asks public [*sic*] to consider the destruction the earth endures to provide electricity. Accept the reprieve we have given the earth by cutting the cord from Moss Landing Power Plant. In defense of mother earth, we say: no thanks to lip service from corporate earth rapist [*sic*] like P.G.&E. direct action not words. Earth day is every day.

The FBI was already on the case, claiming that these sabotages were acts of "domestic terrorism" and therefore under its purview. The FBI mentioned the ENAG statement and its possible link to the Earth First–type flyer that had been circulating in and around Santa Cruz and San Francisco prior to the ecotage, with the printed legend, "Earth Night 1990. Go out and do something for the Earth at night!"

Karen Debraal, the Santa Cruz contact person for Earth First, insisted that ENAG was not affiliated with EF, but praised the perpetrators nonetheless. "I think they are heroes and what they did was great," she enthused. "I wish people would get past their petty inconveniences."

Other local environmentalists, however, felt as though they were collateral damage and weren't above lecturing the culprits. Dan Haifley of Save Our Shores—and speaking also for Ecology Action, the Greens, Forest Forever and the Environmental Council—said, "A couple of macho crazies with chainsaws and guns can ruin much more than a power pole. They can set back the very movement they claim to represent. Being an environmentalist means working gently for the earth and for its inhabitants. It does not mean jeopardizing people's lives and frightening people." Haifley and other local editorialists were furious that the ecotage recalled the painful memories of the Loma Prieta earthquake, from which Santa Cruz County was still recovering one year later.

There were obvious suspects in the case. One was Darryl Cherney. In the week prior to the mayhem, responding to a radio interviewer's question "What would you like to see take place on Earth Day?" he said what he wanted most was for everyone to go without power for one day.

Bari was just as callous in an interview on Berkeley's leftist KPFA-FM, right after the PG&E sabotage. "Desperate times demand desperate measures," she said (which prompted the AVA's Bruce Anderson to ask in exasperation, "What desperate times?"). Later, on the same subject, she put down the "sniveling" rich suburbanites of Santa Cruz who were inconvenienced because their "ice cream had melted" as a result of the power outages—ignoring the obvious fact that the well-to-do were not the only victims.

Two days after the first PG&E tower toppled over in Santa Cruz County, a few of the dozen or so assembled Earth First demonstrators nimbly ascended the cables of the Golden Gate Bridge to within ten feet of the top of the north tower. They had Jiffy-glued the doors to the bridge's internal elevators, making pursuit by the authorities impossible—at least for the time being.

They carried with them a cumbersome 100-foot-long banner they hoped to secure and then unfurl for the morning commute. It read: "Defend ancient forests. No to fossil fuels. Earth First!" Cherney was part of the group but remained below on the roadway.

Ironworkers from the Golden Gate Bridge District had to make the perilous climb up the cables to the struts. They arrived before the banner could be hung out, then "escorted" the demonstrators down. Newspapers reported that Greg King was on his cell phone doing a live interview with local radio KCBS when the ironworkers cautiously ushered him down to face arrest. The rest of the group, brandishing their signs, refused to leave. The siege lasted three hours. The California Highway Patrol and police from around the Bay Area who'd arrived to assist the CHP during the rush-hour chaos arrested the group on "suspicion of creating a public nuisance, vandalism, interfering with a police officer and trespassing."

Two Oakland police officers conducted a search of Cherney's van, and what they found was the final straw between him and Bari: the flyers recommending monkey-wrenching that the FBI had linked to the ENAG sabotage of the PG&E towers in Santa Cruz the previous day. Also in his possession were flyers for Redwood Summer. After the car-bombing, in their briefing to Oakland police, the FBI noted the telling similarity of the language between the flyers in Cherney's possession and the statements of ENAG taking credit for toppling the towers.

Because Cherney had been on the roadway, he too was arrested for trespassing. Police released him the same day, but the damage was done. The headlines linked Earth First not only to the assault on the Golden Gate Bridge, but also to the sabotage in Santa Cruz.

A few days after the bridge "storming," the *San Francisco Examiner* printed a story envisioning dire outbreaks of domestic ecoterrorism. It was fantasy, but it raised the ante on Earth First and fellow travelers. "The Scenario," as the piece was called, began: "Terrorists, whether religious fanatics or political zealots, attack the Bay Area. They plant explosives on the transmission towers of key electric lines. They bomb switching stations. They poison the water." The article went on to discuss the Golden Gate Bridge climb attempt, the Santa Cruz power lines, Earth First! and even Redwood Summer, linking them all by juxtaposition in a compromising way.

DESPITE BARI'S PRESS RELEASE renouncing tree-spiking, the FBI never bought her commitment to nonviolence; so it was not surprising that the bureau was interested in her and Cherney. But Bari could not acknowledge her own contribution to her predicament. She raged against her now ex-lover—first, for permitting the search of his van, and second, for being so stupid as to leave it full of the incriminating flyers. Cherney's crime was getting caught. At the Oregon Environmental Law Conference where she denounced tree-spiking, Louisiana-Pacific's director of security, Frank Wigginton, had taken a video of Bari handing out the same flyer.

To make matters worse, Cherney's logorrhea whenever he got

near the media had led to a virtual admission that he was the author of the flyer. He told the *Santa Cruz Sentinel* that the poster "was made in direct response to the Earth Day hype we felt was kissing the butt of corporations." Defending the perpetrators, he went on to predict that in twenty years, "the eco-terrorists will be looked upon as heroes."

He was "running his mouth," as Bari said. And she said plenty more than that, according to writer David Harris, who witnessed a bristling argument between the couple in a San Francisco restaurant shortly after Cherney's release from police custody following the bridge caper. "Their relationship was crashing," Harris said. "It was a stormy argument. She threw a fit about him being caught with all that incriminating stuff that ended up in the hands of the Oakland police.... In that relationship she wore the pants. I got a strong sense that Darryl was groveling."

Harris and others had many concerns about the summer project—beginning with the name "Mississippi Summer in the Redwoods," which appeared to equate the smallish environmental movement to the civil rights struggle in the summer of 1964. (He approved the name change to Redwood Summer.) But now there were far more serious criticisms being leveled at the whole enterprise, principally with the danger in bringing hundreds or even thousands of young people into a rural area and pitting them against a logging community that already felt pressured by the loss of jobs. Some viewed the invasion of youth as a deliberate attempt to create violence, and not, as in the civil rights movement, to defuse it.

Her critics said that Bari might be powerful on the podium inspiring the troops, but she didn't really have a plan for housing or feeding them or providing them with legal help before and after the series of demonstrations scheduled at various logging sites in Mendocino and Humboldt. Money had begun to come in from many supporters who liked her ideas, but most of them could more easily part with dollars than with the time and commitment needed to sustain a movement. Critics charged that Bari's ambitious plans were not backed up by any follow-through, that she was "flying by the seat of her pants." As David Harris said, "They had no sense of what a huge undertaking this would be. They were used to being The

Organization in a little community of long hairs and then creating press opportunities—all on a small scale."

BARI HAD SET UP SEVERAL SECRET meetings in Ukiah and Branscomb with gyppos and loggers and lumber mill CEO Art Harwood to lobby them for an agreement to subdue potential hostility toward her followers.

She shared the summer plans and briefed the loggers so they'd know what to expect, underscoring her own no-spiking pledge. But these meetings, attended by only a handful of gyppos and logging folk along with a handful of her own EF allies, failed to impress even some of her fellow Earth Firsters who believed she and Cherney had already so alienated the logging community that there was no way to reduce their animosity.

Bari never saw it that way. She felt that each person in the timber industry whom she won over marked a victory for her working-class alliance. Moreover, she felt she would overcome the organizational problems that others were grousing about. She believed the Seeds of Peace people in Berkeley, once they were on board, could provide plenty of food and temporary housing and latrines, and she was in touch with attorney Susan Jordan to consult on Redwood Summer legal issues. It was only May; she had a few more months before Redwood Summer began.

Bari attended her last critical meeting for her timber-industry alliance on the night of May 22. She parked her car across the street from the meeting at a Willits café and locked it. She'd brought Utah Phillips, the IWW graybeard and folksinger, to the meeting; he and fellow folkie Dakota Sid and their women were flopping overnight at her Redwood Valley digs before the trip to the Bay Area the following day to meet at the Seeds House in Oakland. There were twenty or so people at the secret Willits meeting with the handpicked timber representatives. The sides came to an agreement: in return for no eco-tage of the timber industry's equipment; there would be no head-bashing of Redwood Summer demonstrators. The several loggers and gyppos at the meeting in no way spoke for the whole industry. Still, Bari was elated. She stayed up until 2 A.M. that night, giving a radio interview, making phone calls, issuing orders to the mostly women workers on Redwood Summer, and then joining her overnight guests in spirited singing of protest songs while they knocked back a few beers.

Mike Sweeney would baby-sit his girls while Bari headed south to the Bay Area to take the next organizational step on the path leading to Redwood Summer—securing the Seeds of Peace and other allies' commitment to participate as cosponsors. Bari, Cherney, George Shook, Utah Phillips and his wife, and Dakota Sid held a brief press conference at the MEC in Ukiah at noon on the 23rd, before caravanning to the Bay Area.

When Judi parked in front of the MEC, she locked her car door because she was carrying Stenberg's tools in her trunk. At her Redwood Valley home the night before, she hadn't locked the car. She had assumed she was on safe ground.

THIRTEEN

UP UNTIL THE MIDDAY MOMENT on May 24, 1990, when Bari's Subaru hit the pothole on MacArthur Boulevard and set off the motion device of the pipe bomb in her car, she had measured the last forty-eight hours as a success. From the meeting with the logging folk in Willits, to the Redwood Summer endorsements she had nailed down from Seeds of Peace allies, to the truce in her current working relationship with Darryl Cherney—all seemed testaments to her organizing and negotiating skills. Only her and Cherney's road show slated at UC Santa Cruz remained for her to finish up with a flourish.

Then the bomb altered everything forever.

Judi never lost consciousness as she waited for the Jaws of Life to free her from the car. Terribly injured and frozen in trauma, she listened to Cherney's declarations of love while he tried to reassure her that she would not die. She later said she had believed she would—the pain was that extreme.

Once she was extracted from the car, the ambulance took her to the county trauma center at Highland Hospital in Oakland, where she was examined and prepped for surgery to remove the car seat spring along with other debris forced up inside her by the antipersonnel pipe bomb's explosion. While she lay on the gurney outside the operating room, two Oakland police officers questioned her, pressing her to confess that she had carried the bomb intentionally and to name any co-conspirators.

If the police interview at that moment seemed cruel, it was nonetheless in keeping with police practices to extract "death-bed confessions," which are legally admissible in court after a patient dies. They hoped to clear up the car-bombing and find out who else might have been involved with one interrogation session.

Bari would remember the officers' badgering while she lay helpless, and she remained bitter about it long after she recovered. The police finally got around to officially arresting her while she was under the knife. Both she and Cherney were charged. Bail was set initially at $9,000 for Bari, $12,000 for Cherney.

The Oakland/Piedmont municipal judge, Horace Wheatly, responding to police requests, subsequently raised the bail to $100,000 for each based upon additional police information (although the amount was less than the Oakland Police Department requested). Both activists were charged with knowingly transporting an explosive device in Bari's car.

The day after the bombing, May 25, the OPD put out their version of events at a press conference. Lieutenant Mike Sims began, "The evidence is strong they were transporting this device and that's why they were arrested. We believe it [the bomb] went off accidentally." Asked how he knew they were knowingly transporting the bomb, Sims said with breezy assurance, "Based on our determination of the placement of the device in the car, we believe they should have known it was there."

The Oakland Tribune quoted the same unnamed sources referring to nails they'd found in Bari's premises on the Redwood Valley property as being a likely match with those in the antipersonnel pipe bomb. The report, a scant two days after the car-bombing, showed that the police and the FBI had been very busy indeed. The day of the bombing, the authorities carried out extensive searches in Berkeley, Oakland and Santa Cruz, and requested court permission for special night searches of Bari's and Cherney's Northern California homes because they worried about possible destruction or removal of evidence.

Later that night, the Oakland police and the FBI held a joint secret session in which they put their evidence on the table along with their hunches. Oakland police now shared the inventory of material they'd found in Cherney's van on the Golden Gate Bridge the previous month. Both the presence of the two Oakland cops on the bridge the month before and their offering up the list of contents of Cherney's van right after the car-bombing would later be viewed by the conspiratorially inclined Bari as evidence of a sinister plot against her and Cherney.

They listed a metal toolbox that held bluish-gray duct tape (something that had been used to bind nails to the pipe bomb). They found plastic pipe nipples with metal end caps and six to eight pieces of one-half-inch rebar, twelve inches long and sharpened at one end—a "road-spiking kit to blow out lumber truck tires," the cops called it. They also found red wires and alligator clips that they viewed as suspicious.

In a strange footnote, the cops found what they considered an alarming entry in Cherney's datebook marking the imminent arrival in San Francisco of Soviet premier Mikhail Gorbachev on June 3. The FBI quickly notified the Secret Service, which dispatched one of their agents to the scene. The FBI notes of the outcome dryly commented, "Secret Service did not consider this notation to constitute a threat to a protectee."

BARI'S ARREST BY OAKLAND POLICE meant that she was, while a patient, also a prisoner. Shortly after her surgery, while she was still unconscious, the police moved Bari to Highland Hospital's in-house "jail," a secure nursing ward for especially violent patients and others deemed flight risks. Bari, of course, was in no condition to flee. Her incarceration there was punitive (although attorney Susan Jordan would later point out that it could also be seen as a protective interim measure before "security" could be organized among Bari's followers). It was Bari's doctors who protested most strenuously. Oakland police relented; within the hour she was returned upstairs to a normal bed and room. But Bari would later talk about her detainment in the hospital jail, however brief, as one more crime by law enforcement against her.

Once medics had treated Darryl Cherney for his facial lacerations and determined that his deafness in one ear was only temporary, he too was arrested. He was taken from Highland Emergency to the city jail. Acceding to his request, police gave Cherney a cell by himself. He hand-wrote an account of the bombing in the decorative, kitschy style of printing he employed in his political posters and flyers—with little round circles to dot the i's. He named his leading candidates for the bombing—Neo-Nazi Party boys from Fort Bragg—and gave a simple recitation of his and Bari's motivation for putting on Redwood Summer: "My name is Darryl Cherney and I belong to a group named Earth First. Judi Bari, the driver of the car, and myself have become deeply involved in fighting the timber companies over the rapping [sic] of our forest lands."

Cherney was his usual loquacious self in conversations with the police. He wanted them to know they were wrong about him and Bari. People had threatened her repeatedly. She and he were a threat to the logging industry. He wanted the cops to know that. Finally he asked for a lawyer, but not before, as one cop put it, he'd been "talking his head off." By contrast, Bari, disciplined even in her narco-pain trance, had already said she wouldn't talk without an attorney.

Susan Jordan is a general criminal defense lawyer with a practice split between Mendocino County (where there are plenty of dope defense cases) and the Bay Area, where she leaned toward high-profile left-wing cases when she could get them. Immediately after hearing the police scenario identifying Bari and Cherney as would-be terrorists who had accidentally bombed themselves, she tried to get in to see Bari, whom she had previously counseled pro bono on legal issues relating to Redwood Summer. On the basis of the earlier contacts, Jordan claimed that Bari was still her client and that she had a right to see her and act in her behalf. She finally found a judge willing to make it official.

The wiry, tough-talking attorney had one famous case—really, her only big one—under her belt at that point: the Inez Garcia trial. Garcia, a fiery Chicana, was a rape victim who had tracked down her assailant (whom she knew) hours after the assault and gunned him down. Jordan was known to identify with her victimized female clients, and Bari, a bomb victim accused of being the perpetrator, fit the bill. She was incensed over the FBI and OPD issuing accusatory press statements while Bari was still in surgery. She complained loudly that the law enforcement authorities were in a rush to frame her client.

Jordan also sought to keep any friends of Judi's from popping off their mouths to the press.[*] She had always disliked the media, according to a handful of Bay Area journalists who had dealt with her before. She didn't want any well-intentioned Earth Firster compromising her client. Shutting down all cooperation was consistent with Jordan's left-wing hostility to law enforcement and the media, but the move was also good lawyering to protect her client.

AT THE MENDOCINO COUNTY SHERIFF'S Office in Ukiah the night of the bombing, Sergeant Steve Satterwhite volunteered during a phone conversation with Oakland police to stake out Bari's place in preparation for the arrival of an FBI/Oakland investigative team. He knew Bari's and Sweeney's Redwood Valley property and headed out there to keep an eye out for any unusual activity before an official search took place.

As Satterwhite watched from his car, he suddenly saw a light go on at the Bari compound. He saw a short, compact man—it was Mike Sweeney—go into the converted garage and emerge after a while with a large box.

A few hours later, the FBI and OPD officers arrived, having flown to Mendocino in an FBI helicopter. After Satterwhite briefed them, they questioned Sweeney about the contents of the box he'd removed. Sweeney said it was clothes for his girls and said that he was under no obligation to show or tell the officers anything. He added that he'd known they were coming—Susan Jordan had warned him—and he was not going to speak to them at all.

When the officers showed him their search warrant, he handed them the keys to Judi's place. In testimony given later, the police indicated that they didn't feel their warrant covered the former husband's home even though it was on the same tract of land.

In Bari's quarters in the converted garage, investigators found nails and some papers, but no bomb factory. (Bari had already removed the bulk of her papers to the cabin she'd rented on String Creek, outside Willits, where she planned to live when she returned

---

[*]In a recent, guarded interview, Jordan categorically denied ordering Bari's friends and relatives to refrain from talking to the media or law enforcement.

from Santa Cruz.) Still, the nails they found there were enough for Oakland police to assert two days later to an *Oakland Tribune* reporter that preliminary inspection showed them to be a match to the nails affixed to the bomb.

Following the search, the investigative team headed up to Humboldt County to search Cherney's rented home in Salmon Creek. There they encountered more hostility—this time with neighbors and a landlady mocking them by warning that the front door of Cherney's one-room hobbit-like house had been booby-trapped. The agents and officers weren't buying it, once they'd circumnavigated the place and peered through its tiny windows. Nevertheless, they opened the front door with a rope hung on a lead as the onlookers laughed derisively. Once again they didn't find the bomb factory they were looking for.*

Two days after the car-bombing, Louisiana-Pacific's Frank Wigginton called the FBI's Special Agent Frank Doyle. Just two weeks prior to the car-bombing, Wigginton told Doyle, a bomb had been set on the front porch at the LP mill in Cloverdale. Wigginton recalled that the manager complained that someone had, as he quoted him saying, "Dropped garbage all over my porch!" Wigginton questioned the man and realized that the "garbage" was, in fact, debris—papers, wood and some burnt particles.

The bomb was an incendiary device set to explode a can of gasoline with the obvious intent to burn down the mill. The perpetrator had also propped up a crudely lettered large cardboard sign against a nearby tree. It read: "LP screws workers," a typical Earth First sort of graffito. The bomb, however, had fizzled and failed to ignite the gasoline, though it did scatter paper debris on the porch.

It was only much later that people on both sides who were interested in the Bari car-bombing would note that the Cloverdale bomb had been set to go off on the third anniversary of a tree-spiking injury suffered by George Alexander in May 1987, when metal shards from a spiked piece of wood shattered the jaw of the 23-year-

---

*On or around June 25, Oakland police armed with another search warrant conducted a second search of Bari's premises, this time also searching "other structures" besides Judi's garage and seizing vacuum cleaner bags, matches and potassium chlorate.

old Louisiana-Pacific mill worker.[*] Bari had previously interviewed Alexander for the *Anderson Valley Advertiser* and had been moved by his injuries.

JUDI AWOKE AFTER THE SURGERY to find her right leg hoisted up in traction. Her doctors told her she had to lie flat on her back without turning for eight weeks. She had four fractures in her pelvis; her sacrum and coccyx bones were crushed. She had internal bleeding from a perforated colon. A spring from the seat of the car had impaled her right buttock, leaving a deep puncture wound. She had nerve damage that in the future would send shocks of debilitating pain up her legs and back. But she was, she told Bruce Anderson when he later came to visit, grateful at the time that she wouldn't have to "shit in a bag" for the rest of her life as the nurse had warned before the surgery.

She could make small jokes about that and about "Sister Morphine," whose relief she needed constantly to deal with her pain during those early weeks. But while her spirit seemed intact, she was to face a long, difficult recovery and it would be a while before she would know if she could ever walk again. Even then, her right foot would drag and she was never pain-free.

As she began her recovery, Judi once again took stock of her troops along with the publicity her case had garnered. All hell had broken loose after the bombing; the folksingers Utah Phillips and his wife, Joanne, made for Nevada City, where they resided; Dakota Sid left for his home in Grass Valley. As word spread of the incident, everyone up in Mendocino or Humboldt who had ever worked in environmental politics began inspecting beneath their car seats.

And in Berkeley, Greg King, who believed his drink had been

---

[*]By 1990 there had been twelve tree-spikings acknowledged by lumber companies in Northern California alone, according to Christopher Manes in *Green Rage*. Other than the Alexander wounding, there were no injuries, but Manes put the cost to the lumber industry for tree-spiking at $25 million.

laced with LSD the night before the bombing, was so traumatized and paranoid that he drove like a crazy man to get away from the Bay Area and all its phantom bombers and bummers. He was so spooked and scared, he took a long sabbatical from environmental journalism and high-profile Earth First politics.

Anna Marie Stenberg drove to the Bay Area immediately upon hearing news of the bombing. She had gained admission to Bari's room by claiming to the Oakland police guard to be her sister. Bari was then unconscious, so Stenberg left. She funneled the Earth First spin to the media, as did lawyers and other Earth Firsters. She told local TV reporters that one had only to look at Bari's bombed-out car—which she claimed she had done at the Oakland police storage facility—to see that the bomb had been placed under the driver's seat, not behind it. "There was a huge hole under the seat that went all the way to the pedals in front," Stenberg told everyone who would listen.

Karen Pickett and her boyfriend, Earth First cofounder Mike Roselle, quickly organized locals and supporters streaming in from Mendocino and Humboldt. The couple lived in the Bay Area, behind the Oakland hills in the tiny unincorporated hamlet of Canyon, where geodesic domes and other idiosyncratic dwellings were nearly hidden among the redwood groves. Now Pickett, along with Pam Davis, who had sped down to the Bay Area almost as quickly as Stenberg, put together a vigil of some two hundred supporters at Oakland's downtown city jail. They were protesting the lockup of Cherney and the arrest of Bari, and they threatened not to end their noisy blockade until Cherney, at least, was released. (The round-the-clock sit-in abruptly ended four days later, on Monday at 5 A.M., when the OPD ordered the crowd to disperse. A small group remained outside Highland Hospital in support of Bari.)

Susan Jordan immediately passed the word to Anna Marie Stenberg to shut up and stop talking to the media. She also nixed the press conference that Earth First had planned and Karen Pickett had pulled together.

In those early days of Bari's hospital stay, only immediate family were let in, with the exception of Stenberg's ruse and Jordan's access to her client. Two officers were posted as sentinels outside her door.

Writer Fred Gardner had rushed over to Highland when he first heard the news of the car-bombing. Gardner, like his pal and sometime employer, Bruce Anderson, was a generation older than Bari. He had achieved some prominence in the Vietnam antiwar movement as an organizer in the GI coffee house projects where antiwar activists provided haven, politics, and bagels and coffee for Vietnam soldiers. Today he covers pot issues for the *Anderson Valley Advertiser*.

Gardner had few doubts that the FBI was seeking to frame Bari for the deed. At Highland Hospital around midnight the day of the bombing, he found the waiting room to the intensive care ward where Bari lay under police guard. He caught the eye of the cop down the hall and told him he was Bari's brother. "She doesn't have a brother," the cop shot back and threatened to arrest him.

Gardner returned to Highland three days later. He saw two people emerge from Bari's room, and knew instantly that they were Judi's parents. He thought they looked frail and haggard. They had flown out that Sunday, May 27, from Baltimore. They came armed with a list of medical questions compiled with the help of the *New York Times* medical correspondent, Lawrence Altman, designed to help them determine the extent of the damage done to their daughter. The hand of their eldest, Gina Kolata, was behind this questionnaire. It was as close as she dared come without provoking her sister's sibling hostility.

Arthur Bari discussed his daughter's injuries with Gardner, sharing details that hadn't then been made public: "The car springs were blown upwards into her causing some nerve root damage which will be permanent." But there was no spinal chord damage. Gardner spent several hours in the waiting room. He liked the elderly Baris, finding them "gentle, articulate people, and remarkably calm." They asked Gardner to relay their daughter's message to her followers that she would be okay and that they should stay nonviolent.

Gardner answered that if Judi wanted to get a message out, how would they feel about taking a tape recorder in so she could make a statement for the *Anderson Valley Advertiser*? However messed up she was on drugs and in pain, he had no doubt she'd rise to the occasion. They thought it was worth a try. Ten minutes later they emerged with the tape. They handed it over to Gardner and they all said goodbye.

Gardner was at the elevator when Ruth Bari caught up with him. "Judi has one more thing to say," she said, asking for the tape recorder to take back into the room. Arthur Bari, Gardner recalled, thought they were pushing their luck—and he was right. When the Baris came out the second time, the police confiscated the tape.

Gardner drove Judi's parents back to their hotel. Arthur was sanguine about the seizure of the recorder. In the story Gardner filed with Bruce Anderson, he quoted Judi's father as saying, "The policeman may have been under a great deal of pressure. What would his superiors have thought if he let it get out?"

Later that night, as a weary Gardner was just drifting off to sleep, the phone jarred him awake. He lifted the receiver and heard a blistering tirade: "This is Susan Jordan and I am furious with you! You were a schmuck," she railed at him.

FOURTEEN

IN THE EIGHT WEEKS THAT BARI LAY in the hospital, she had a steady stream of visitors once the police relaxed their guard. Although she had to cope with her horrific injuries, she capitalized on the fact that the car-bombing had made headlines around the country, prompting reporters from the mainstream press to seek interviews. She received them in her narcotized state. Despite her pain, she wanted to participate in the media dance with her martyrdom.

Catherine Bishop, a reporter then working for the *New York Times,* was invited by the Bari-ites to do an interview at Highland Hospital. Bishop queried the national desk and got an okay. When she arrived, she noted "all those little minions" of Bari's standing outside her room. They barred Bishop's entrance—despite the fact that she had an appointment—telling her that Bari was indisposed and asking her to go to the waiting room. Bishop was mildly annoyed, but rather amused by the self-importance of all the yes-women, who acted as if they were serving a diva or a movie star. She waited and waited. She then noticed a "little old man" step out of the elevator and get admitted to Bari's room directly.

Moments after he'd gone in, one of the Bari-ites came out to get her. Bishop surveyed the tableau: Cherney stood by the window, holding a guitar; Bari was in bed, wearing her Earth First T-shirt, bra-less as usual. The "little old man" was seated in a chair at Bari's bedside. It was the Archdruid himself, David Brower. He was holding Judi's hand. The two of them were posed for their close-up, with Cherney at the ready with his guitar.

Bari was almost tea-party nice, Bishop would recall: "Oh hi. So nice of you to drop in. Where's your photographer?"

Bishop told them none had been assigned to go with her. Bam! "Brower drops her hand. Cherney puts his guitar back in his case. They were done!"

Bishop, a hardnosed newsie, found Bari "wacky." But for Bari it was a chance to put her spin on the great bombing event, just as the police and FBI had put out their version to the press—a version, as it turned out, they were tinkering with just as fervently as Bari and her own team of spinners.

In Bari's telling, she was the victim of a grand conspiracy. "They're also after the Black Panthers, you know," Bishop quoted her as saying. Bishop answered her, "It's not 1968." But Bari insisted the plot to get her was the same COINTELPRO program that had been launched by the FBI under President Richard Nixon to disrupt and do in domestic radicalism, from the Panthers to the antiwar movement. And furthermore, while it may have seemed that these activities had been laid to rest by the Senate committee hearings chaired by Senator Frank Church in 1976, this did not mean the evil FBI had backed off altogether. Oh no, not by a long shot.

Bishop remarked on one element that was especially bizarre in Bari's rap that day: "Judi Bari was spewing this political line—not: 'I'm going to find the mother-fucking bastard who blew up my pelvis.' She was pretty intense, even on drugs for her pain. It was almost like, 'I'm a martyr, finally.' First she said it was the timber industry people who did this to her, then it changed to the FBI and their conspiracy against labor. But she wasn't mad. It really struck me. It was strange." Bishop thought this was a possible indication that Bari herself wasn't innocent.

Bishop wrote a total of three stories—including one later that summer, on the demonstrations that were part of Redwood Summer. Privately, she also came to think of Cherney, whom she had interviewed, as a possible bomber. "I could believe Cherney could have been involved in this thing. I asked him straight on making the bomb or carrying it knowingly or purposely to hurt Judi. He didn't pass the test for me of a good denial. He was always so desperate to get attention. Maybe he was pissed off at her too."

Bishop did note that Bari, discussing the possibility of being hit again with another bomb, had voiced the fear that if she did, her ex-husband, Sweeney, would end up with their two daughters. "That didn't make her happy at all," recalled Bishop, but when the journalist asked her if Sweeney could have bombed her, Bari denied it instantly and would hear no more of it.

Katy Raddatz, then a *San Francisco Examiner* photographer, accompanied the paper's reporter, Jane Kay, to interview Bari around the same time. Unlike Bishop, Raddatz thought it was cute that Bari posed, all ready with her little fiddle held up under her chin. Raddatz admired her subject's cooperation and cheeky willingness to strike a pose. She climbed up on Bari's bed, straddling her, and shot the picture from overhead—*à la* photo shoots in Michelangelo Antonioni's famous film *Blowup*.

But not all Bari's visitors were media. Many were friends and colleagues in the Movement. Bari's suspicions and concerns seemed scattered and contradictory at times, but ultimately indicated a determination finally to make sense of various theories as to who had bombed her, and then to exploit that thesis for her own political ends.

About a week after Bari's surgery, Mary Moore made her way down from her rustic west Sonoma County home to Highland Hospital to see her friend and political ally. Moore had left her temporary post at the MEC, where she had been "doing the money" as it began rolling in to support Bari.

While Moore had lost the intimacy with Bari they'd once shared when residing in Sonoma County, the two women still said "little fingers touching" to one another and then hooked their pinkies together in a little-girl gesture symbolizing their bond, no matter what political disagreements might momentarily arise between them.

At Bari's hospital bedside, the motherly Moore was filled with pity. As she would later describe it, Bari's diminutive frame looked even more childlike with her leg raised in traction. The circles beneath her eyes were even darker now, making her gaunt face a haunted portrait. And while with others Bari might seethe in righteous indignation at her enemy the FBI and plot to counter them while receiving the media like a royal, to Moore she blurted out her soul's concerns.

Bari referred back to the confession Moore had made to her

early in their relationship that her children had been taken away from her by her ex-husband decades earlier because she had taken a black lover. For her part, Bari again expressed her own fears of losing her children in a fight with Mike Sweeney. The couple's battle for custody, she told Moore now, might be shifted permanently in Sweeney's favor just because she'd been arrested after the car-bombing, and even if she were proven innocent, the bombing itself, Sweeney might claim, made her a dangerous mother. Moore noted that Judi did not speak of any fear of prison, of permanent disability, or even of the collapse of Redwood Summer and her own leadership in a political movement—only her worry that her ex-husband might use the bombing to take her children from her.

It was something solely between the two women and not for consumption by the gofers and sigh-sisters now acting as Bari's praetorian guard. (With the police no longer right outside her door, the friends of Bari believed, as in *The Godfather,* that their *capo* was still in mortal danger of further assassination attempts.)

Few of these attendants knew about the custody fight. Stenberg knew, of course, because she and Judi frequently conversed about their marriages on the phone late at night; but Bari's other EF friends knew nothing about this (or at least, if they did know, refused to say so publicly). Even in the hospital after the trauma of being blown up, Bari compartmentalized her private life, keeping it very separate from her political activities. The ongoing struggle with Sweeney was still the most secret of all her wars.

Publicly, Bari named "Nazis" from Fort Bragg, in cahoots somehow with timber interests and aided by the FBI, as her would-be assassins. But to Bess Bair, a friend and former colleague, she confided what seemed to her listener to be her most wrenching fear, one she could only whisper softly so that none of the other Earth First guardians in her hospital room would hear.

Bair, a.k.a. Rosie Radiator, was a tap dancer who had led armies of her dance students tapping across the Golden Gate Bridge for its fiftieth birthday in 1988, as well as in radical public performances that expressed the exuberant politics of San Francisco's hip culturati. She had previously performed alongside Bari and Cherney, and was also involved in the redwood wars. She counted herself a friend and supporter of Bari's. (When Judi was strapped for money, Bair and her boyfriend had arrived on her doorstep to deliver free firewood.) So when Rosie heard about the bombing, she came to Highland Hospital. Like everyone else coming to see Bari, she had to make an appointment.

They talked, Rosie sitting close by Judi's bed. "Do you have any idea who did this to you?" she asked after learning the extent of the injuries.

Bari leaned over, grimacing with pain, her head turned toward her listener. In a hoarse voice bordering on a whisper, she said, "I know who did it. It was my ex old man."

When Rosie left, she felt terrible. She sensed that Bari had no intention of naming her husband publicly, that she would simply live with her dark suspicions. Rosie came back subsequently for another visit to show Bari she'd opened a checking account in Bari's name to raise funds for her recovery. She handed over a check made out to Bari for several hundred dollars. Rosie's main mission that day, however, was to get Bari to issue the call to her listeners and sympathizers to make sure to vote for California's Proposition 130, also called the "Forests Forever Initiative." "All you need to do is make a voice tape," Rosie urged her.

The Forests Forever Initiative, the mainstream ballot measure hammered out by parts of the timber industry working with the Sierra Club, would be on the fall ballot.[*] Rosie felt the publicity and groundswell of sympathy for Bari around the car-bombing could catch a lot of voters up in the cause of the redwoods. The initiative constituted a workable moratorium on logging old-growth timber and mandated a sustainable-yield harvest, although it certainly didn't give the radical environmentalists everything they had wanted.

"Fuck elections," Rosie says Bari responded. "I'm going to get the FBI." Her chief nemesis when she talked to Rosie a few days earlier—Sweeney—had been displaced by the bureau.

Rosie left, and never offered to work with Bari again because of this refusal to use her current notoriety in support of the environ-

---

[*] Also on the November 1990 ballot was Proposition 138, the so-called "Big Green," a companion piece of legislation that would have codified and streamlined a single statute affecting industry and agribusiness, making California the most environmentally strict state in the country. Both were narrowly defeated.

mental measures. She tucked away her friend's accusations about Sweeney, along with her puzzling intention to get the FBI instead, as some bizarre disconnect.

Rosie was puzzled by what she had heard largely because she was overlooking the possibility that Bari had only briefly considered the idea that Sweeney was guilty and then dismissed it. Later on, in fact, when Steve Talbot raised the possibility of Sweeney's guilt to her, Bari was unequivocal in asserting his innocence. Writing in the *Anderson Valley Advertiser,* she said:

> My ex-husband and I have a cooperative relationship in our divorce, and he has no motive to bomb me. Mike was taking care of our children at his girlfriend's house when the bomb was planted.... I know my ex-husband didn't do it because he couldn't look me in the eye if he had.

WHILE IN THE HOSPITAL FIGHTING her way to recovery, Bari was running through a long, paranoid list of possible perps. First it was timber and the Fort Bragg "Nazis." Then, to Rosie, it was her ex-husband. Months later, at a meeting with Ukiah law enforcement officers, she even named David Kemnitzer, her "host" for the sleep-over in Oakland the night before the car-bombing.[*]

The one constant in her accusations was the FBI. Judi had cause to be critical of the bureau. In the years to come, even the Alameda County district attorney would quietly criticize the G-men's handling of the case.

Within minutes after news of an explosion on MacArthur Boulevard had crackled over the police radio, the FBI was all over the car-bombing. Special Agent Timothy McKinley would later say he'd been driving around on his lunch hour looking for a little apron for his daughter to wear in a costume for her school play when he heard

---

[*]There was yet another person whom Bari would name—although as an FBI agent rather than as the specific agent of the bombing. That was Irv Sutley. There may have been a method in maligning him. If the disputed solicitation to murder Sweeney had indeed come from Judi, she may have felt that by fingering Sutley as an FBI agent who may have been a part of the conspiracy to bomb her, she would be neutralizing any accusations he might someday make about the murder-for-hire scheme.

of the explosion. Realizing he was not far away, he called into FBI headquarters and learned that the two victims "were subjects of an FBI investigation in the terrorist field." He immediately headed to the site of the bombing to join the investigation.

What the FBI knew or thought they knew about Bari and Cherney determined their theory of the case, starting from the premise that the pair had knowingly transported the bomb. The FBI agents would brief officers and investigators of the Oakland Police Department as well as the Bureau of Alcohol, Tobacco and Firearms who converged on the bombing scene to begin the investigation.

Much of the story line for law enforcement resulted from the early arrival on the crime scene of one of the bureau's top bomb experts, Special Agent Frank Doyle. ATF would normally have been the agency in charge of the investigation because of the bomb, but the FBI—and Doyle—took over by asserting that this was a case of domestic terrorism.

In briefing the less experienced Oakland police and assuming the leadership role in examining the shattered car, Doyle was doing what came naturally. He was a hazardous device technician who had been assigned to the International Domestic Terrorism Squad for the previous twenty years and served as the FBI's expert witness for testimony on bombs in federal, state and local courts. He was considered good enough at what he did to teach seminars for all law enforcement groups, both within and outside of the FBI Academy.

Doyle and his co-investigators claimed that the gaping three-foot-long hole in the floor of Bari's Subaru indicated that the bomb had been positioned behind, rather than under, the driver's seat. When the police and the FBI found a smashed guitar case and a shredded blue towel, they theorized that Bari had knowingly set the items on top of the bomb to conceal it.

The FBI also stated early on that the cache of two kinds of nails in the trunk of Bari's car would prove identical to those that had been duct-taped to the pipe bomb, enhancing its destructiveness as an "antipersonnel device."

It was a hurry-up kind of assessment—the nails in the trunk of the car and the nails on the bomb must be related to one another and therefore confirmed the theory that Bari had prior knowledge of the bomb she carried. In its haste to make the case, the bureau ignored the fact that the nails in the bomb were finishing nails and those in the car's trunk were roofing and framing nails. Moreover, Anna Marie Stenberg would soon apprise Oakland police that all the tools and nails in the trunk of the bombed car actually belonged to her, as she'd been doing carpentry for Bari on her new String Creek residence, and Bari had put them in the Subaru trunk for safe keeping.

After hours of examination at the scene, police trucked Bari's car to a storage lot near their headquarters. The car seat, damaged by the Jaws of Life which released Bari from the wreckage, was removed, thus muddying the issue of the bomb's placement.

Seven and a half hours after the bomb exploded, the FBI and the OPD held their own powwow to share information that would provide an overview of the case and a direction for the investigation. It is clear from the notes of Sergeant Myron Hansen, an Oakland cop who sat in on the briefing, that the FBI agents had made some strong assumptions about the car bomb based on disparate information: from the bureau's case against Dave Foreman and other Earth Firsters in Arizona the year before, and from the Earth Day sabotage of the power transmission towers the previous month in Santa Cruz, along with the posters taken from Cherney's van during the Golden Gate Bridge takeover. The FBI cited the Earth First actions to bolster its developing case that the car-bombing was just another step in a terrorist campaign. The scenario they passed on to the *Oakland Tribune* assumed that Bari and Cherney would either hand off the pipe bomb to other mischief-makers in Santa Cruz to blow up an environmental eyesore, or, less likely, actually plant the bomb themselves.

At that evening's conference in Oakland there were thirteen men from the FBI and ten from the OPD. Special Agent John Reikes, a veteran FBI agent, told the assembly that there was an Earth First conspiracy to take down power lines. "It started over one year ago," he said, according to notes taken by OPD's Sergeant Hansen. Earth Firsters were bombing power lines in Arizona, Reikes said, and the FBI had determined there were ties between the group in the Southwest and others in Marin County (but no mention of Mendocino or Humboldt). The Arizona group's ultimate plans, added Reikes, were to come to California and "take down nuclear power lines." The agent went on to talk about Earth First's activities in Mendocino, saying that for the last two years they'd been tree-spiking up there. Then, on April 23, 1990, came the downed power lines in Santa Cruz; the poles and the tower had been cut. Reikes reported that the Earth Night Action Group (ENAG), heretofore invisible, had taken credit for the downing of the lines. (It's clear that the FBI viewed ENAG as simply an Earth First front.) The next fact that Reikes proffered was that Bari and Cherney were, as Sergeant Hansen's notes attest, "supposed to go to Santa Cruz tonight. *Possible target was Moss Landing power plant.*" (Italics added.)

The FBI found the couple's very destination suspect because Santa Cruz had emerged as a hot spot for environmental sabotage. In 1987, members of the radical Animal Liberation Front had set fire to a Santa Cruz lab doing research with animals. In a later FBI internal memo, Earth First—with Bari and Cherney leading—was blamed for vandalism at a Sonoma County military recruitment center, but with no explanation of how that determination had been made.

Almost immediately after laying out their theories, police put stories out to the media presenting Bari and Cherney as perpetrator-victims. Early in the investigation, anonymous police sources gave the *Oakland Tribune* a peculiar scenario that went beyond their contention that the Earth First duo had transported the bomb. The story in the *Tribune* read in part: "To drum up sympathy for their cause, the suspects planned to detonate the device in the car while they were at a Santa Cruz rally, making it appear they were the targets of an attack by logging interests."

It was an interesting theory—a rigged assassination attempt to dramatize the recruitment drive on the Santa Cruz campus; and certainly, given the outsized ambitions of Bari and Cherney and their appetite for publicity, it was within the realm of possibility. But even though she was a self-acknowledged "media slut," it seems highly unlikely that Bari would have knowingly transported an armed bomb with a timer and a motion trigger for several hundred miles.

It was not impossible that Bari had knowingly carried the bomb as part of the Earth First plans to interrupt power to the Diablo Canyon nuclear plant, but there would never be any way of proving it because law enforcement had botched some of the evidence so

badly. Alameda County district attorney Tom Orloff, while acknowledging the bungled evidence, nevertheless continued to insist years
later that there was certainly "reasonable cause" both for the initial
arrests of Bari and Cherney and for the broad search warrants the
police and FBI sought, including nighttime searches of Bari's and
Cherney's domiciles up north, of the Seeds House and various vehicles. "If you feared there might be other bombs, as the police did,
the evidence was enough under the circumstances to get the warrants," Orloff said.

Indeed, armed with the local warrants, police had raided the
Seeds House, where they rousted the residents, knocked one of the
communards to the ground and detained everyone they could get
their hands on. Then the FBI and the OPD went on to search Kemnitzer's home. They theorized that the bomb had been armed the
night before at that site and, suspecting more bombs, confiscated
Kemnitzer's daughter's innocuous soldering kit for jewelry and
glass-making as suspicious material. The FBI also searched EFers in
Santa Cruz.

There was still another crucial factor that influenced the FBI's
early presumption of Bari's and Cherney's culpability. Special Agent
Phil Sena disclosed that he'd received a message from an informant
in Santa Cruz who had been developed by the FBI in the aftermath of
the Earth Day ecotage of the PG&E towers. Sena said the Santa Cruz
source had warned that "heavy hitters" would be heading down
from up north, planning an "action"—presumably a bombing or
other dramatic act of ecotage. While the tip was enough to activate
FBI vigilance and to bolster the scenario of the car-bombing they
had laid out for Oakland police, it was insufficient as evidence, especially since the FBI could not identify the source without
jeopardizing him or her.

Of course Bari's defenders, upon learning of the putative
source, belittled it and the theories of the case that went with it. In
discovery motions on the civil suit that Bari and Cherney filed
against the FBI and Oakland Police Department in federal court the
year after the bombing, their attorney—the courtly, reed-thin Dennis Cunningham—never learned the name of the informer, but he
gained some sense of who she was (the informer was a woman). The
tipster, said Cunningham years later, had emerged from a "ring of

activists the local cops had suspected in the PG&E sabotage." Cunningham said the source did more than just talk to police: "she ran her mouth." Recalling the subpoenaed documents he'd read as part of discovery, Cunningham said that "the actions against the power tower and the poles were hatched in her living room. She was going with one of the guys even though she was married at the time—a weird husband." He further identified her as having a past history as an informer, alleging she had served in the Army and had once been married to a man in military intelligence. Cunningham and his later co-attorneys tried to find out more about the tipster, since they felt it was germane to the FBI's and the police's reasons for arresting Bari and Cherney for the car-bombing; but they were disappointed. "We were blocked from finding out anything more about her by the judge," said Cunningham.

The police and the FBI would hold to their original view of the case—that Bari knowingly transported the bomb—even after having their case handed back to them on a platter of humiliation in the judgment arising from Bari's civil suit a decade later.

THE CRIMINAL INQUIRY BECAME considerably murkier when, five days after the car-bombing, Mike Geniella, a reporter for the *Santa Rosa Press Democrat*, received what would become known as the "Lord's Avenger letter" (because it signed off, "I am the Lord's Avenger"). Geniella had made himself the paper's go-to guy covering logging issues in Mendocino and Humboldt Counties. He'd met Judi, argued with her, and found that she proved useful in alerting him to issues and demonstrations. He had publicized Earth First actions and got the numbers right on acres of redwoods threatened. He was a natural recipient for this letter, which would play such an important role in the case.

The letter-writer took credit for the Bari car-bombing and the Cloverdale arson device. It was a bizarre, artfully written screed combining real technical knowledge with biblical jargon. The FBI believed it showed accurate knowledge of both bombs. The author was also familiar with Bari's schedule. Moreover, he proved sufficiently conversant with the Bible to get his quotations correct.

And there were quirky writing tics—the lavish use of capital letters, for one—that struck observers.

With stilted language and a highfalutin tone, the Lord's Avenger begins, "I built with these hands the bomb that I placed in the car of Judi Bari. Doubt me not." Then he promises to tell the "design and materials such as only I will Know." The writer talks about his intent to "spread the message spoken by the bomb" and why he attempted the murder of Judi Bari: "This woman is possessed of the Devil. No natural Woman created of our Lord spews Forth the Lies, Calumnies and Poisons that she does with such Evil Power." The Avenger then sets the scene at the November 1988 clash of pro- and anti-abortion activists outside the family-planning clinic in Ukiah. "The Lord cleared my Vision and reveal this unto me outside the Baby-Killing Clinic when Judi Bari smote with Satan's words the humble and Faithful servants of the Lord who had come there to make witness against Abortion. I saw Satans [*sic*] flames shoot forth from her mouth her eyes and ears...." He goes on to quote Timothy 2:11 for its anti-feminism: "Let the woman learn in silence with all subjection. But I suffer not a woman to teach, nor to usurp authority over the man, but to be in silence."

The Avenger lays out a conspiracy not just to kill Bari, but to defame her with the "LP Screws Workers" sign deliberately left as an Earth First calling card for the Cloverdale mill bomb. At first, he says, he was "Weak," his faith in God so lacking that he was afraid to attack Bari directly. Instead, he says, he tried to bomb the Cloverdale mill to "bring infamy down on Judi Bari." He then describes that bomb exactly as "1 1/2 inch galvanized pipe with galvanized end caps candle wax on threads. One cap drilled so wires could go to the igniter match heads inside a model paint bottle to be set off by flashlight filament. Epoxy glue in the drill hole." The full description includes the plywood box and the one-gallon gas can with its 70:30 mixture of gasoline and oil. The Cloverdale bomb had a pocket watch with the minute hand gone, the Avenger accurately discloses, with a small "hex head screw" drilled into the lens, a 9 volt battery, a light switch "for safety, a light socket for Test lamp." And when the hour hand hit the screw, "the bomb exploded."

But in fact, the Cloverdale mill bomb failed to go off. Then, the Avenger writes, "the Lord told me Use not Indirection." He decided that Bari herself "must be struck down," the Cloverdale bomb having proved inadequate to stop her.

He says he placed the bomb in her car "whilst she was at the meeting with the loggers," referring to the hush-hush conference the night before she left for Berkeley that only a few outsiders knew about. He then gives the specifics of the car bomb—somewhat different from the Cloverdale bomb because it didn't use gasoline but employed potassium chlorate and aluminum powder in a 3-to-1 ratio. He mentions three sizes of finishing nails taped to the bomb's exterior, and the pipe taped to paneling, all of which, he writes, fit "under her seat." Again, as with the Cloverdale device, there was a pocket watch, a safety switch and an empty light socket. But this time there was a "motion switch of 2 bent wires and a ball."[*]

The Avenger writes of nearly despairing during an unforeseen delay of the bomb's ignition—that is, within the twelve hours on the watch face—but says the delay served his purposes even better: "The hour hand Moved. But it did not Explode! The Lord had Made another Miracle. He had stopped the hand of the watch by His Divine Intervention.... For two nights and two days the hand was stayed until the Demon was joined in her car by the VERY SAME man who had helped her Mock and Insult the Faithful outside the Abortion Clinic.... PRAISE GOD!" The reference, of course, was to Darryl Cherney.

In keeping with the Christian fundamentalist argot of the letter, the Avenger also rails against Bari and her followers for their sacrilegious paganism. He was making an example of her "so that others would Cringe with Fear.... Now all who would come to the forests and worship trees like gilded Idols have been Warned."

The Lord's Avenger letter became the key to solving the bombing mystery. The author's identity became a subject of intense speculation. Few people were gullible enough to believe the Lord's Avenger was actually Bill Staley, as the fundamentalist anti-abortion posturing of the letter seemed to suggest, but the police

---

[*] As it was later described by a private investigator hired by Bari, the ball bearing was part of the motion device that would detonate the bomb once the timepiece had armed it. The ball's escape from its mooring in a depression on the surface of the device would send it caroming to make contact with metal points, raising the spark from the filaments that would ignite the gunpowder to explode the bomb.

interviewed him anyway over the next weeks, finally declaring him not a suspect.

Anonymous letter-writing seemed to have become a subplot all its own in the Judi Bari saga. In January 1989, almost four months prior to the car-bombing, the so-called "Argus letter" was sent to Ukiah police chief Fred Keplinger. (It would also be referred to as the "snitch letter" because it ratted on Bari.) The letter wasn't released by authorities until a year after the bombing, when it was turned over to documentary filmmaker Steve Talbot almost as an afterthought. It begins:

> Dear Chief Keplinger:
>
> I joined Earth First to be able to report illegal activities of that organization. Bari and the Ukiah Earth First are planning vandalism directed at Congressman Doug Bosco to protest offshore oil drilling. Earth First recently began automatic weapons training. Bari sells marijuana to finance Earth First activities. She sometimes receives and sends marijuana by U.S. mail. On December 23 she mailed a box of marijuana at the Ukiah post office.... If you would like to receive confidential information on short notice to make possible an arrest on federal charges at a U.S. post office next time she mails dope, please do the following: Place an advertisement in the "Notices" section of the classified ad section of the Ukiah Daily Journal.

The writer says he will reply by telephone and identify himself as "Argus." To back his contention that Earth First was doing weapons training, he included a photo that was a near-twin of the one that ran on the cover of the *Anderson Valley Advertiser* with Bari holding an Uzi-like weapon in a pose that was an imitation of Patty Hearst as the SLA's Tanya.

Bari began leveling very public accusations against Irv Sutley as the author of the "snitch" letter and as an FBI operative, since he had already openly forwarded one of the Bari Tanya photos to Bruce Anderson at the AVA. (Sutley would always maintain his complete innocence, pointing out that Pam Davis, who took the photos, routinely made duplicates; and further, that Bari had copies herself, which were accessible to anyone at her home, including Mike Sweeney, since Bari didn't lock her door except when entertaining male guests.) Bari also accused Sutley of having once witnessed her mailing pot "to a friend" back East, a charge Sutley denies, although he admits that he did ask Bari about getting some pot, but nothing came of it.

Both the Argus letter and the Lord's Avenger letter prompted some observers to note a similar literary vein, setting off speculation as to who might be the authors and what their motivation was. In the case of the Argus letter, sent prior to the bombing, it seems clear that someone was out to invite police scrutiny of Bari for dealing, a "crime" as common as squirrels on the North Coast. The charges of military training seemed to be based upon knowledge of Sutley's bringing guns to Cherney's quarters, but no one shot his guns that day and Earth First never engaged in military training.

The Argus letter displayed the same literary affectations as the Lord's Avenger's, but with a seemingly different purpose: The Argus letter seemed designed to provoke police action against Bari and Earth First. The Lord's Avenger letter on its face seemed designed to refocus the police and FBI investigation away from Bari and Cherney, both of whom could not have written the letter since Bari was hospitalized and Cherney was still in the Oakland City Jail.

FIFTEEN

IN THE COURSE OF THEIR EARLY INVESTIGATIONS, the police and the FBI came up with nothing other than their original thesis—that Bari, or Bari and Cherney were the culprits. In fact, the case against Bari had begun to unravel almost immediately, at least based upon FBI assertions that the bomb was positioned behind, rather than under, her seat in the car. (Even Bari's surgeon at Highland Hospital stated that his patient's injuries were consistent with a bomb exploding under her, not behind her.)

Investigators were also forced to eat crow about their assertions that the nails affixed to the pipe bomb—as an antipersonnel measure—matched the nails eventually recovered from Bari's Redwood Valley home. Initially, in order to obtain the search warrants, they had listed the two kinds of nails found in the Subaru's trunk—carpenter and framing nails—as a probable match. Later on, after one agent's assertion that the nails recovered from Bari's Redwood Valley home were manufactured in identifiable batches in the low thousands (making the case that they could easily tie those nails to the bomb), the FBI were forced to admit that the nails were churned out in the millions, making exact matches virtually impossible.

The Alameda County District Attorney's Office knew the evidence it had was insufficient to win a conviction against Bari and Cherney, especially as the FBI theory of the bomb placement began to unravel. In July, nearly eight weeks after the arrests, the DA declined to press charges against the pair. It was a pragmatic decision: Oakland's case against the Earth First leaders was too weak to fly in court, and the last thing the DA's office needed was a political trial they would lose.

And while it didn't become public knowledge until a decade later, Susan Jordan had been trying to cut a deal of limited immunity for anything Bari might say in return for cooperation with law enforcement. The FBI refused to grant it. "We're not set up to grant immunity in victim interviews," Special Agent Phil Sena commented later that year. Jordan responded by advising Bari not to give any interviews with police or the FBI. Her refusal to talk without immunity confirmed her guilt to some in law enforcement and made some of her old friends who would later break with her—like Bruce Anderson—wonder what exactly she knew and was withholding.

It was a question that never occurred to Judi's hardcore supporters. From the beginning, there was an orchestrated campaign to proclaim the innocence of Bari and Cherney while protesting against the government's version of the crime. In the weeks following the bombing, dozens of activists—political and environmental sympathizers, including the usual celebrities of leftist causes—bombarded Washington with letters in support of Bari and calling for an investigation.

Representative Ron Dellums, the radical black congressman from the East Bay; Tom Bates, the left-wing state assemblyman from Berkeley; and Representative Don Edwards, a liberal Democrat from San Jose, all called for an investigation into the FBI's handling of the case. They were critical of the bureau, although their joint statement did not appear until after July, when the district attorney declined to press charges.

And Bari herself, holed up in her Highland Hospital room with its homey decorations on the walls and her coterie of devoted Earth First attendants, made it clear that despite the letter from the Lord's Avenger, she, at least, still believed the FBI was involved.

The letter was a smart piece of obfuscation, Bari asserted—too smart for anyone other than the FBI to have written. "The Lord's Avenger letter was very skillfully used," she told Beth Bosk in 1995. "It's literature. It's so well written, nobody I know can write that good." At another point, however, she insisted it was "a classic COINTELPRO letter; it was so well written." She described the writer as "misogynist," singling out the focus on her "pro-abortionist activity." As she said, "I've done one clinic defense in my entire life, and that was it."

But Bari was wrong when she claimed she didn't know anyone who could write well enough to have produced that letter. Three people who had been present at the anti-abortion rally were writers: Anna Marie Stenberg's ex-husband, Mike Koepf; Bruce Anderson; and Mike Sweeney.

The finger-pointing with regard to the letter would go on for over a decade. Koepf would later charge that Bruce Anderson had written the Avenger letter, saying he did so to get his pal Bari off the hook. (The FBI examined the typewriters of both men and found that these machines hadn't been used to type the letter.)

Stenberg herself believed that Koepf might have written it. After all, he had penned a novel, and he wrote for Anderson and the AVA until the two had a falling-out. Koepf, moreover, had been a Green Beret first class with special military skills, and had kept a sheath of army materials that included bomb-making manuals around Stenberg's place before the pair split up. She argued that Koepf hated Bari because of her influence in getting Stenberg to break up with him. Stenberg gave the police information about Koepf's manuals.

But Anderson dismissed any suggestion that Koepf might be the Lord's Avenger: "Where's his motive?" And he laughed at the idea that Koepf might have tried to murder Bari.

Bill Staley, the model for the Lord's Avenger character, was interviewed by FBI agents. Staley offered to take a polygraph test, but it never came to that. The FBI, along with Bari herself, never considered Staley to be the bomber.

Mike Sweeney, on the other hand, seemed a possible fit. He had been at the anti-abortion rally. (Darryl Cherney would later tell Beth Bosk that Sweeney had been pressed into service as a photographer to record the moment when, as he and Bari anticipated, Staley's activists would attack Bari's group in response to their provocative lyrics—but instead they turned to prayer.) He had sufficient writing skills to craft the Lord's Avenger letter. Besides his experience writing for the *Stanford Daily*—as well as *Checkout* and *Wildcat*, the alternative union newsletters he had put out in San Diego—he had even tried his hand at a novel, in which, rather tellingly, the main character is a female radical activist. "Eliza Devlin," a member of the fictional "Defenders of the Earth," bears more than a passing resemblance to Judi Bari (with an obvious nod to the fiery 1970s Irish radical nationalist, Bernadette Devlin). More to the point, in Sweeney's novel she is murdered by a fundamentalist Bible-thumper named "Mick de Vito," who is almost an exact match to the real-life anti-abortion rally leader, Bill Staley.

It is not known when he wrote the novel, but after Sweeney ascended to the post of recycling czar for Mendocino County at the end of the 1980s, he fired off memos about garbage issues for the next couple of years to his colleague Carol O'Neal. Loath to throw away used paper of any kind, he wrote on the flip side of his literary opus for the garbage communiqués. O'Neal saved some of the most telling material. It was after O'Neal and Sweeney had had a bitter falling-out—and after Bari's death in 1997—that O'Neal, by now living in Southern California, finally released the old memos to Stenberg, with Sweeney's drafts of his novel on the pages' reverse.

Sweeney had long since ditched his roman à clef. The question remains: when had he undertaken this literary endeavor? Clearly it was after the anti-abortion rally in the fall of 1989. But was it before his ex-wife's car-bombing? If he had been tinkering with such a novel before that event, he most certainly abandoned his project afterward, realizing that it might cause authorities to question if it was a case of art imitating life, or vice versa.

THE POLICE AND THE FBI PORED OVER the Lord's Avenger letter. So did Bari's lawyers and the investigators they hired. The FBI, acknowledging the letter's claims, thought the Cloverdale and Bari car bombs were so similar they might well have been constructed by the same person.

The Lord's Avenger gave a detailed description of the car bomb, the wires and their coloring, the timepiece, and said he had placed it in the car when Judi was still in the Ukiah meeting with the loggers. But the motion device that triggered the bomb was armed by the revolution of the hour hand on a watch. Since there were only twelve hours on the face of the timepiece, the bomb should have exploded during the trip to the Bay Area.[*] The Lord's Avenger explained the anomaly by asserting that the bomb had simply mal-functioned and exploded later than planned, attributing the malfunction to the Lord's will. During the delay of the timing device, Cherney became a passenger in the car with Bari, allowing the Lord to get two targets instead of one.

Most of the investigators—law enforcement, Bari's private detectives and forensic experts alike—for a long time held the opin-ion that the timeline dictated by the clock device eliminated Sweeney as a suspect. Certainly he had an alibi for the time during which the bomb was theoretically placed. In fact, he had three separate alibis covering the putative timeline of the bomb: he was at his desk work-ing in the Mendocino Environmental Center in downtown Ukiah; at home on the Redwood Valley property with his children (whom he was caring for while Bari was scheduled to appear at the Santa Cruz gig); and last, with his two daughters and his girlfriend Meredyth Rinehard at her house.

But more than a decade after the bombing, a meeting be-tween two Bay Area investigators—both of whom had worked at different times for Bari or her lawyers—brought about a discovery that would expand the time window in which the bomb could have been placed, wide enough to include anybody in Mendocino County as a potential bomb-maker.

Josiah "Tink" Thompson, a former college professor turned sleuth, had been hired by Bari after she filed her legal case against the FBI and the OPD. Along the way, Thompson made a mockup of the car bomb, feeling confident that as a former Army demolition expert he had the design down pat, based on documents from the FBI's own forensics.

Thompson also worked subsequently for the defense of the Symbionese Liberation Army's Kathleen Soliah—a.k.a. Mary Jane Olson—for conspiring to bomb parked Los Angeles police cars in 1975. One of Thompson's collaborators on that case was forensics

---

[*]Once the single hand of the timepiece made contact with the plastic that was sol-dered onto the watch face at 9 o'clock, and with the bomb's manual on/off switch set in the "on" position, the motion device would come into play. The tiny ball bear-ing, set in a depression, would pop out to complete a circuit of exposed wire and filament to spark the powder and detonate the bomb.

expert Mark Shattuck, a bioengineer with a doctorate from Stanford whose testimony relates to bombings, car crashes and how people get hurt.

Shattuck had also worked on the Bari case before the charges against her were dropped, and when he met with Thompson years later to talk about the Soliah investigation, they naturally reminisced about the earlier case. During their discussion the two men focused on the Bull's Eye pocket watch that was used in the Bari bomb, and discovered that it had a regulator on the back that could slow down the watch's action from the twelve-hour limit of the clock's face to twenty-four hours *and even slower,* simply by mechanically bending back a metal piece (once the second hand had been removed, which in fact was the case with the watch used in the Bari car bomb). It meant that someone in Mendocino County could have planted the bomb before Bari and her caravan traveled to the Bay Area. (The Lord's Avenger wrote that he had placed the bomb during the Willits logging powwow the night before Bari's departure to the Bay Area, a claim that law enforcement officials had discounted because of the presumed twelve-hour limit on the timing device. But even that site in Ukiah is dubious, since Bari said she'd locked her car before the meeting—a precaution she never took outside her own home in Redwood Valley, where she spent the night after the Ukiah meeting.)[*]

ANOTHER DIMENSION OF THE car-bombing that would help to sustain the ten-year civil suit filed by the Earth First pair—and fuel Bari's depiction of the FBI as a sinister plotter, with the Oakland Police Department as its dupe—revolved around the chief FBI bomb expert, Frank Doyle. As his role became clearer, in depositions obtained in the suit that Bari and Cherney filed a year after the bombing, a curious coincidence was uncovered. Doyle had been the main instructor

---

[*] Police documents and FBI memos make it clear that law enforcement investigators interviewed Sweeney and sought examples from his typewriter at the MEC. (They also looked at typewriters at the Ukiah Public Library, hoping to find a match to the Argus or the Lord's Avenger letter.) The police bought Sweeney's alibis. As the case dragged on, no one from the FBI or the police again considered him a suspect.

at a "bomb school" the FBI had put on in Eureka on Louisiana-Pacific land just two weeks prior to the car-bombing.

Frank Wigginton, the security chief at LP and a former sheriff, had cordial—even crony—relations with law enforcement in the area and had been in charge of finding suitable land for the FBI school's bombing demonstrations. LP's clear-cuts were perfect: the open spaces and the area's status as privately held land removed the chance that members of the public might wander into range by mistake.

The bomb school had been held under the auspices of the College of the Redwoods in Eureka every year for four years prior to the car-bombing, sometimes two or three times a year for police from all over the region, giving instruction in different kinds of bombs in the context of terrorism.

The FBI's spokesman, Andrew Black (whose e-mail tag is "sleuth") describes the bomb school as routine, "part of the FBI's mission teaching police and sheriff's officers in schools around the country. Where the bomb school is held varies from year to year. It's not that mysterious." But during and after her long recuperation, Bari had a different view. In fact, Doyle became the lynchpin in her theory that the FBI had played a role in the attempt on her life. She spent the next seven years doing research into such matters as Doyle and the bomb school, and taking depositions in her civil suit; she was able to quote chapter and verse on her case. It was typical of Bari that she would marshal even the most ridiculous points to bolster her conspiracy allegations against Doyle and the FBI.

"Now in the bomb school," she told Beth Bosk in her best pedagogical style in their interview several years after the bombing, "the instructor [Frank Doyle] told the class that when people bomb each other, they very rarely place the bomb inside the passenger compartment—because it's allegedly so hard to break into a car...so bombers strap the bomb underneath the car, or place it in the engine compartment." When Bari learned that the FBI had demonstrated several bombs that were placed *inside* the cars, she immediately developed a scenario in which the FBI was "creating virtually the same crime scene that was about to happen in Oakland a month later."

When she wasn't analyzing the bomb-school class that Doyle ran, she demonized him, as she did all her potential enemies. "He's a very scary guy," she said. "He's sneery [sic] and sarcastic.... Frank Doyle kind of impresses me as a rogue element."

At the scene of the bombing in Oakland two weeks after the bomb school, Special Agent Doyle did lead the Oakland police officers in interpreting the evidence, at least according to a statement made later by Sergeant Myron Hansen, himself a graduate of the 1990 bomb school. Hansen said that he "wasn't about to tell him [Doyle] anything different" when he asserted that the bomb had been placed behind the passenger seat. Experience may have blinded Doyle: generally, a bomb inside the car meant it was being transported knowingly by the perpetrator. But other witnesses that day placed the bomb somewhere between the front and back seat, and underneath—not, as Doyle said, behind the front seat and visible.

To Bari, this was not a mistaken assumption but evidence of a conspiracy. She felt the same about the rest of the sloppy FBI and police work that characterized the investigation. Bureau agents' failure to forward parts of the bombed Subaru to the FBI lab, for example, as well as the failure to investigate various crude death threats that Bari and Cherney received prior to the bombing, were proof of sinister intent. But no investigation is perfect or always by the book, and the Bari-ites, none of whom would consent to interviews with the OPD or the FBI, stitched together law enforcement mistakes in a conspiratorial web that was good enough ultimately to sway a civil jury, but which most in the media and the legal community regarded with skepticism.

All the interviews done by law enforcement in and around Mendocino came to naught. In 1993 they finally dropped the investigation, admitting they'd come up with "insufficient evidence...which could lead to identification of those responsible for this act...."

The memo from the FBI San Francisco office to the local U.S. Justice Department attorney, John Mendes, concluded, "This investigation was hampered from the start by the extraordinary circumstance in which the victims refused to cooperate and provide information which could help solve this crime." According to the U.S. bylaws governing domestic terrorism investigations by the FBI, it was also time to throw in the towel. FBI jurisdiction was given 180 days; another 180 days could be granted upon request. But it was never meant to be an open-ended, ongoing FBI operation.

The bureau tossed the case back to Oakland; Oakland eventually dumped it on the Willits police. As another FBI memo would note, by 1992, Oakland had a triple-digit homicide caseload. And, after all, Judi Bari had survived. There were other crimes to solve.

SIXTEEN

JUDI WAS RELIEVED WHEN HER SISTER GINA offered to take the girls for the summer following the bombing. But neither her serious injury nor Gina's generosity could soften the resentment that Judi bore toward her older sister. And for her part, Gina would never mention the car-bombing or take a public stand on who might have done this to her sister.[*] But she took her nieces during the summer of 1990—as she had done before. No doubt Gina was hoping that the small doses of sanity and comfort—that bourgeois nourishment so reviled by Judi—in her Princeton household would give the girls strength to cope with what lay ahead.

With her daughters gone, and criminal charges against her dismissed by the district attorney, Bari was now free to work on her rehabilitation and her FBI conspiracy theories. After nearly eight weeks in the hospital she was released to a rehabilitation center in Santa Rosa that had been scouted by a Bari-ite named Robin Latham, acting at the behest of Anna Marie Stenberg and with a physician's recommendation. Latham had demurred at first, telling Stenberg she thought that Bari disliked her as she had once been very insulting and dismissive of her. Stenberg had to assure her that Bari would be grateful now.

Bari made progress, gradually moving from wheelchair to

---

[*]When Gina Kolata was on a book tour in California in the spring of 2000, I shared a quiet moment with her just before her reading in a Berkeley bookstore, and asked her if she endorsed her sister's conspiracy theory linking timber and the FBI as being behind the car-bombing. Kolata looked pained at my question. She waved her hand in a dismissive gesture and murmured a barely audible "I don't think so."

walking on crutches for limited time periods. While she was staying in the facility, Sweeney demanded they close the deal on the house that Bari had finally agreed to after the bombing, a deal one of her erstwhile private investigators would characterize afterward as: "Judi now has the kids; he has the property." Bari later told documentary filmmaker Steve Talbot that the very day before she'd left Mendocino County for the Bay Area Seeds of Peace meeting and the Santa Cruz engagement, Sweeney had angrily demanded that she turn over the Redwood Valley property to him, waving the papers in her face. He pressured her again during her rehab in Santa Rosa. Bari acceded to the deal—Sweeney would repay the $45,000 loan from Bari's parents that they had used to buy the property, plus interest—but it galled her that he pressed her to sign when she was still vulnerable.

Nights were her worst time. The nerve pain ran up her leg to her lower back. On one of Darryl Cherney's visits, she was hurting so bad she asked him to spend the night in the hospital with her. He told Talbot he had held her and sung songs to her while she cried. She referred to herself as Jekyll and Hyde—okay in the afternoons but turning monstrous at night from her agonies.

Bari left the rehab facility at the beginning of August, moving to a "safe house" in Cazadero, a former logging hamlet of about one hundred souls in Sonoma County. Her friends continued viewing their heroine as in need of protection from a would-be murderer still out to get her. Prior to staying with them, Bari had never met the Quaker couple and their teenage children who now gave her sanctuary. The woman was a registered nurse and so offered Bari medical as well as spiritual refuge.

She left her cloistered safety in Cazadero on August 14, driven by Anna Marie Stenberg, for a rally in San Francisco on the front doorstep of the Federal Building to protest the FBI at its regional headquarters. Bari's eyes still looked hollow, receding into those huge dark circles, and her tiny body was twisted with pain, but she was heartened by the crowd of loyalists that Mary Moore and others had rounded up. They cheered wildly for her, seated in her wheelchair. Raising a defiant fist at her government nemesis inside the granite building, she delivered her analysis of the FBI's "conspiracies" to frame her. She also told the crowd that her ex-husband,

Mike Sweeney, had already made a mockup of the car bomb (designed from information given out by the FBI and detailed in the Lord's Avenger letter) to demonstrate that it could fit under her Subaru seat.

When Betty Ball saw that device on July 23—at Susan Crane's Ukiah home, where the mockup was alleged to have been constructed by Sweeney—she freaked out and called the police. Local and state agencies quickly converged on the scene and the California state bomb squad gingerly took it outside and blew it up. Although the device was a harmless replica, Sweeney's obvious ability in constructing the dud was duly noted by some of Bari's friends. Sweeney later denied he had made it, but a tape recording of Bari's speech reveals that she clearly told the rally at the Federal Building that he had.

It was a good, fiery speech that day, but despite hints of her old powers, Bari had plainly chosen the role of martyr over that of environmental activist. She still referred to the need to save the redwoods, but her obsessive subject was herself and what "they" had done to her. Now she named new enemies to replace the gyppos who exploited Mexicans and underpaid loggers, or the corporate logging CEOs or the "camos" who took right-wing paramilitary training in the woods. She inveighed against the FBI, summoning up a litany of COINTELPRO horrors committed against the Black Panthers and the antiwar movement, and placing herself as the latest victim.

Not long after the rally, Bari called Bruce Anderson and asked if he would take her out to String Creek, where she would soon move into her new place. The tiny band of settlers who would be her neighbors at the outpost on the one-lane road just three and a half miles outside Willits hosted a picnic in her honor so she could get acquainted.

Anderson found her precautions in giving directions to her safe house unnecessarily elaborate. "She told me that once I got to Cazadero I was to go to a phone booth and call and then she'd give me directions—like I might have been followed." But he was impressed with how beautiful the safe house was and how genteel her hosts.

When he took her to her future home, Anderson thought this was Bari's first time visiting String Creek. But she had been stealthily moving her belongings and her papers out there over the weeks leading up to the car-bombing, and thus she'd probably met at least a few of her neighbors. Certainly her landlords—John Phillips and Joanne Moore—were quite familiar to her, the latter having been her lawyer in the settlement with Sweeney.

Phillips had been working to get the cabin habitable for Bari during her recuperation. Her old friend from Maryland, David Katz, would later put in solar panels so she could have electricity and some other comforts. The cabin would remain primitive by middle-class standards, but cushy compared with the tents, lean-tos and hovels occupied in remote Mendocino and Humboldt.

Everyone pitched in to welcome and help the victim who would now be living among them. Anderson was genuinely touched by the new neighbors' concerns for Bari, but he thought it madness for her to move to such a remote place given that someone had been out to kill her. It simply wasn't safe in his opinion, and he told her so. In comparison with her overly elaborate precautions directing him to her safe house in Cazadero, her blithe disregard for her safety in moving to String Creek seemed irrational. He finally yelled at her that there wasn't even a chain across the dirt lane to block a car from getting up there and across the creek to her place. On a dark, wet night, nobody would hear anything.

"She blew me off," he would say years later. "You'd think as a mother who was going to have her girls staying with her she'd be more concerned after someone had tried to kill her. But she wasn't frightened in the least." During the welcoming picnic, he began for the first time to doubt seriously her various theories as to who bombed her and began to wonder if she herself was the bomber.

Once Bari was ensconced in the foggy seclusion of String Creek and sufficiently repaired, her daughters returned from Princeton to join her. The contrast between Aunt Gina's "bourgeois" home and their mother's funky digs out in the damp wooded valley of String Creek could not have been more dramatic. Although friends and supporters had worked to fix it up, Judi and the girls now resided in a dark, two-room cabin that was off the grid of county-supplied power and water, and where, at least during the long rainy season when solar panels were useless, they could look forward only to erratic heat from a wood-burning stove, and to lugging heavy propane canisters to fuel the refrigerator. (An outhouse was in use until a toilet and a simple shower were finally rigged in an indoor bathroom.)

The girls shared a tiny bedroom. There was a small piano for them to play. Judi slept in the loft once she had healed enough to make the climb up a pull-down ladder.

Although Lisa would later gratefully remember Aunt Gina's generosity, upon her return from Princeton she flattered her mother's animus toward her sibling by tattling that Gina had a personal shopper! It was exactly the kind of detail her mother would seize upon as proof of her sister's bourgeois corruption.

Once her girls were with her again, Bari lobbied the Mendocino County School District and got a double-wide trailer classroom installed in the tiny valley. She was barely a 15 or 20 minute drive from Willits, and String Creek, with only a couple of school-age kids, had far fewer children than other areas where the commute to schools could be up to an hour in each direction. But Bari got what she wanted because of the countywide sympathy generated by her injuries and her newfound fame.

In the first days of Bari's move to String Creek, Anna Marie Stenberg's son Zack Stentz had come up from Santa Cruz to take care of her. It was more than a duty: Bari had become both a friend and a mentor to him and his best friend, Lisa Henry. The two UC Santa Cruz students, who had been the primary organizers for Redwood Summer on the UCSC campus, signed up for shifts, staying out there in the cabin to nurse her through an ongoing recuperation. It meant being nurse, cook, maid and, occasionally, whipping boy—or girl.

Others came out to visit, too. Bari had won herself a new following among Mendocino County women, according to Bruce Anderson, who visited with her on Wednesdays after he took copy for his newspaper to the printer in Willits. Most of the new sympathizers hadn't really known Judi before the bombing. Several of these women signed on to take care of the patient and help her in her "business" affairs over the months to come. Many of this group had not come out of Earth First. They saw Bari as a victim and a feminist heroine whom they had to tend and nurture.

Initially, of course, the overwhelming business at hand, aside from caring for Bari herself, was organizing Redwood Summer without her. While participation in the event was going to fall short of the many thousands of youngsters that Bari and Cherney predicted would show up, there was an outpouring of money from all over the country and new support, particularly from residents of Mendocino who were moved by what Bari had suffered and ready to turn out for—in many cases—their first demonstrations since the Sixties and early Seventies.

Pam Davis was running herself ragged setting up the first base camp for the Summer in Honey Dew, northwest of Garberville in the Mattole watershed in Humboldt County. Much of her effort went into smoothing out potential trouble spots. "The community was saying, like, 'Who are these people?' I told them we were here to check in and we talked to people on the front porch. I told them we're in their community but that we weren't here to wreck their lives." There was little trouble, Davis recalled, except for "some locals who drove by shooting." The demonstrators took such threatening behavior in stride. Besides, no damage occurred.

The plans for Redwood Summer were to mount little sorties, hardly demonstrations at all, interspersed with outreach and followed by larger gatherings later in the summer. Once the demonstrations moved south from Humboldt County, the second base camp for Redwood Summer activists was set up at Branscomb, in Mendocino County, on the logging road between Laytonville and the coast above Fort Bragg. While demonstrations at lumber business offices or out at logging sites were often met with hostility, there was also an effort to disarm loggers by serving doughnuts and coffee. EFers chatted up the loggers at these events, even if later the two sides met as implacable enemies.

On June 6 at the so-called Tailed Frog Grove near Arcata, demonstrators engaged in a cat-and-mouse action to impede cutting at the 160-acre Pacific Lumber site. Loggers reportedly dropped their saws and charged uphill, tackling two Earth First photographers and scattering demonstrators. When protesters regrouped at the site later, sheriff's deputies arrested eight of them. Released in a remote area, the activists were, according to one local environmental newspaper report, "harassed for hours by angry loggers."

On June 19, four young men calling themselves the "Squirrel Brothers" did a two-day tree-sit in a Pacific Lumber old-growth site near Fortuna. They came down when a PL climber deputized by police went up and slashed their food supply.

A much larger hostile encounter on June 20 was in the logging company town of Samoa, west of Arcata in Humboldt County. This had been the plan all along for Redwood Summer: to put on one big demonstration per month, with the rest of the summer punctuated by small informational pickets, tree-sits or nonviolent resistance actions in the woods, or blocking trucks and logging equipment at mills or wood chip plants.

In Samoa, the hostile locals gathered outside the Louisiana-Pacific pulp mill gates to confront some five hundred demonstrators at a well-publicized Earth First rally. The crowd cheered when Bruce Anderson, acting as MC, introduced Darryl Cherney with the line, "He bombed in Oakland, but he's a big hit up here!" Rosie Radiator tap-danced; and writer Alexander Cockburn, echoing Judi's line, called for an alliance between environmentalists and workers. When the demonstrators moved to block the logging trucks just as the TV cameras were rolling, the police waded in, arresting more than forty of the activists.

That July there were also informational pickets in Willits, at Chamberlain Creek along Highway 20, and even in the bedroom suburb of Mill Valley in Marin County. Redwood Summer activists also strung huge banners across the Skunk Line railroad between Willits and Fort Bragg, endorsing the upcoming forest initiatives on the November ballot. And a four-hour Redwood Summer peaceful picket line in front of the Louisiana-Pacific chip mill in Calpella, north of Ukiah, was met by fifty or so women and children of logging families organized under the "Yellow Ribbon" banner. The women and children chanted "It's okay to be a Logger!" and "We are the victims."

On July 6, Redwood Summer got a shot in the arm when the California Department of Forestry ruled that Pacific Lumber's proposed logging might endanger the marbled murrelet, whose habitat was the redwood groves. Just two weeks before, the federal government had declared the spotted owl to be a threatened species, a move that buoyed environmentalists to hope that thousands more acres of forests in the Pacific Northwest might be saved.

The headline event of Redwood Summer was to be a march

right through Fort Bragg, population six thousand, on Saturday, July 21, to stage a rally at the front door of Georgia-Pacific. Maribelle Anderson, whose family owned a small local logging company, organized a Community Solidarity Day in Fort Bragg on the same day.

The pro-logging families gathered at one end of the town on the high school football field, decked out in their yellow shirts and sporting yellow ribbons denoting logging solidarity. Their slogans included "We need wood products, not another Woodstock," and they sported bumper stickers like "EAT SPOTTED OWL FOR DINNER."

At the other end of town the Redwood Summer supporters rallied near the Georgia-Pacific mill, downing free Ben & Jerry's ice cream and dancing in the street to music played from a flatbed truck. As 1,500 of them marched to the front gate of Georgia-Pacific on Main Street (Highway 1) in the center of town, they were met by some 600 helmeted police, sheriffs and highway patrol officers representing over 30 law enforcement agencies and separating them from about 200 angry young loggers. The police kept the two groups apart, despite the confined space, and maintained the peace rather well.

Steve Talbot was there, writing a story on Redwood Summer for *Mother Jones* magazine, almost a year before he went to work on his documentary PBS film on the bombing of Judi Bari. He described the event even years later in positive terms as almost a dialogue: "There was an open mike on that flatbed truck in the middle of town. There were cops on all the roof tops and cops keeping a couple of hundred locals away from the environmentalists and people were heckling the speakers and some loggers got up to the mike and talked about the damage they'd seen done to the woods and the streams. But the enviros let them get up and talk. And I thought, okay, maybe something is actually going to happen here."

A final mass demonstration was held in August, a march through the town of Fortuna, across the road from Pacific Lumber and their company town of Scotia. The whole event had grown out of a mini-Woodstock episode, a hippie-by-the-river affair at Willow Creek where Earth First had set up a base camp for the Redwood Summer crowd. From there, the group spontaneously decided to march through Fortuna, site of the PL sawmill and the major employer in town. Unlike Fort Bragg, there were no bohos or hippies anywhere among the natives to ameliorate the blatant hatred for environmentalists.

Talbot regarded that demonstration as ill conceived and dangerous: "It was suicidal to march through that town with those banners. They got out of town by the skin of their teeth by calling the demonstration short." Some 600 of them had marched between rows of about 400 logging-industry stalwarts who jeered, pelted them with eggs, tomatoes and rocks, and were threatening to tear them apart. Bruce Anderson described it as "leading lambs to the slaughter." The Fortuna march demonstrated to Talbot, at least, that "beyond Judi and a couple of others, these were not great and strategic minds."

Redwood Summer was a mighty effort on the part of Pam Davis, Darryl Cherney, Kelpie Wilson, Betty Ball, Anna Marie Stenberg, Roanne Withers, Karen Pickett and others, most of them women who, following Bari's lead, were responsible for what she referred to as "the feminization of Earth First." But the Earth First movement itself gained only a few permanent activist converts, although it no doubt raised consciousness about the plight of the redwoods. Talbot estimates that no more than two or three thousand youngsters had answered the call to Redwood Summer actions. The cutting went on as it had before, and both the Forests Forever and the Big Green initiatives, which would have imposed limits to forest cuttings in accord with sustainable-yield goals, lost in the November election.[*]

BARI HAD REMAINED IN THE BACKGROUND during Redwood Summer, watching it all slip away. She was smoking marijuana constantly

---

[*] Gail Lucas of the Sierra Club, who had been a major force in the Forests Forever campaign, pointed to the $12 million campaign mounted by the timber industry against both of the green initiatives. She saw Earth First and Redwood Summer as playing a big part in the defeat of the proposals. "I don't think it has been helpful," she told newspapers at the time, "because it allowed the industry to focus on Earth First and take the light away from over-cutting."

now—only for pain, she'd insist—a habit she would continue up to her death.

While Redwood Summer sank without sparking the mass movement that Bari had anticipated, her own myth was taking wing. People wanted to support her. Bruce Anderson received one check for her at the *Anderson Valley Advertiser* for $5,000. That was just the beginning: "People didn't know where to send it. I forwarded all the checks—amounting to eight or nine thousand dollars—to the MEC for her. Of course, none of it was accounted for or declared. People just wanted to help her."

But she became increasingly hard to help. In his weekly visits to her cabin, Anderson noticed her "diva-like" behavior. (He likened Bari to Barbra Streisand.) He found her particularly cruel toward her protégé and caretaker Lisa Henry.

"I pulled up one night. I was meeting Talbot there at dusk," Anderson recalled. "Lisa was trying to fit a canister of heating oil into its place and having difficulty with it. Judi totally berated her. 'You're fat. You're ugly. You're stupid,' she yelled at poor Lisa. The poor kid just stood there sobbing. She was barely nineteen years old. She'd been Judi's contact down at Santa Cruz, and she really worshipped Judi. But then, the minute Judi sees us it was Jekyll and Hyde, friendly banter."

Zack Stentz, who was best friends with Lisa Henry, blames most of Bari's abusiveness on her pain. "It was heartbreaking to be around. I would spend the night there in the room with her sleeping on the floor in a sleeping bag. She would be shuddering and crying out. She felt it was like electrical shocks running up her whole body. I massaged her back and legs."

Henry and Stentz were part of a rotating team of people staying full-time with Bari. In keeping with UC Santa Cruz's off-the-wall "alternative studies," Henry had actually finagled course credit in her social work class for a proposed five-month sojourn at Bari's cabin. But she left Bari's service "very upset" and well before her "course" as Bari's nursemaid was completed.

A long time later, when Bari's health improved, she invited Stentz and Henry to dinner at the cabin. She fixed what Stentz described as a "really complicated recipe—eggplant lasagna and very good too." All was forgiven, but in the meantime Lisa Henry had changed her major and moved to Illinois to live a different kind of life from the one she had seen in Bari's service.

It was in the summer of 1991, Zack Stentz recalled, that his mother, Anna Marie Stenberg, had a falling-out with Judi. Stentz saw the two as "very strong, very stubborn women who had deeply cared about each other but were very angry with each other—for whatever reason." Their quarrel tugged at his loyalties and polarized two Mendocino camps that had once been in the same coalition: "Sonoma County people and people on the coast remained friends with my mom; the people in Willits and Ukiah stayed friends with Judi."

LATER IN 1991, BARI RETURNED to the Highlander Research and Education Center in Tennessee—this time for a weeklong gathering billed as a healing retreat for individuals who'd been severely injured for their Movement activities. United Farm Workers union cofounder Dolores Huerta was one participant. (Her spleen had been ruptured by a blow from a police baton during a 1988 demonstration against the policies of presidential candidate George H. W. Bush.) Brian Willson, who'd lost his legs after lying down on the train tracks at the Concord Naval Weapons Station, was another Highland guest. Huertes and Willson would become Judi Bari fans. But others whispered criticism of Bari after her visit, asking why she'd requested a litter to carry her from place to place while at other times she'd manage to walk outside without help to smoke her pot.

Back home, Bari's harsh ways with people continued to generate criticism. Bruce Anderson recalls that Bari drove another helpful caregiver away, a woman named Melissa Roberts who at the time was also an IWW officer, and who assisted Bari in obtaining a $25,000 grant from the union to do an investigation of the car-bombing. The reason for Bari's attack, according to Anderson, was that "Melissa refused to fudge figures for grant applications."

The money was supposed to be for union affairs. Bari had in fact reconstituted the Wobbly local she founded with Anna Marie Stenberg in 1989 and solicited new members. Carl Hammarskjold, a onetime beat reporter for the tiny *Independent Coast Observer*, was one of those who signed up. Initially, the local's meetings were billed as

IWW meetings. "Then," Hammarskjold explains, "with the expanded membership in the union, they voted the $25,000 grant money to be given to Bari," who then dubbed the group the "Wobbly Bureau of Investigations." Some of the attendees during the few months he went to the meetings were Bari and Cherney, naturally, but also AVA contributor Fred Gardner, Pam Davis, Tanya Brannan and some of her female political activists, known as the Purple Berets.

Once the group had the money, Hammarskjold notes acerbically, all the talk about the IWW union was soon over. Now it was full-time on Bari. Over and over again she stressed the line that the attack on her was part of a conspiracy to disrupt Redwood Summer and that it had all the markings of an FBI COINTELPRO operation. She pressed everyone to read the bible of COINTELPRO conspiracy lore, *Agents of Repression: The FBI's Secret Wars against the Black Panther Party and the American Indian Movement,* by Ward Churchill and Jim Vander Wall, who argue that FBI campaigns against domestic radicals didn't end after the Frank Church hearings in 1976, but continued and intensified, culminating in investigations of Central American activists.

For Hammarskjold, these were simply propaganda sessions. He says the group wasn't spending the $25,000 stipend from the IWW to investigate, although they ostensibly had three areas of investigation: the FBI, Irv Sutley as an "FBI patsy," and a search for the typewriter that had produced the Lord's Avenger letter. They were having political pep sessions for Bari that ended for Hammarskjold when, he says, both Pam Davis and Bari asked him to leave and not attend future meetings. "Everyone suspected everyone else of being an FBI agent, more and more, especially after reading the book on COINTELPRO. I was in my early twenties at the time, just out of a private college, wearing khakis, and I guess that made me not very trustworthy from their perspective."

It was the same old Bari, still expelling people, just as she had back in her student antiwar days when she accused a fellow activist of being an FBI agent, and just as she had early in her career as a North Coast environmentalist when she pushed Sequoia out of the tiny new Ecotopia chapter of Earth First, and just as she had from her sickbed when she rid herself of various attendants who were performing the most personal chores. She finally broke with her old friend Mary Moore as well, when Moore's lover at the time, Kwazi Nkrumah, a former steelworker and Black Panther, offended Bari in an article he wrote in the *Sonoma County Free Press* warning against the very kinds of accusations of FBI infiltration and agent-mongering that Bari had been leveling recently at Irv Sutley.

And after a year of Bari's close confidences with Steve Talbot, his film *Who Bombed Judi Bari?* was aired on PBS on the anniversary of the car-bombing. Talbot said that while Bari's attorneys were grateful for the film's proving once and for all that the bomb was under the seat and that the nails found at her home and in the trunk couldn't be matched to the bomb itself, Judi herself was enraged at Talbot for introducing the Santa Rosa airfield bombing with Sweeney as lead suspect, thus offering him as candidate for the car-bombing as well. Although she had told Talbot about the airport bombing, Bari felt betrayed when Sweeney was cast in a negative light. She denounced Talbot in an AVA article entitled, "Who Bombed Steve Talbot?"

Bari's greatest political rift in the post-bombing period was one that had been percolating ever since she publicly denounced tree-spiking. She wrote to Earth First cofounder Dave Foreman to explain her position and her plans. In an article in the AVA in April 1991, she said that Foreman had written back "stating emphatically and passionately why he disagreed with me." But despite their differences, she noted, "he respected my work and thought I was 'a hero who will be remembered 100 years from now.'"

Foreman was indeed unhappy with Earth First—at least as it was now being led by Bari on the North Coast. He didn't like hippie tree-huggers who were antithetical to his Rednecks for the Wilderness. Worse were the Marxoids, like Bari herself, who were turning an environmental force into one waging what he denounced as "class warfare."

He broke with Earth First in a public letter he and his wife, Nancy Morton, released to the media in the summer of 1990. They were leaving the group that he, more than anyone else, had brought into being, and in the open letter he decried a situation in which wilderness protection had veered sharply toward "left-wing social causes." Yet he still believed in guerrilla tactics—monkey-wrenching—and he still saw the human race sourly, calling it a "human pox," a pestilence pushing the world to "the threshold of biotic terror" through its rampant development.

Foreman and his wife also expressed their dislike for Earth First's increasingly countercultural leanings. On this he wasn't that far apart from Bari herself. But Judi was amused at the hippie culture that transmogrified environmentalism into a pagan religion, and she was willing to work with it; he wasn't. "We feel we should be sitting at the bar of a seedy honky-tonk," the letter read, "drinking Lone Star, thumbing quarters in the juke box, and writing this letter on a bar napkin." He would tell one interviewer, tongue in cheek, that he wanted to start a new organization and call it "Bubbas for Bambi," but his disaffection—particularly from Bari's Marxist/ Maoist style of environmentalism—was real.

He set out his arguments more fully in his 1991 *Confessions of an Eco-Warrior.* He stressed that the roots of Earth First were in the conservative American tradition of the Founding Fathers. "It is absolutely essential to understand that Earth First! did not emerge from the anarchist movement, or from the left," he wrote. He insisted that its antecedents were the Sierra Club, Friends of the Earth, the Wilderness Society and even the National Audubon Society. He complained of a "new" Earth First, and especially what he described as the "strong faction...on the West Coast that finds its place more with the left than with the conservation movement and is inspired more by the writings of Abbie Hoffman than those of Edward Abbey." There could be no doubt about whom he was writing.

Foreman might even make room, he said, for these latter-day lefties as shock troops were it not for the fact that "excessive internal debate about style, strategy, and substance leads to infighting from the real job—fighting the vandals looting the riches of this Earth." He complained that his movement was "now dominated by anti-capitalist rhetoric and an overwhelming emphasis on direct action to the exclusion of other Earth First! techniques. I am not an anarchist or a Yippie. I am a conservationist. I believe that human overpopulation is the fundamental problem on Earth today." Then he concluded, "In other words, I am no longer part of the Earth First! movement. I no longer represent it and I am no longer represented by it."

Bari didn't take the message lying down. She wrote a scathing review of his book in the AVA in 1992. She attacked Foreman's misanthropy (although it was only slightly more passionate than her own at times) and also, somewhat less grandly and rather ludicrously, the fact that he had omitted Cherney from the list of Earth First musicians who had inspired him. Battling back at him, she wrote: "Rather than confront the hard, controversial issues, Foreman lobs vague accusation at us 'class struggle social justice leftists' that he claims have 'infiltrated' Earth First! He doesn't mention the controversial right-wing stances he has taken, such as advocating the starvation of Ethiopians and the closing of borders."[*] She closed bitterly: "So I'll return the compliment you gave me last year, Dave. You're a hero who will be remembered 100 years from now. But the movement has passed you by, and it's time to step aside. Work elsewhere where you feel more comfortable. But quit bashing those of us who are still on the front lines."

Bari did go to hear Foreman reading his new book at Copperfield's Books in Sebastopol. Bruce Anderson attended and was surprised that she sat mildly in the audience. Foreman, in turn, was welcoming. The two chatted afterward, agreeing in principle to forgo further attacks on one another and keep their differences private.

Bari acknowledged the split between her group and her Earth First opponents with surprising candor in an article she wrote for the AVA dated March 3, 1992, entitled, "Showdown at the Earth First! Corral." The fight began, according to Bari, when the EF journal printed an article that called for "dressing up as a hunter and going out shooting other hunters." Along with others in her Ecotopia chapter of EF, Bari wrote to the journal denouncing the article and withdrawing their names on a "contact list" regularly published in the journal until the issues were settled.

It was getting down to the nitty-gritty of who exactly Earth First was going to be: a nonviolent public group committing civil disobedience with publicly acknowledged leaders like Judi Bari; or the eco-ninjas, an anarchist secret cabal of monkey-wrenchers who

---

[*]In December 1990, Foreman was quoted in *Mother Jones* as apologizing for his statements on AIDS and starvation in Ethiopia as nature's way of thinning overpopulation. "My comments were horribly insensitive and superficial," he said. "I sympathize with people suffering from AIDS."

operated independently and anonymously to sabotage development that threatened pristine wilderness.

In the article, Bari quoted liberally from letters denouncing her. One writer said, "If you are not tough enough for Earth First! then I suggest you join the Sierra Club or the Audubon Society. If that is too radical, try the Green Party." Another dismissed Bari's arguments against tree-spiking as "humanistic nonsense," arguing further, "Of course a few humans are endangered. So what! Plenty of damn humans here. The death of a few activists is not important in the evolution of Gaia. Are you warriors or whiners? I'd trade a hundred of you for one spiker."

For Bari it was easy to dismiss those who were advocating outright murder of hunters. This smacked of armed revolution, she wrote, a step she believed—putting on her old Marxist analyst's cap—was "premature." (The word seemed to imply that at the proper moment, she might go out and join them!) But it wasn't just the call to arms against hunters that stuck in her craw. She had a laundry list of slights from the *Earth First! Journal*'s editors: they didn't print her articles or—horrors—they edited them or shortened them. She accused them of hiding behind a rotating-editor system in which no one was answerable for editorial policy.

Because of the arguments raging back and forth, it was decided to hold a conference in Portland to settle the editorship and policies of the *Earth First! Journal*. In the early spring of 1992, Bari traveled there with a contingent of loyalists from Ecotopia EF who were firmly under her control. On their way up, her group (as she put it coyly in her AVA account) "discussed the fact that the FBI was certain to be at the conference"—her way of establishing the line they were to take in the days ahead. In her own telling, it backfired. Other than her group, most of the EFers were sick and tired of listening to Bari's FBI bogeyman paranoia.

At the Oregon campground, where more than one hundred people in attendance divided into two warring camps, Bari made her case that all the dissension was being spread either by the FBI or by unwitting saboteurs. She insisted that EF support her suit against the FBI. She whined about the journal's treatment of her, contending that the editors had contributed "to [her] isolation" by failing to publish the work of Ecotopia or even to publicize her suit against the FBI. "I have to admit," Bari later wrote with pathos, "that it is galling to hear people blithely dismiss the work for which I was horribly maimed and nearly killed. And I have to admit it started to get to me."

She also complained of "a vile misogynist attack" against her in the *Earth First! Journal*. The writer, a Southern Californian named Ken Shelton, called a feminist diatribe that Bari had published late in 1990 "an excrementicious [*sic*] piece of eco-femme idiocy." He further dismissed Redwood Summer as "a truly maggot-gagging, ignominious display, effective in saving precisely zero old-growth redwood trees." Shelton concluded, "Give us a break, Bari. Behind every aggressive white male, stands a pampered female, wheedling, whining, and conniving, clamoring for more comforts and commodities."

Despite her appetite for struggle, the conference soon became unbearable for Bari, especially when a woman she had considered a friend declared that the problem was Bari's "hostility." At the lunchtime adjournment, Bari found herself "too weak to walk back to the lodge where lunch was being served." Then this same putative friend twisted the knife, in Bari's telling, by advising those who had come to Oregon with her that their job was to be "nurses": "You need to treat Judi like a patient. Worry about her food and her comfort. Don't be putting ideas in her head!"

Bari felt she was in a "loony bin." It was even worse after lunch when she took her place in the ritual EF circle in her own special chair, placed to accommodate her injuries. At one point when she felt badly treated by the group, she pulled her sleeping bag over her head. She knew people saw her as having "lost it," and melodramatically defended herself: "You all are not taking seriously anything you've heard here. You've watched me deteriorate. I can no longer participate effectively, I'm out!"

As she concluded in the article she wrote for Bruce Anderson upon returning home from the meeting, "So the FBI won, and I certainly played my role in helping them do it. I ended up isolated and discredited."

SEVENTEEN

WHILE BARI WAS STILL OFFICIALLY UNDER ARREST right after the bombing, her attorney, Susan Jordan, employed private investigator Sheila O'Donnell and bomb expert Mark Shattuck to examine the evidence in an attempt to free her client. A few years after the charges were dropped, Bari commissioned her own investigation, hiring Josiah "Tink" Thompson with money from the donations that were pouring in, and with the IWW grant specifically earmarked for such a purpose.*

One by one, Thompson said, Bari's pet suspects were eliminated as candidates for car-bombers: the FBI, Irv Sutley, David Kemnitzer, anti-abortionist Bill Staley, the right-wing neo-Nazi "Stompers," loggers from Fort Bragg, and anyone else named from the timber industry. There was always the possibility that a disgruntled Earth Firster or anonymous local haters had tried to do her in, but Bari's various investigators remained skeptical.

One of the investigators admitted he'd harbored suspicions about Sweeney from the outset and believes his views were shared, if not expressed, by some of Bari's legal team. Another investigator says that he even accompanied Susan Jordan to the Ukiah police after the case was closed by the FBI and Oakland, to urge that the investigation continue. Whether anyone expressed suspicions about

---

*Greenpeace, the environmental group, largely contributed to the first investigation, then reportedly balked at paying O'Donnell money she claimed was still owed. O'Donnell then refused to write up her notes unless payment was received.

Sweeney at that meeting is debated.[*] (However, one of the investigators still believes that putting a bomb in Bari's car that far ahead of the blast would have put Sweeney's girls at risk, and thus was unlikely to have been done by the girls' father.)

One person that Bari's team did definitely eliminate as a suspect was Judi Bari herself. Knowing her, they were certain she could not have been so stupid as to ride with a bomb under her seat that had its switch in the "on" position—or the "off" position either, for that matter. With a motion device as well as a timer, it was too dangerous. Because her team believed that Bari was innocent, and because its members were politically to the left, they were outraged by the charges filed against her by the OPD and the FBI. But as professionals they were also highly critical of the official negligence and rush to judgment they had seen in many of their other cases.

Over the next few years, many attorneys worked for Bari and Cherney: Jordan, Bill Simpich and Douglas Horngrad represented them for the arrest. When the civil suit was filed a year after the bombing, a stream of lawyers—including Marvin Stender and Paul Harris, the latter having once represented Black Panther Huey Newton—were associated with the case over the next decade, while the dedicated Dennis Cunningham stayed for the duration.

The defendants named in the civil trial filed by Bari and Cherney at first included the Mendocino County Sheriff's Office and the former head of the FBI's San Francisco office among others, but were eventually narrowed down to the Oakland Police Department and individually named agents of the FBI.

Cunningham was the main attorney, joined by Bob Bloom once Marvin Stender vacated. They did the pretrial work, awaiting the arrival of their star courtroom attorney: Tony Serra, a gray ponytailed, avowed pot-smoking, leftist lawyer (played by James Wood in the 1989 film *True Believer*) who describes himself as a "performance artist" in the courtroom. (Serra does no pretrial work on cases, leaving

---

[*]Susan Jordan claims she has no "specific recollection" of the meeting but says vaguely, "I may have met and don't remember." She insists that she has "remained very interested that some law enforcement agency investigate." In her and others' view, law enforcement "just quit." "I think they wanted to nail Judi with it and when they couldn't they said 'we're done.'"

that to his firm or to other attorneys.) During the Bari-Cherney civil trial, Serra joined the tag team of fellow litigators Bloom and Cunningham to bring their suit to a successful, if improbable conclusion.

Early on in the civil suit preparations, Bari signed on as a hired hand, working hard in her own behalf. She got superlative marks from Cunningham for her paralegal work. He said she may well have missed her calling as a lawyer.

Bari was not a big reader of literature; she didn't go to films. But she knew chapter and verse the history of the contemporary left and its legal battles with the FBI and law enforcement. To be working side by side with Cunningham and Bloom (both of whom had represented the Attica Prison inmates in their successful suit after the 1971 uprising) and to josh with lawyers for the Black Panthers was gratifying because it placed her in the same arena with the left-wing legal heroes of her youth. The fact that now they were working on her case reinforced her own dedication. She made a point of knowing the case backwards and forwards. This was *her* life. Her Earth First work began to pale in comparison.

She participated in depositions in which she challenged witnesses—cops and FBI agents—as if she were a lawyer herself. ("Not in evidence," she snapped during one such encounter.) And during the deposition of Special Agent Phil Sena in 1994, Bari waded in, covering Cunningham's back, as it were, when she thought the FBI attorney, Joseph Sher, was about to speak out of turn:

Cunningham: "We've been given to understand that the FBI, and you in particular, were in possession of some information as of the 24th of May, 1990, to the effect that..."

Bari snaps [as Sher is about to interrupt]: "Let him ask it before you object."

A chastened Sher replies, "I was going to do that."

Bari pored over testimony and documents up in her String Creek cabin loft at all hours of the night. She didn't shrink from the minutiae of reading endless transcripts and depositions for small variances and slip-ups, searching for weapons that could be used by the attorneys who would carry her case forward.

ON MAY 28, 1992, BARI MADE a rare appearance as the headliner for a rally and march by the "Albion Nation," an affinity group of environmentalists in and around Albion Ridge and the Albion River, but including environmentalists from all over Mendocino. The event capped nearly two months of struggle over a redwood grove near Albion that was dubbed "Enchanted Meadows" by its champions. The hundred or so activists demonstrating against Louisiana-Pacific employed the usual tactics: tree-sits, road-blocking and self-chaining to heavy equipment.

After months of demonstrations, LP had had enough of the disruptions. It was Frank Wigginton's idea, he claims, as head of LP security, to hit the demonstrators preemptively with Strategic Litigation Against Public Participation (SLAPP) suits—a tactic used by corporations around the country to halt the spate of lawsuits generated by employee whistleblowers and by activists of various stripes. The SLAPP suits filed by Louisiana-Pacific sought damages from the defendants to compensate for the lost income of the company and the workers due to the interruption of business.

"They were killing us," Wigginton says. "They were stopping our ability to harvest our lumber. I told my boss he had to file suit individually to get them. We sued them for trespassing or interfering with lawful business and put a monetary value on it—this many men that were stopped, this much time and money lost in production. It was great sport!"

Bari, Bruce Anderson, Beth Bosk, Roanne Withers and Anna Marie Stenberg were just a few of the named defendants. The group of activists turned around and, with their attorneys, countersued.

Bari was arrested for trespassing on that May 28 in Albion. Anderson maintains that her arrest was largely symbolic: she had simply stepped over the orange line painted across the road to mark private LP property, and the deputies arrested her, moving her some thirty feet to book her at their mobile arrest trailer, and then immediately released her.

Wigginton had noted that she was using a cane while she participated in the demonstration. He says he was concerned enough to warn her to be careful; "I didn't want her to get hurt."

Bari waited a year after her arrest to file her own lawsuit against LP, also naming Wigginton and the Mendocino County Sheriff's Office, claiming she'd been "manhandled" by two sheriff's deputies and falsely arrested, and that her daughter Lisa had suffered "trauma" simply by having witnessed her mother's arrest. She asserted that she first suffered back injuries when the deputies moved her, neglecting to mention any lingering pain from the car-bombing. The lawsuit stated that her constitutional rights to free speech and equal protection had been violated. Bari claimed she was "forcibly walked across the orange line" against her "explicit wishes not to trespass and to avoid arrest," and then she "fell down."

Bruce Anderson, who was present at Albion, scoffs at that account: "She walked purposely and was arrested fairly." He and others saw the suit as one more instance of the old Sweeney/Bari scamming through nuisance suits against deep pockets—in this case, the County of Mendocino—to bleed them for cash. It worked. Bari received a quick $5,000 settlement.

Prior to that lawsuit, she had convinced most of the Enchanted Meadows group to drop their countersuit against Louisiana-Pacific in return for LP's agreement to drop the SLAPP suits. But there were holdouts—Bosk, Stenberg, Anderson and five others—who all believed their countersuit was important enough to see through to the end. They felt betrayed when Bari settled with LP and then convinced so many of the others to do the same. Her action destroyed the group's solidarity, scotching any chance, as Roanne Withers put it, to draw "national attention to predator corporations and what they are doing to the country's remaining forests."

According to Withers, Bari played on the group's collective worry that because LP had sued for astronomical amounts in damages, the homeowners among them might lose their houses should their case fail. But even some of those without such assets had been swayed by Bari's lead.

Ironically, four years later LP capitulated to the holdouts. The timber corporation was facing huge attorney's fees and it was not at all certain that the company would prevail, even though, as Withers pointed out, SLAPP law says you have no right to trespass even if it involves free speech. "We were able to prove harassment and ambiguous property lines, for starters," Withers says.

All the awards from LP were earmarked by the recipients for environmental goals (unlike Bari's $5,000, which she saw as her own). Stenberg designated her cash award for restoration funds for Elk Creek. Bosk gave the 100 acres of the lower portion of Enchanted Meadows she'd won as a preserve. All in all, this victory was achieved with no thanks to Judi Bari, in the view of Withers, Anderson and the other holdouts.

IN HER AFTERLIFE FOLLOWING THE bombing, Judi Bari had become a famous personality all over the North Coast and well beyond. She had a weekly two-hour show, *Punch and Judi*, on the FM community radio station, KZYX in Philo, which opened with the signature voice of Tracy Chapman singing, "Don't you know they're talkin' about a revolution…. " She made frequent appearances on Berkeley's KPFA, flagship of the leftist, listener-sponsored Pacifica Foundation's network. After her split with former allies like Anderson, Stenberg and Moore had become public, Bari proved adept at keeping them off those particular wavelengths.

Even the fashion magazine *Bazaar* printed a flattering profile of Bari, an anomaly for a publication devoted to chic, given Judi's braless hippie style. The article, exploring FBI and timber conspiracies against her, was spoon-fed by Bari to the author. Other publications did Bari profiles in the same vein. She was being transformed into the Mother Teresa of the North Coast forests.

But Bari's focus was now almost entirely on herself and her federal lawsuit. Even the *Bazaar* article noted her myriad files and boxes of materials stashed in the little alcove under her sleeping loft, testament to the all-consuming attention she gave to her case. She was spending equal time doing depositions and fundraising—for her legal case, rather than for the redwoods or Earth First.

She also took care of her daughters. She was now able to cook dinner for them; pork chops and mashed potatoes were on the menu the night the *Bazaar* reporter visited. And she still made her rounds about the county—in better style now, behind the wheel of her newly purchased four-wheel-drive Dodge station wagon. She had her regular hangouts, popping in at the Downtown Bakery in Healdsburg, whose proprietress, a former Chez Panisse staffer, remembered how haunted Bari looked, how dark the circles under her eyes. In Willits she hit another hippie café as a regular, enjoying her status as local celebrity.

But in the years since the tragedy, Bari's relationships to others changed—in her own telling, for the worse, although not for a minute could she admit her own responsibility for the quarrels that ended some of her deepest friendships.

In the second and last interview with Beth Bosk's *New Settler* in 1995, Bari ascribed her alienation from old allies to the after-effects of the bombing:

> Pain has changed my life in a lot of ways. Levels of pain I didn't know existed, I experience every day. Not only is my back broken (which leaves me with a constant low-level pain), but I also have this nerve damage that makes the nerves to my paralyzed foot randomly fire, and when they fire, it feels like an electric shock. There are two places it does so in my foot, and sometimes, it does it in the back of my leg. The back of my leg hurts more because it is a larger area, and because my foot's paralyzed, it can't contract. But in the back of my leg the muscles actually contract and I can't move when it does that. The level of pain of that is so horrible.
>
> People who used to hold my hand in the hospital saw me experiencing that pain; it was excruciating. Now I've learned to not change my expression. I've learned to tolerate those episodes (which last anywhere from 3 to 10 seconds—those zaps of electric shock-like pain). I've learned to tolerate them without changing my expression because I've discovered that it warps my relationships with people so much.
>
> My relationships with people have been destroyed by the bombing anyway. It's very hard for me to have an equal relationship with anyone.

Bari said her pain made "other people so uncomfortable" that they avoided her, although this assertion seemed to be contradicted by the coterie of mostly women who massed around her in the aftermath of her injuries. She insisted that her relationships had been altered by "this weird kind of notoriety that I've gotten, where anything that I say has more weight than it deserves: if I express an opinion, it's considered a pronouncement. I can't relate to people as equals because they won't relate to me as an equal."

But many who once were close to her claimed that she had become a tyrannical diva. Even Beth Bosk succumbed to Bari's elevated status when she called her an "icon activist" in the post-bombing interview. Bari responded with theatrical self-pity: "People have these incredible standards of behavior for me. And if I meet them, I am resented for being too saintly; and if I don't meet them, I'm vilified for not being saintly enough. And nobody can look at me without thinking of the bombing. I can't just be myself."

The one friendship she pined for openly was that of Bruce Anderson. Bari's description of the arc of their relationship acknowledged they had fallings-out "over feminist issues." She had stolen and then destroyed AVA issues, reacting to a drawing in the paper that offended her feminist sensibilities. Anderson was furious, but he says the two had patched it up well before the bombing.

For Bari, the real breach opened when she read in one of Anderson's columns that "fair-minded people" might readily think that Bari had bombed herself. Bari also translated Anderson's criticisms of her into the charge that she had "a horrible personality."

"It was devastating to read that," she told Bosk. "I cried for days. I didn't want to talk to anybody. I loved Bruce Anderson and at the time of the bombing, he was one of the closest people to me in the world." Bari could not tolerate Anderson's departure from her line on the car-bombing—that it was timber and the FBI. (She would have been less pleased when, after her death, Anderson's suspicions began to turn to Sweeney, largely as a result of conversations with Steve Talbot, who, in researching his documentary, was approached by several people close to Bari who pressed him to investigate her ex-husband.)

Bari had one other revelation for Bosk. It was her candid and embittered admission that she had lost her sexual desire. "Since your [sic] famous for asking everyone about sex, I'm going to volunteer that one of the unspoken results of the bombing is that it has ruined my sexual response. I don't have any. That part of me is numb. If this had happened to a man, nobody would expect them to perform sexually. They blew my butt up and all else associated." It was sexist, she seemed to be implying, that she, unlike a similarly afflicted man, was still being expected to perform.

She wrenchingly described how cruel men (and also women)

made passes at her when she was still recuperating. In her telling, it was her very physical vulnerability that prompted these sexual overtures and she admitted she was still angry about it. She was angry too that men disappeared from her life once she was no longer sexually responsive. This reinforced her view that most men were sexist and sexually predatory.

Bosk interjected her own bizarre line of questioning, bringing up the scene in the 1978 film *Coming Home* in which the character played by Jane Fonda, after performing oral sex on the paraplegic Vietnam vet played by Jon Voigt, looks up and asks, "Can you feel that?" Bosk then quotes Voigt in character answering in a blissed-out state, "No, but I can see it," leaving the door open for Bari to volunteer if anyone had performed such sexual mercies on her. When Bari didn't pick up on the cue, Bosk continued more decorously, "Did the blast destroy the ability that necessitates the trust it takes to be overwhelming in love, and therefore sexual with someone else?"

Bari answered simply: "I don't know, because I haven't had the opportunity." She admitted that she feared she had lost her "sexual attractiveness—because my body became distorted…. There just are not very many men in my life anymore. I don't have many friends that are men…. It changed very many things, and it left me with a sadness, in a way. And in a way, it left me with a sense of relief."

Adoring women seem to have filled the vacuum left by the withdrawal of men from her. She had always previously made fun of many of the types of women she was now attracting—poets, practicing Buddhists, sympathetic women who were not necessarily activists but who saw Bari as a feminist icon, just as Bosk had suggested. These women embraced her more closely now that she wore martyr's wings.

Indeed, Bari now claimed—not wholly persuasively for those who had known her well—that she was truly nonviolent as she had never been before the bombing. This went down well with the county's feminist poets, self-appointed "goddesses," backyard ecologists and artisans who now celebrated and befriended her. Many of these women had never taken to the old Judi-in-your-face provocative activism, viewing such a posture as violent and male-identified. Now they enjoyed the newly quiescent Judi; they rallied around her and nursed her through her final illness.

BARI HAD SUFFICIENTLY RECOVERED from her injuries to resume her daily life for several years when, in the summer of 1996, she discovered a lump in her breast. She had never had regular mammograms; she didn't even have checkups with her nominal doctor at the Willits clinic. When she took her girls in for care, it was usually at the county emergency room. In this she was like many hippies on the North Coast who lacked medical insurance and distrusted "Western medicine."

But Bari did go in to the clinic in Willits when she found the lump. According to one doctor familiar with her condition, the lump was "obviously a cancer; not a simple lump, but an angry lump." Bari was referred to a specialist and advised to make an immediate appointment for surgery, but as the doctor recalled, "She didn't show up for appointments, insisting she was not going to ignore everything else in her life just to take care of the lump."

Finally she was convinced to see the specialist. Routine lab work was done and revealed metastatic breast cancer. Her liver enzymes were elevated, indicating that the cancer was systemic. It was a death sentence.

At that point, Bari's doctors pressed her to have the cancer cut out to extend her life. She refused treatment until months later, in November. By then it was too late to operate. After she'd gone public with the disease that winter, she did agree to undergo radiation treatment—but only to mitigate her pain.

She told Mike Geniella, in one of her last interviews with the press, that she had sampled herbal concoctions, spiritualism and the occult as alternative medicine—what most mainstream doctors, and certainly someone like her sister Gina Kolata, who had written extensively in the *New York Times* about new and effective mainstream medical treatments for breast cancer, would regard as quackery. She was smoking marijuana almost constantly—including the time weeks before she died when she appeared at a local high school, sat in the front row and mockingly lit up big joints in front of the community, daring anyone to challenge her. Bari told Geniella the pot helped ease her pain. She finally sought experimental antibody infusion treatment at the University of California Medical Center in San Francisco, but she had a bad reaction to the therapy and it was discontinued.

Throughout her illness, even up to the last weeks in the String Creek cabin, Bari worked on the transcripts of depositions for her civil trial. She had also continued fundraising for her case, work she'd begun while recuperating from her car-bombing injuries. Mark Scarmella, who works with Bruce Anderson on the AVA, visited Bari at her cabin and saw what he described as "incredibly sophisticated fundraising sheets that were equivalent to the most elaborate data systems today on computers, but Judi had done it all by hand." He watched while she spread out before her large expanses of graph paper systematically recording donations to her cause: names on the left, color-coded across the top to list mailings, responses, donations and "do not notify" indications. ("She didn't want to waste any money contacting anyone who had not responded to the first mailings," Scarmella recalled.)[*]

In Bari's last days she transferred her terminal care to Sharon Paltins, a medical doctor who also did alternative treatments out of a clinic in Laytonville. Paltins had come out of the Hog Farm collective and still had strong ties to the nearby commune. By going public with her disease, Bari inspired a new round of sympathy—even from some ostensible enemies with whom she had clashed. Thus she was touched when, out shopping one day when she was still ambulatory, she ran into Marilyn Butcher, the county supervisor who had lectured her that she'd brought the Redwood Summer death threats upon herself. Butcher impulsively hugged her. Such human moments softened some of Bari's bitterness. She was also touched by sympathy letters from some in the logging industry, including several CEOs.

And even the men who, she'd sadly told Bosk, had all drifted

---

[*] Bruce Anderson and Scarmella found that, according to filings with the California State Department of Corporations, over $1 million had been raised as of 2000 for the Redwood Summer Justice Project, which was founded to fund the Bari/Cherney civil suit.

away after she recovered from the bombing now drifted back in her final days to say goodbye or to hang out or to do a service for her. David Drell, for example, came by and planted flowers around her cabin for her to enjoy.

The person around her more than anyone else at the end was young Alicia Littletree, her anointed successor and amanuensis. Littletree, virtually straight out of high school, organized the stream of visitors who came to pay their respects. She also helped Bari with paperwork. Littletree (her Earth First nom de guerre) had grown up in a hippie enclave on the Northern California coast, and had done her first tree-sit while still in high school. After meeting the ailing Bari, she devoted herself to her care and presided over her days in String Creek as her life ebbed away.

Lisa Bari later claimed somewhat resentfully that the little cabin was so full of visitors she could not even get her own time with her mother; there were fights over access to her mother with all the participants fawning and sad.

Bari's main concern in her last days, other than the civil trial, was setting up her estate and securing her legacy. She named her old Sonoma County activist friend Darlene Comingore as her executor. Walt Penny, Bari's ex-fiancé from Baltimore, came out and helped with setting up a foundation for Bari's estate. Bari was also actively seeking someone to do an authorized biography of her life. She offered it to the writer of the *Bazaar* profile, but was turned down.

Her pal Mike Geniella of the *Santa Rosa Press Democrat* did a final, sympathetic big spread on the cancer-ridden Bari when she was still able to get around. He watched her perform the prosaic chore of baking a pie, and noted the pride she took in doing so. She struck Geniella as being at peace with her coming death.

Nine days before Bari died, KZYX held an hours-long tribute to her on her old *Punch and Judi* slot. She was at home listening as praise poured in from around the county. Green Party gubernatorial candidate Dan Hamburg called in along with a host of others, but not Bruce Anderson or any of the former friends or colleagues she'd driven away in the past years. She expressed gratification that she'd been able to hear such warmth and praise, likening herself to Huck Finn listening to his mock funeral. But the old angry self reared up again just a day or so before her death, when Mike Sweeney showed up at night at her cabin. Reportedly she roused herself from her sickbed and screamed at him to get off the property. He left, and complained about it over dinner with one of his few friends in the county.

Near death, Bari was still trying to control her image. She wanted obituaries to list her occupation as "revolutionary," bedside witnesses said, not "environmentalist." And, she repeated the words of the legendary IWW organizer, Joe Hill, just before he was executed in 1915: "Don't mourn. Organize!"

During the last week of her life, Judi's parents and her sister Martha flew out from Maryland to say goodbye, staying at a motel in Willits. Gina Kolata was not invited and she stayed away. In fact, Judi was adamant to her family and friends that she wanted Gina barred from attending her funeral. Judi died early in the morning on March 2, 1997.

Rather amusingly, she had told her people that she didn't want any "ohm-ing"—Buddhist chanting—over her dead body, or any other "spiritual bullshit." No one dared try it, not even the avowed Buddhists who had cared for her in shifts before she died.

She had her way in everything except regarding her older sister. In the end, Lisa disobeyed her mother and invited her aunt to come to the memorial on March 9. Gina attended, but didn't speak or mix much with Judi's friends, and she stayed in the background as youngest sister Martha put on a slide show of Judi's life. Bagpipers played and a potluck was held in Willits out in the park under some tall redwoods; then they all moved in a procession several blocks to a community hall to hear speakers. Mumia Abu Jamal, the Philadelphia Black Panther on death row for murdering a policeman, sent his condolences.

Bari's death received national coverage. Tributes poured in from environmentalists, and friends like Betty Ball were widely quoted: "Some holes can't be filled. Judi was the most brilliant strategist and the greatest imp I ever knew."

Steve Talbot, summing up Bari's legacy later on, expressed the ambivalence of many who had been close to her during the critical years of the timber wars on the North Coast. "That was Judi at her best," he said, "trying to form this alliance and being someone who really had the ability to mobilize people and get them moving together in the right direction. But then there was Judi at her worst—infighting—among this little incestuous world of people...."

It was true of Judi to the end.

EPILOGUE

IN JANUARY 2001, DARRYL CHERNEY PAID two bucks for a fork with Irv Sutley's DNA on it. He got it from a waiter at a Garberville eatery where Sutley had just downed his burrito before heading to a little public forum on the Bari case. Cherney and the Bari-ites were pinning their hopes on a match between the DNA recovered from Sutley's saliva and that on the envelopes or stamps of the Argus snitch letter, the so-called Second Warning threat letter, or the Lord's Avenger letter.

This was only one of the bizarre happenings in the scramble to assert rival interpretations of the car-bombing that resurfaced with renewed vigor after Bari died and long after law enforcement agencies from Oakland to Willits had given up on the case.

One of the more serious efforts to solve the mystery came from Ed Gehrman, a Piercy schoolteacher with a history of activism in leftist causes. Gehrman was an unlikely investigator. In the early 1980s he took a leave from his work as a small-town teacher and came to the Bay Area to work in the anti-nuke movement, joining up with the Livermore Action Group that opposed the University of California's Livermore nuclear research facility. Gehrman, in fact, first encountered Bari on demonstrations protesting U.S. weapons shipments to Central America in support of the Contras. He had been inspired by Bari's 1990 Redwood Summer campaign, as he put it, to "answer the call to action." And, like so many who had enlisted in the cause because of Bari, he was horrified by the car-bombing. He was swayed by reports and speculation that appeared the year after in both the AVA and Steve Talbot's documentary about Bari—

specifically, that Irv Sutley was a "provocateur," a snitch or, as Bari had asserted, an agent working for the FBI. And Gehrman bought her thesis that timber and the FBI were involved in the bombing.

One day Gehrman happened to run into a close friend and political colleague who counted himself in Sutley's corner. He asked his friend how he could continue to support Sutley.

His friend responded, "Eddie, you need to talk to him yourself. Listen to what he has to say. Sutley's not an agent."

So Gehrman's investigation began with his long interviews with a cooperative Sutley, followed by months of checking out his story. Gehrman looked into the get-together after the abortion rally and the photos taken of Bari as "Tanya"; into Bari's claims that Sutley had accompanied her to the post office when she was mailing pot; and into the alleged solicitation to kill Sweeney by Pam Davis on Bari's behalf. He also checked out Sutley's claim that he could not even type at the time the Lord's Avenger letter was written because of severe injuries to his shoulder dating back to his days as a warehouseman (injuries subsequently corrected by several surgeries).

Sutley was telling the truth, Gehrman at last concluded. (Steve Talbot ultimately agreed with Gehrman). His views were bolstered by the results of a voluntary 1994 polygraph test administered to Sutley in Los Angeles by former Secret Service agent Joseph Paolella, a licensed polygraph examiner. The polygraph test was arranged at the behest of private eye Jan Tucker, a longtime friend of Sutley's whom he knew when both were stalwarts of the Peace and Freedom Party. The examiner asked four questions:

- Did you receive any payment from law enforcement agencies to be an informant against Earth First or Judi Bari? (Sutley's response was "no.")
- Were you solicited by Pam Davis to kill Bari's estranged husband, Mike Sweeney? (Sutley's response was "yes.")
- Did you write the "Argus" letter to the Ukiah Police Department in 1989 or 1990? (Sutley's response was "no.")
- Were you involved in any way with the bombing of Bari's car on May 24, 1990? (Sutley's response was "no.")

Paolella signed off on Sutley's truthfulness on all the questions.

Gehrman also analyzed the Argus letter, as well as Bari's accusation that Sutley had snitched on the pot mailing. All in all, it was an impressive amassing of interviews, evidence and arguments.

Gehrman then went a step further, dangling the whole messy story and the conflicting charges before Vassar English professor Don Foster, who leads a double life as an "attributionist" scholar and a pro bono consultant for the FBI. Foster first came into public view when he confirmed the identity of the Unabomber (based upon the latter's manifesto). He also outed Joe Klein as the "anonymous" author of *Primary Colors*, and weighed in less conclusively on the Jon-Benet Ramsey case.

Foster agreed to take a look at the three letters in the Bari case—the Lord's Avenger, the Argus and the Second Warning—and apply his systematic analysis to those letters in comparison with known writings and/or interviews of many of the main characters in the Bari saga. These included: Bari herself, Cherney, Sutley, Sweeney, the FBI's Richard Held and Frank Doyle, Anna Marie Stenberg's ex-husband Mike Koepf, Steve Okerstrom (whose "fellerbunchers" were torched), the anti-abortionist Bill Staley, Sahara Club "Stompers," timber company spokespersons and "various" mill workers. He would also look at writing or interview transcripts by various journalists, police officers and local activists.

Foster concluded that of all these, Sweeney's writing examples had multiple similarities—far more than the other samples—to the three letters. There were so many points of likeness, in fact, that Foster asserted that Sweeney was the "plausible author of the Lord's Avenger letter." He went further: Foster identified Sweeney as the best candidate, among the group he looked into, for author of all three letters. (It must be noted, however, that he was working with writing samples, or copies of writings, by these various people that were hardly equal in volume or kind.)

There is no legal standing to any of Foster's findings, which were published in *Flatlands* magazine in February 1999. And attributionism is hardly an exact science. Foster himself helped define this discipline by employing his own computer program to count how many times, for example, a writer used certain word combinations or exhibited certain verbal tics and other idiosyncrasies. He believes that no two people display the same overall characteristics in their writing, and that such a process results in a unique portrait. He gives a work or works an exhaustive analysis, but this analysis is limited to whatever written material to which he happens to have access.

While attributionist analysis has been dismissed by some critics, Foster's findings in the Bari case are interesting nonetheless. He began his case by showing that all three anonymous letters he was studying—Lord's Avenger, Argus and Second Warning—shared a host of idiosyncratic stylistic and textual traits; nine points in common were named. His case for the likelihood of Sweeney authoring all three includes the following points:

- "The Avenger types and writes very much like Judi Bari's ex-husband," notes Foster. "The Avenger letter is single-spaced; his mailing envelope double-spaced (as is true also of the Argus letter). Sweeney in 1992 wrote to Jon Shepard. The letter is single-spaced; the mailing envelope is double-spaced."
- "Like Sweeney, both Argus and the Avenger avoid breaking and hyphenating words at the right-hand margin...."
- "Like Sweeney, the Avenger frequently omits the comma before the *and* or *but* in a compound sentence."
- "Sweeney's manner of capitalization is compatible with that of the anonymous documents. For example, both Argus and Sweeney unnecessarily capitalize "communist" as if it were a proper adjective like 'Marxist.'..."
- "Sweeney sometimes uses unnecessary initial caps to highlight sarcasm, just as all three of the anonymous letters do."
- Foster points out that Sweeney often capitalizes entire words, as for example in an article titled "Recycling Tips": "...can ALSO be dropped off...there ARE limits...but it's NOT necessary...WATER SOLUBLE adhesives...." Foster comments, "This stylistic feature is evident throughout the Sweeney documents, most frequently in unpublished writings where the capitalized words cannot be ascribed to editorial intervention. The same device is used by the 'Lord's Avenger' ('The VERY SAME man...PRAISE GOD!' etc.)."
- Sweeney often uses infinitives—for example, "to try to nego-

tiate"—where many Americans would say, "try and negoti-
ate" or "try negotiating"; the Avenger writes "try to abort"
instead of "try and abort" or "try aborting."

- Sweeney habitually writes "all the" instead of "all of the," as
in: "All the sinister implications" (12/1/90). The Avenger,
says Foster, "duplicates Sweeney's practice": "All the forests
that grow and all the wild creatures..."
- Foster points out that Sweeney, in his role as recycling czar,
issues bulletins repeatedly accusing opponents of "lies" and
"lying," which he links with "poison": "In the end these *lies*
will rebound in WMI's favor.... But like all the rest of these
lies it did succeed in *poisoning* rational discourse..." (2/2/91,
italics Foster's). Sweeney urges his readers not to "let anyone poison your mind" with the "*lies*," "slander" and
"falsehoods" that his critics are directing against him
(5/5/92). The Avenger, says Foster, employs a similar vocab-
ulary: "[He] describes Judi Bari as a 'Demon' and a 'Devil'
who 'spews Forth...*Lies,* Calumnies, and *Poisons*...to sew [*sic*]
Confusion'" (italics Foster's).

Foster acknowledged that his analysis was not conclusive
because he didn't have literary examples from other figures compa-
rable in length and complexity to those he had from Sweeney. Not
surprisingly, however, his published case provoked Sweeney to
protest that he was the victim of a McCarthyite "smear technique."
Writing on his own website, Sweeney accused Foster of being "an
old-fashioned charlatan who could have walked right out of the
pages of a Mark Twain novel. He was able to pass himself off as an
expert literary detective for several years (to the indignation of legitimate scholars) until he exposed himself as a fraud." What Sweeney
had in mind was the JonBenet Ramsey case, where he said that Foster "got caught offering himself to both sides...first telling the
mother that he knew "absolutely and unequivocally" that she was
innocent, and then turning around and telling the police that he
could identify her as the perpetrator...."

Yet Foster was not alone on the matter of the Bari bombing.
Making the case against Sweeney had become something of an
obsession in some quarters of the Mendocino community, particu-

larly among the *Anderson Valley Advertiser* readership and the paper's publisher, Bruce Anderson. Over many decades, Sweeney had managed to alienate many people in the community, both by his personal abrasiveness and by his political decision to trade in his former radical credentials for a job as a recycling bureaucrat.

But in fact, despite the prosecutorial attitudes toward him, there was never any evidence against Sweeney that would pass muster in any court of law, nor, say his defenders, in the court of public opinion either. Anderson and others have repeatedly called for law enforcement to act against him, but no one in the police departments of Oakland or Mendocino or in the FBI has ever believed there was sufficient cause to do so. Those looking for signs of Sweeney's guilt are reduced to looking at what he hasn't done rather than what he has.

ON JUNE 11, 2002—TWELVE YEARS after the pipe bomb exploded in Judi Bari's Subaru and five years after her death from cancer—the jury in her and Darryl Cherney's civil suit found that Oakland police officers and FBI agents had wrongly arrested and blamed the pair for the car bombing in order to silence their environmental and political speech.

The case, which had been filed a year after the bombing, had dragged on interminably with pretrial motions and maneuvers before finally being scheduled for the fall of 2001. There were eight amended versions of the lawsuit filed by the plaintiffs and two pretrial motions that landed in appeals court. The final suit named the FBI and the OPD, individually suing three Oakland officers and six FBI agents. By the time it was heard, several defendants in both organizations had already retired.

The last postponement of the trial after eleven years came when plaintiffs argued that the terrorist attacks on the World Trade Center and the Pentagon might prejudice the jury against Bari and Cherney because Earth First's history of ecotage would evoke the still vivid memories of the 9/11 terrorism. Judge Claudia Wilken agreed and moved the trial to the spring of 2002. Wilken came under scrutiny by both camps for the long delays and pretrial motions, as well as for her rulings in court. Which side was she on? The question was bandied about by observers involved in the case. She was rumored to be a former leftist, and many believed that the delays she allowed favored the plaintiffs; but she stood firm in her decision to rein in the breadth of inquiry of the plaintiffs, ruling out any discussion of COINTELPRO or past FBI overreach.

At the time, this was a big blow to the Bari team. Bari and her lawyers had counted on showing that the local FBI, then headed by Richard W. Held, had been secretly investigating Earth First *before* the car-bombing, with the intention of disrupting and destroying domestic radical activism. But Held himself was granted immunity by a higher court and removed as a defendant in 1997. This decision was appealed and upheld. Bari's supporters had to settle for parading a fifteen-foot puppet depicting Held in black-and-white prison stripes around the Federal Building plaza outside the courtroom, where Earth First held its rallies for the Cherney and Bari case.

Such rallies became an issue inside the courtroom because some of them took place during the deliberations, and jurors had to pass through the soapbox theatrics of the partisan crowd. Jurors also had to listen to Tony Serra and other members of the legal team address the crowd as they passed into the Federal Building through the plaza. When the defendants' attorneys complained about the circuslike atmosphere outside the court and how it might influence the jurors, Wilken ruled against them—an indication to some of her critics that she might be favoring the plaintiffs after all.

On the other hand, her ire was aroused when attorney Bob Bloom still seemed to be arguing COINTELPRO, despite her ruling. But then she turned around and actually permitted Cherney to drag out his guitar and serenade the jury with his ditty, "Spike a Tree for Jesus," supposedly to make attorney Dennis Cunningham's point that the song was innocuous rather than an incitement to violence. The judge and members of the jury wore tiny smiles during the wacky performance.

Then, after twelve years of delay and six weeks of the trial itself, the jury took seventeen days to deliberate before returning with a resounding verdict in favor of the Earth First plaintiffs. The jury awarded the two environmentalists $4.4 million (Bari's portion going to her estate), contending that the plaintiffs' rights had been violated by six of the seven defendants (three FBI agents and three Oakland police officers).[*]

Even Bari-ites were surprised. Darlene Comingore, the executor of Bari's estate, told the *Oakland Tribune*, "It's really beyond our wildest dreams—the jury got it." And while Cherney told reporters that he, for one, wasn't surprised at the outcome, one journalist who had faithfully covered the trial almost daily countered, "If you were looking in his face that day, it told a different story."

Martha Bari put out an exultant statement which she claimed spoke for her family, but again, Gina Kolata was mum. (Bari's mother, Ruth, suffers from Alzheimer's disease and is cared for in a nursing facility.)

Both sides appealed—the defendants for obvious reasons, and Cherney to protest the pretrial dismissals, not just of Richard Held but also of the Willits police and Ukiah sheriffs. And in what seemed like an empty gesture at the time, Cherney announced a $50,000 award for the arrest of Pacific Lumber/Maxxam's Charles Hurwitz, but nothing for information leading to the arrest of the car-bomber.

Cherney may now have the chance to put his money where his mouth is—both by paying a reward for the arrest of Hurwitz and by putting up a reward to nab the bomber.

On April 21, 2004, negotiators for the U.S. Department of Justice finally agreed to a settlement in the long-running civil suit carried on by Bari's estate and Cherney. The agreement stipulated a cash reward of $2 million to the plaintiffs paid out by the FBI, and a dispersal of the $2 million won from the City of Oakland (which had not made any moves to appeal the civil trial jury's awards, but neither had the city paid any monies, waiting for a resolution from their codefendants, the FBI). In return for the FBI agreeing to forgo any appeals, the attorney negotiating for the plaintiffs, Jim Wheaton, agreed to drop any further claims either for attorney's fees or for further damages.

These fees for the legal team headed by Dennis Cunningham are substantial, covering more than a decade of legal work. Oakland

---

[*]Shortly after the verdict, an East Bay criminal attorney reported that Judge Wilken had admitted to a group of women that she was shocked at the plaintiffs' wholesale victory and at the high monetary awards set by the jury.

city attorney Maria Bee, representing the police, said of the deal, "It's a good resolution in that it saved the city several million dollars of exposure for attorney's fees and appellate costs.... [T]he legal fees were as large as the judgment" The FBI tab before the settlement would have matched that. Oakland will pay out its share of the judgment in four annual installments of $500,000.

Attorney Wheaton, who had been hired by Cunningham to handle the out-of-court negotiations with the FBI, gloated to reporters, "This is a huge victory for the environmental movement and the First Amendment. I think this is the largest verdict ever against the FBI. I don't think there has ever been a settlement this large for someone who wasn't shot or killed."

Court documents reveal that Bari's attorneys will get nearly 40 percent of the $4 million settlement, or roughly $1.4 million. The $1.7 million going to Bari's estate, after taxes and the Redwood Summer Justice Project take their share, will leave her daughters with between $350,00 and $400,000 each. The Redwood Summer Justice Project, which pressed the Bari case both before and after she died, now maintains the Judi Bari website (as well as providing something of a sinecure for her old pal, Purple Beret leader Tanya Brannan).

In the public eye, the case has always been perceived through the distorted lens first crafted by Bari herself in her scattershot accusations. She never minded embellishing her list of possible perps to include the FBI as part of the car-bombing conspiracy, even though at other times (speaking to Beth Bosk, for example) she dismissed the notion. But after she had raised the specter of an FBI plot to get her, even her own denials weren't enough to stem that particular rumor.

The very weekend after the settlement was announced in April 2004, when this writer toured the Point Reyes Bird Observatory in Bolinas on a hot Sunday morning, several fellow birders on the tour, upon learning of this book, expressed the view that the successful outcome of the civil trial for Judi Bari and Darryl Cherney that week must have been proof that the FBI was somehow involved in the attempted assassination. They didn't seem to glean from news reports that the civil case ruled only on false arrest and denial of First Amendment rights by law enforcement agents as a result of their post-bombing action of characterizing the pair as terrorists, a smear that had a chilling effect upon their rights of speech. It was a view I've heard many times over the course of researching the book.

BEFORE THE FINAL SETTLEMENT this year, however, nothing had been done to solve the crime of the car-bombing. Even after winning the civil case in 2002, Cherney made a feeble effort to get his prime suspect, Irv Sutley. Cherney delivered the fork he'd bought from the restaurant worker with Sutley's DNA on it—the one Sutley had used to eat a burrito—and delivered it to an unnamed lab that compared it with the envelopes and contents of the Lords' Avenger, Second Warning and Argus letters.

The results of a previous DNA test on the Lord's Avenger letter revealed that there was a woman's saliva on the envelope and a very small recoverable sample of a man's DNA on the letter itself—prompting Bruce Anderson and others to say that any DNA testing of Mike Sweeney should also include testing of Sweeney's girlfriend at the time of the car-bombing.

All the lab results, including Sutley's, were then "interpreted" for the Bari-ites and Cherney by a Bay Area DNA specialist, Ed Blake. In a rather cryptic analysis, Blake reportedly said that there was a 300-to-1 chance that the Argus letter had been penned by a male relative of Sutley's, but only by someone "up or down" from him—that is, a father or a son, but *not* Sutley himself. Upon hearing these results, Sutley quipped, "I have no children, unless I fathered Sweeney and didn't know about it—*because I would have been only three years old!*" At the time of the letter, Sutley's father was disabled and homebound, and had suffered several heart attacks. (He died in 1998.) And while frustrated observers of the case, like Bruce Anderson, publicly call for the subpoenaing of all suspects' DNA to compare with the Lord's Avenger envelope, a senior law enforcement official noted that such subpoenas can be issued only with "probable cause," a standard that, so far, has not been met.

There seems little chance of any reopening of the case—the FBI's jurisdiction ended after the City of Oakland declined to press charges against Bari and Cherney. Where jurisdiction for a crime is divided—did this one belong to Willits, Redwood Valley or Oakland?—cases often languish. Willits police claim they don't have a big city's resources to do an investigation. Oakland was besieged with a triple-digit homicide rate and had to concentrate on murders and drug wars, which meant that cases like the car-bombing had to be shelved, especially when the victims and their closest supporters refused to cooperate. Bari's family—her parents and sisters—did not seem to be pressing the case, either. And even if the author of the various letters could be determined absolutely, this would not necessarily prove who set the bomb.

THERE WAS A POLITICAL VACUUM on the North Coast after Judi Bari died. It had begun to develop with the end of Redwood Summer, seven years earlier. It was as if the bombing and the removal of the leading activist had let all the air out of the balloon of energy and high expectations, which are the mainstay of any political movement.

And then along came Julia "Butterfly" Hill. She had hit the North Coast in 1997, the very year that Bari died. She'd had a little college and some retail experience, and she crafted jewelry. She had one of those quick conversions to Earth First typical of North Coast hippies, and was fired up to do a tree-sit.

Butterfly had never been political before. Her father was an itinerant preacher who sermonized under tents, roaming for years with his family in a trailer before finally settling in Arkansas. Julia was raised a fundamentalist, whereas Judi Bari was raised in a secular Marxist household. The contrast could not have been greater. Yet it was Butterfly who filled the void that Bari left, and became more famous.

At twenty-three years old, she was a tree-sitter with a face and figure ready for the big screen (for a while there was talk of Winona Ryder playing her in the movie certain to follow). Butterfly acquired her fame by sitting in the crown of a 200-foot-high redwood for two long years—the record for tree-sits. Early on, Darryl Cherney was her media rep, hectoring newsies to take note that even at sixty days she'd set the record for living under the forest canopy.

She was the most ardent preacher of anthropomorphism in a territory full of New Agers. She named her tree "Luna" and imbued it/her with a kind of tragic, mothering personality. "My spirit led me here and I meant to stay with it," she said two months into her sit. And later, "I could see all her [Luna's] scars and wounds from fires and lightning strikes. I was making a spiritual connection...." When Pacific Lumber started logging a nearby ridge and hauling the logs out by choppers, she told *San Francisco Examiner* reporter Eric Brazil, "I found myself crying a lot and hugging Luna and telling her I was sorry. Then I...was being covered by sap pouring out of her body from everywhere, and I realized, 'Oh, my God, you're crying too.'"

Butterfly came down from her tree finally at the end of 1999 when an agreement was struck with Pacific Lumber establishing a small no-cut zone with Luna at the center. The company also donated $50,000 to ecological research.

A bit of lunacy indeed, cried Earth Firsters including the by-now soured Cherney and redwoods veterans like Pam Davis, who belittled Butterfly for not crediting all the tireless Earth First support crews who schlepped away her excrement and brought her food and everything else she required. Old-time EFers and others called her a "corporate sellout" and a "self-promoter." Still others were critical that she'd sold out for fifty grand and only saved one tree and a few "pecker poles," as Judi used to call the smaller redwoods. In the view of longtime environmental activists, she should have fought instead to secure a whole ecosystem.

And because of Butterfly's focus on Luna, it was inevitable that this tree would become a target for the enemies of the no-cut crowd. In November 2000, while Butterfly was visiting relatives out of state for Thanksgiving, Luna was attacked with a chainsaw, sustaining a deep, life-threatening gash.

"I feel this vicious attack on Luna as surely as if the chainsaw was going through me," Butterfly said, overcome with tears. It was feared that the tree would topple over with the first high wind, but Luna was fitted with a steel collar and seems to be holding its/her own. Meanwhile, Butterfly's foundation got another hefty infusion of cash in the wake of the murderous assault.

Butterfly now drives a Lexus SUV (according to the Earth First grapevine) and lives in the pricey East Bay hills, maintaining an office in Oakland to house her own Circle of Life Foundation. She is a money magnet. ("If Judi Bari had looked like Julia Butterfly she would have been unstoppable," Bruce Anderson observes.) These days she outdraws Ralph Nader. And, in reaction to criticism from environmentalists who say she siphoned money from competing organizations, she now divides the gate with other local good-cause groups.

AT&T sought to cash in on the comely tree-sitter with a TV ad depicting a willowy young thing who, indeed, looked a bit like Butterfly, perched up in the treetops on a canvas platform using her wireless AT&T to stay connected. Butterfly sued in 2000, charging that her image had been misappropriated for commercial interests, and she won.

Cherney and Earth First turned on Butterfly when she became a superstar. But whom did Cherney represent next (aside from himself)? Behold La Tigresa, the forty-something "performance artist" who, wearing a faux tiger-striped sarong, bares her breasts at logging sites in hopes of disrupting the cutting. La Tigresa, a.k.a. Dona Nieto, began her career by standing alone and bare-breasted on a roadside, reciting poetry to any of the loggers who would listen, occasionally screaming "rape!"—instead of the traditional "timberrrrr"—when she heard the sound of falling trees. Stunned loggers summoned the sheriff's office, complaining that, among other things, they had to listen to her poetry. ("I am the goddess, I speak now from the mouth of all women...in the creases of my inner thighs lies your salvation, get down on your knees and worship me.")

Cherney has recently announced a leave of absence from his activism. He has said he wants to write the screenplay for his own biopic, as well as travel—take a rest—to recharge whatever batteries are left. He has taken off in the winter season before, to India or other exotic destinations. But he has yet to collect any of the money award for the deal he negotiated with OPD that both sides drop their mutual appeal (OPD because they had lost the suit; Cherney because he wanted to include more defendants). As of this writing, the FBI has not precluded its own, separate appeal to the civil trial.

IN THE WAKE OF BARI'S DEATH, Earth First all but disappeared, save the *Earth First! Journal* and an ongoing Redwood Summer camp staged in Humboldt, a pale reflection of the original that mounts a few tree-sits. (But Roanne Withers says there is now a fresh crop of youngsters who have recently joined the movement, who seem inspired to do some good legwork on timber harvest plans.) Even the ecotage has changed from Dave Foreman's days, when wit often informed the group's actions. A new offshoot of the radical environmental movement has turned away from Bari's public confrontational demonstrations and toward the secret cabal of Earth Liberation Front's (ELF) explosive violence against everything from SUVs and housing developments to genetically altered crops. Now ELF has been joined in vandalism, sabotage and just plain violence by the Animal Liberation Front, targeting people, restaurants and corporations that do animal research or simply raise, sell or serve foie gras. Many authorities believe the two groups overlap.

While this cannot all be directly attributed to Judi Bari's legacy, there are those in the movement who believe that Bari blew an opportunity to further the environmentalist cause when she diverted attention and money to her fight with the FBI and police agencies, who, after all, had never gone forward with the charges against her. Still, she remains enough of an eco-icon for the town councils of Oakland and Arcata recently to proclaim a "Judi Bari Day"—Arcata on her birthday; Oakland on the anniversary of the car-bombing.

Many people still hold the mistaken belief that the Bari-ites won in court by showing that the FBI was complicit in the bombing, rather than—along with the Oakland police—merely guilty of false arrest and slander. Bari would have liked the mix-up just fine.

NOTES

Chapter 1

1 *Walking Rainbow:* Interviews of Patricia Kovner and Pam Davis.

2 *Finnish Communists and co-op movement:* Interview of Margaret
Lima Wilkinson, daughter of IWW and Communist Party boss
of Northern California, Mickey Lima; also information from a
1978 stay at the Lima summer retreat in Mendocino County,
where I first learned of the Finnish Communist and co-op connection and other local lore from the Limas' next-door neighbors
Oscar and Bea Ericson—he was Finnish, she a Russian-born Jew,
and both had been in the Communist Party.

3 *Pace of logging in the Northwest and Canada:* I am indebted to
David Harris's *The Last Stand* (Times Books, 1995) and William
Dietrich's *The Final Forest* (Simon & Schuster, 1992) for background on the threatened regional forests and general history of
logging in the huge Northwest bioregion.

3–4 *Disciplined paralegals:* Interviews of David and Ellen Drell, and
Roanne Withers; telephone interview of Betty Ball.

3–4 *Michael Huddleston and Stephen Day:* Interview of Patricia
Kovner; interviews of Huddleston and Day in *New Settler,*
December 1989.

4 *Profitability of virgin redwoods:* Dietrich, *The Final Forest;* Judi
Bari's writings; interview of Tim Hermack of the Native Forest
Council.

4–5 *Greg King and Darryl Cherney:* The story of their early fight
against Maxxam is from Harris, *The Last Stand;* Jonathan
Littman's profile of Cherney in *California* magazine, June 1990;
interviews of Andy Caffrey in 2000 and 2001.

6 *Ecotopia description:* Ernest Callenbach, *Ecotopia* (Banyan Tree
Books, 1975).

6–8 *Walking Rainbow and the idea for Redwood Summer:* Interviews of Pam Davis and Patricia Kovner.

8–11 *Seeds of Peace House and Bari's sleepover:* Interview of David Kemnitzer, 2000.

9 *David Brower, "Archdruid":* Interviews and briefing with journalist Mark Dowie, who has profiled Brower.

11–13 *Descriptions of bomb and witnesses:* Oakland Police reports; also from Beth Bosk's interview of Bari in *New Settler,* 1995; post-bombing interviews of Bari in the *Anderson Valley Advertiser;* and interview of David Kemnitzer, among other sources.

Chapter 2

15–17 *Bari family background:* Many of the details of Bari's childhood and family came from an interview of Judi's older daughter, Lisa, in the spring of 2000; also from Beth Bosk's interview of Bari in *New Settler,* May 1990, prior to the bombing; from Bari's former friends Bruce Anderson and Anna Marie Stenberg; and from many newspaper and magazine interviews and stories. The details on Ruth Bari's mathematics career came in part from a short biography of Ruth Bari written by her daughter Gina Kolata and posted on a website devoted to women in mathematics, and from official university websites.

17–19 *Sibling rivalry between Judi Bari and Gina Kolata:* Interviews of Lisa Bari and Mark Dowie. Dowie also wrote an article on Gina Kolata for the *Nation,* July 6, 1998.

18 *Gina Kolata's Catholicism:* Interview of Mark Dowie.

19 *Bari's resentment of Kolata for never acknowledging her:* Interviews of Bruce Anderson, Anna Marie Stenberg, and a confidential source.

20 *Bari's drug use:* Bari in *New Settler,* May 1990; Jonathan Littman in *California,* June 1990; interview of Bruce Anderson.

20–22 *Bari's student days: New Settler,* May 1990; interview of David Katz.

23–24 *Bari's move to Buffalo House, joining union:* Interviews of David Katz and Mark Dowie; Russell and Sylvia Bartley's interviews of Judi Bari in 1990.

24–25 *More union activities:* Interview of David Katz; Jonathan Littman in *California,* June 1990; *New Settler,* May 1990.

26 *Bari meets Sweeney through union:* Bartleys' interviews of Bari, 1990; *New Settler,* May 1990.

NOTES

Chapter 3

27   *Mike Sweeney as "political heavy":* Interviews of Mary Moore and Bruce Anderson. Sweeney "was good in those days": Russell and Sylvia Bartley's interviews of Bari, 1990.

27–28   *Mike Sweeney's background:* Interviews of Lisa Bari, Steve Talbot and David Helvarg. (Talbot also gave me access to his interviews of confidential sources who were at Stanford with Sweeney.) Also, Bartleys' interviews of Bari, 1990.

28–29   *Bruce Franklin, "Every day, Joseph Stalin...":* Recalled by David Reid.

29–30   *Venceremos, Bruce Franklin, ambush of prison convoy and the SLA:* Vin McLellan and Paul Avery, *The Voices of Guns* (G. P. Putnam's Sons, 1977); and the House Committee on Internal Security publication, "Political Kidnappings," August 1973, from the so-called Ichord hearings (named after the committee chairman, Sen. Richard Ichord). On the evolution of Bruce Franklin from Revolutionary Union through Venceremos: Interview of Steve Hamilton.

Chapter 4

33   *Mike Sweeney as potential father:* Interview of Mary Moore; Russell and Sylvia Bartley's interviews of Judi Bari, 1990.

33   *"She fell in love with him...":* Interview of David Katz.

34   *Bari's domestic life, garden:* Interviews of Mary Moore and Pam Davis; and Bari in *New Settler*, May 1990.

35   *Bari's antipathy toward Cynthia Denenholz:* Interview of Steve Talbot.

35   *Denenholz complaints about Sweeney:* Post-divorce court filings.

36   *Sabotage of Denenholz's water system:* Interview of Steve Talbot; trial brief from Bari and Cherney's civil suit against the FBI and Oakland Police Department, noting investigation of Sweeney for pump sabotage with reproduced FBI memorandum dated 7/31/90.

36–38   *Mary Moore, SONOMore Atomics, Whisper, and Bari introduction to the Atomics as Sweeney's new girlfriend:* Interview of Mary Moore.

39   *Pam Davis's background and her friendship with Bari:* Interview of Pam Davis.

39–41   *Santa Rosa airfield and arson "bomb":* Interview of Steve Talbot; also transcripts from his PBS documentary, *Who Bombed Judi Bari?* On the political organizing that Bari and Mike Sweeney did to fight the proposed expansion of the airfield: Bartleys' interviews of Bari, 1990. Suspicions about Sweeney: from letters written to Steve Talbot by Bob Williams, who had a business at the airfield. According to my interviews, Bari told Talbot and Anna Marie Stenberg that Sweeney committed the Santa Rosa airfield arson bombing.

42–43   *Domestic abuse in the Sweeney/Bari marriage:* Interviews of Mary Moore, Toni Novak, Anna Marie Stenberg and David Helvarg, along with a confidential source, a female friend of Bari's who asked for anonymity.

44   *Bari and Sweeney's 1982 organizing and suit against Hewlett-Packard project:* Interview of attorney Susan Brandt; Bartleys' interviews of Bari; interview of Adrienne Swenson (participant in organizing); local newspaper accounts; later, Susan Swartz, *Santa Rosa Press Democrat,* May 25, 1990.

44–45   *Bari and Sweeney's suit against Caltrans:* Interviews of Peter Fisk and Irv Sutley.

45   *Sweeney's withdrawal from radical politics*: Bartleys' interviews of Bari.

45   *Goodbye party for Bari:* Interview of Mary Moore.

Chapter 5

49–50   *Feminists of Albion Ridge:* See Kate Coleman, "Country Women," *Mother Jones,* April 1978.

50   *Mills in Branscomb:* Interview of Art Harwood, president of Harwood Lumber.

51   *Hog Farm:* I visited the Hog Farm with Patricia Kovner during their rock-and-roll weekend at the end of summer.

52   *Heroin cult in Mendocino:* Interview of Roanne Withers.

52   *Garberville after harvest time:* David Harris, *The Last Stand* (Times Books, 1995).

52   *Pot grown on public lands:* Steve Chapple, *Outlaws in Babylon* (Longshadow Books, 1984); also for estimates of annual marijuana crop in the Reagan era.

54   *Bari flashing a carpenter's union card:* Interview of David Raitt.

54–55   *On yurts:* Interviews of David Raitt and Will McAfee.

55   *Bari being made a foreman:* Interviews of David Raitt and Will McAfee.

55–57   *Bari's story of her epiphany about the redwoods:* There are many sources for this, beginning with the interview of Bari in *New Set-*

tler, May 1990; the story was repeated by such Bari fans as David Drell.

57–58   *Larry Chaulk's version of the virgin redwood slab story:* Interview of Larry Chaulk.

Chapter 6

59–61   *Bari involved in Pledge of Resistance:* Susan Swartz, *Santa Rosa Press Democrat,* May 25, 1990; interview of Bari in *New Settler,* May 1990; interview of Will McAfee; Russell and Sylvia Bartley's interviews of Bari, 1990, which also relate Bari's pushing for more militant activism.

61   *Demonstration at the El Rancho Tropicana:* Interview of Will McAfee.

61–62   *Sweeney's emotional abuse of Bari and the spec house as a reflection of their crumbling marriage:* Interview of a confidential source who visited the household and was a close confidant of Bari's at the time.

63   *MEC building, owned by John McCowen:* Interview of Bruce Anderson.

63–68   *Earth First! beginnings:* Primarily Susan Zakin, *Coyotes and Town Dogs* (Penguin, 1993); Mark Dowie, *Losing Ground* (MIT Press, 1995); Dave Foreman, *Confessions of an Eco-Warrior* (Harmony Press, 1991); and various EF histories in magazines and newspapers from the period, including the *Earth First! Journal.*

68–70   *Darryl Cherney's past and his arrival in Humboldt:* David Harris, *The Last Stand* (Times Books, 1995); profile of Cherney in *People,* November 11, 1996; and interviews of Julie Verran and Andy Caffrey.

70–71   *Meeting of Greg King and Cherney, and the demonstration at the Sally Bell:* Harris, *The Last Stand.*

71–72   *Pacific Lumber:* Harris, *The Last Stand.*

71–72   *Sustainability of the forests:* The Wilderness Society, *Defining Sustainable Forestry,* ed. Aplet, Johnson, Olson and Sample (Island Press, 1993).

72–73   *Chipko "tree-huggers":* Thomas Weber, *Hugging the Trees: The Story of the Chipko Movement* (Viking, 1988).

73–74   *Tree-sit lore:* Interview of Andy Caffrey.

74–75   *Cherney's headway in Earth First:* Interview of David Harris; and Harris, *The Last Stand.*

75   *Bridgewood Motel and Cherney:* Interview of Julie Verran.

Chapter 7

77–78   *Cherney meets Bari: New Settler* has the account in two versions: one in the May 1990 interview of Bari, the second in an interview of Cherney in March/April 1997; there are accounts in many interviews that Cherney gave to newspapers, magazines and electronic media; also, interview of Pam Davis.

78   *Cherney's role model, Abbie Hoffman:* Cherney's website had long encomiums to the late Yippie leader, but this former Yippie who ran in the streets in antiwar demonstrations in New York with Hoffman during the late 1960s thinks Cherney had a way to go before he could match the master of the Yippie gesture. Both Hoffman and Yippie cofounder Jerry Rubin didn't have to hector the media for attention: the media couldn't resist.

78   *Dynamic duo:* Interview of Patricia Kovner; Susan Swartz, *Santa Rosa Press Democrat*, May 25, 1990.

79   *Proximity of Sweeney's trailer to Bari's converted garage:* Interviews of Steve Talbot and Irv Sutley.

79   *Congressional campaigns of Eric Fried and Cherney:* Interview of Irv Sutley.

80   *United Farm Workers boycott:* Interview of Irv Sutley; interview of Cherney in *New Settler*, 1997.

80   *Demonstration against James Watt:* Interview of Cherney in *New Settler*, 1997.

81–82   *Cahto fight history:* Primarily from interview of Patricia Kovner, but also references in both the Bari and the Cherney interview in *New Settler*, as well as interview of Michael Huddleston and Steven Day in *New Settler*, 1989; and interview of Art Harwood.

82   *Sequoia and Bari relationship:* Interview of Patricia Kovner. Bari's comments on Sequoia: interview in *New Settler*, May 1990.

83–86   *Cahto and forestry board demonstrations:* Interview of Patricia Kovner; interview of Bari in *New Settler*, May 1990; Russell and Sylvia Bartley's interviews of Bari, 1990.

86   *Keeping of phone lists:* Interviews of Patricia Kovner and Mark Scarmella.

86   *IWW and Mickey Lima:* Interview of Margaret Lima Wilkinson; author's 1978 visit to the Lima family's Fort Bragg property.

86–87   *IWW seminar at EF rendezvous and the "mudhead Kochina":* Bari in *New Settler*, May 1990.

88–90   *Survey of logging companies, GP, the unions and the fall of wages:* Interview of Roanne Withers; Judi Bari, *Timber Wars* (Common Courage Press, 1994), a collection of Bari's writings for the

Anderson Valley Advertiser, in which the title article, "Timber Wars," traces the recent history of logging on the North Coast.

90–94 *Meeting Anna Marie Stenberg, the PCB spill at Georgia-Pacific and forming Local 1 of the IWW:* Interview of Anna Marie Stenberg.

Chapter 8

95–96 *Bruce Anderson teaming up with Bari:* Interview of Bruce Anderson.

96–97 *Humboldt County supervisors' meeting, Greg King and Darryl Cherney:* David Harris, *The Last Stand* (Times Books, 1995).

97–98 *Bari's organizing in the bars of Mendocino:* Interviews of Bruce Anderson and Anna Marie Stenberg. On Bari's relationship with the Pardini brothers: from her own comments in *New Settler,* May 1990.

98 *Organizing loggers "bogus":* Interviews of Bruce Anderson and Andy Caffrey.

99 *Babysitting Lisa and Jessica:* Interviews of Anna Marie Stenberg and Pam Davis. (Sweeney often took care of his daughters, but a neighbor in Redwood Valley also frequently babysat for Bari.)

99 *On Jessica being closer to Mike Sweeney:* In the Bartleys' 1990 interviews, Bari complained that Sweeney "stole custody" of Jessica.

99–100 *Bari as multipurpose organizer:* Bari in *New Settler,* May 1990; Bari, *Timber Wars;* interviews of Patricia Kovner and Lanny Colter.

101 *Abuse in marriage:* Interviews of Anna Marie Stenberg, confidential Mendocino County source, Bruce Anderson, Mary Moore and Toni Novak; also, a confidential source around Bari's later civil suit repeated Bari's expressed fear of Mike Sweeney to David Helvarg.

101 *More accusations of rape by Bari after divorce:* Interviews of Bruce Anderson, Anna Marie Stenberg and Steve Talbot.

Chapter 9

113–14 *At the chip mill:* David Harris, *The Last Stand* (Times Books, 1995).

114 *Bari and musicians at EF rendezvous:* Interview of Kelpie Wilson.

114–16 *The "Whitehorn riot":* Harris, *The Last Stand;* interview of Patricia Kovner; Bari interview in *New Settler,* May 1990; Bari, *Timber Wars* (Common Courage Press, 1994).

116–17 *Navarro tree-sit and truck-ramming of Bari's car: New Settler,* May 1990, for Bari's description of accident; interview of Pam Davis, on seating in the car and skepticism about Bari's view that it was deliberate.

117–19 *Classroom culture wars in Laytonville and Branscomb:* Interview of Art Harwood, who also provided news clips on *The Lorax* book fight from national press, including *People,* and letters of complaint from employees of Harwood Lumber.

119 *Kids' demonstration at Olivet Elementary School:* Susan Swartz, *Santa Rosa Press Democrat,* May 25, 1990.

121–22 *Candy Boak and the skunk oil:* Harris, *The Last Stand.*

122 *"Every place we went, they went…":* Bari on *New Settler,* May 1990.

122–24 *Anti-abortion demonstration at Planned Parenthood Clinic in Ukiah:* Quotations of Bari's description are from *New Settler,* May 1990; also, interviews of Irv Sutley, Bruce Anderson, Anna Marie Stenberg and Zack Stentz; and Jonathan Littman's piece on Cherney and Bari in *California,* June 1990.

124–25 *Sutley's guns and the Bridgewood Motel sleepover:* Interviews of Irv Sutley and Julie Verran.

Chapter 10

127–29 *Irv Sutley, Pam Davis and Bari:* Interview of Irv Sutley.

129–30 *Sutley told his ex-wife about the murder solicitation:* Interview of Toni Novak.

130 *Confirmation that Bari told Stenberg about seeking help for her "Sweeney problem" and mentioning Pam Davis's problems being solved:* Interview of Anna Marie Stenberg.

130 *Bari dismisses murder solicitation charges as "a joke":* Audiotape of KZYX radio show.

130–31 *On Bari and Cherney's crumbling relationship:* Jonathan Littman in *California,* June 1990; interview of David Harris; interview of Anna Marie Stenberg.

131 *Bari on breakup with Cherney, "There is a barrier to how close…":* Interview in *New Settler,* 1990; interview of Bruce Anderson; Russell and Sylvia Bartley's interviews of Bari, 1990.

Chapter 11

133–34 *Arrest of Dave Foreman on conspiracy charge:* Susan Zakin, *Coyotes and Town Dogs* (Penguin, 1993); and newspaper accounts.

134–35 *Suspicions of Bari and Cherney in the wake of the Unabomber:* Interview of Julie Verran.

135–36 *Bari's paranoia:* Interviews of Julie Verran and Bruce Anderson.

136–37 *Bari trip to Highlander Center:* Interview of Anna Marie Stenberg; Zakin, *Coyotes and Town Dogs.*

137 *Bari on revolutionary violence:* In *New Settler,* May 1990.

NOTES

138   *$5,000 reward posters by Cherney:* Harris, *The Last Stand.*

138–39   *Threatening letters to Bari and to Betty Ball:* Trial brief for Bari and Cherney's civil suit against FBI and OPD.

139–40   *Bari's response to Oregon Environmental Law Conference and letter urging her to renounce tree-spiking:* Interview of Anna Marie Stenberg; Russel and Sylvia Bartley's interviews of Bari, 1990.

141   *Fellerbuncher "sabotage":* Steve Talbot's PBS documentary, *Who Bombed Judi Bari?;* Bari, *Timber Wars;* interviews of Steve Talbot, Bruce Anderson and Mike Koepf.

141   *Lieutenant Satterwhite and Supervisor Marilyn Butcher's rebuff of Bari's appeals regarding death threats:* Bari, *Timber Wars;* and her depositions in the Bari/Cherney civil trial brief.

Chapter 12

143   *Bari's growing irritation with Cherney:* Interviews of David Harris and Steve Talbot; Bari interview in *New Settler,* May 1990; Russell and Sylvia Bartley's interviews of Bari.

144–47   *Earth Day 1990:* Roundup of events from newspaper accounts; most of the descriptions of the sabotage in Santa Cruz are from the *Santa Cruz Sentinel;* Golden Gate Bridge action, arrests, terrorist "scenario" from the *San Francisco Examiner;* also depositions and exhibits in the Bari/Cherney civil trial brief.

146   *"Desperate times ..." quotation:* Interview of Bruce Anderson.

148   *Witnessed argument between Bari and Cherney:* Interview of David Harris; also Bari's own complaints to Russell and Sylvia Bartley, to various friends including Steve Talbot, Bruce Anderson and Anna Marie Stenberg, and later to Lisa Bari.

148   *Changing the name Mississippi Summer in the Redwoods to Redwood Summer:* Cherney, in *New Settler* interview with Beth Bosk, said the original name was chosen to cash in on the newly released movie *Mississippi Burning.*

148   *Critics of Bari's planning:* Interviews of Andy Caffrey and Roanne Withers.

149   *Secret meeting with loggers and gyppos:* Interview of Art Harwood; David Helvarg and Steve Talbot's accounts, as told to them by Bari.

149   *Bari locking car at the meeting with loggers:* Bartleys' interview of Bari; interview of Anna Marie Stenberg.

Chapter 13

151–53   *Accounts of the bombing, the evidence, the bail:* Newspaper accounts; Oakland Police reports (part of the Bari/Cherney civil trial brief); the *Anderson Valley Advertiser;* and Bari's later recollections in *Timber Wars* (Common Courage Press, 1994), and in interviews by Russell and Sylvia Bartley, 1990.

153–54 *Cherney in Oakland jail:* Oakland Police reports.

155–56 *Bombing investigation, the nails, Sergeant Satterwhite, etc.:* Police reports; Bari/Cherney civil trial brief; and newspaper accounts.

155 *Bari having removed her papers to String Creek:* Interview of Anna Marie Stenberg; Bartleys' interview of Bari.

156 *Pacific Lumber Cloverdale mill bomb:* Interview of Frank Wigginton; and police reports. "LP Screws Workers" sign: Interview of Bruce Anderson, who said the MEC always kept a stockpile of such signs on hand for Earth First actions.

156–57 *Tree-spiking of mill worker George Alexander:* Bari, *Timber Wars.*

157 *Bari's injuries:* Copies of Bari's medical records, courtesy Steve Talbot; Bruce Anderson's interview of Bari from her hospital bed, in *Anderson Valley Advertiser.*

157 *"Sister Morphine":* Bruce Anderson's interview, *Anderson Valley Advertiser.*

157 *Utah Phillips et al. leaving town:* Interview of Cherney in *New Settler,* 1997; and investigations by Steve Talbot and David Helvarg.

157–58 *Greg King paranoia:* David Harris, *The Last Stand* (Times Books, 1995).

158 *Anna Marie Stenberg driving to Bay Area:* Interview of Anna Marie Stenberg.

158 *Karen Pickett, Roselle and Earth First vigil for Bari and Cherney:* Newspaper accounts; and interview of Anna Marie Stenberg.

159–60 *Fred Gardner and Bari's parents, and Susan Jordan:* Interview of Fred Gardner.

Chapter 14

161–63 *Catherine Bishop visit to Bari and stories she wrote:* Interview of Catherine Bishop.

163 *Katy Raddatz and Bari posing:* Interview of Katy Raddatz.

163–64 *Mary Moore and Bari's fears about child custody:* Interview of Mary Moore.

164–66 *Rosie Radiator and Bari's naming Sweeney as bomber:* Interview of Rosie Radiator, a.k.a. Bess Bair.

166 *Naming of David Kemnitzer as possible suspect:* Interview of David Kemnitzer, who himself first told me of Bari's accusation; also Russell and Sylvia Bartley's interviews of Bari, 1990.

166   *Alameda County district attorney's quiet criticism:* Interview of Tom Orloff, Alameda County district attorney.

166–67 *Special Agent Timothy McKinley's account:* Copies of police and FBI reports as part of the official Bari/Cherney civil trial briefs.

167   *Background on Special Agent Frank Doyle and jurisdiction:* Interview of Andrew Black, FBI press liaison.

167–69 *Investigation of the bombing:* Pieced together from depositions by Oakland Police, FBI agents and police notes that are part of the record for the Bari/Cherney civil case.

169   *Law enforcement "theories" of the case told to* Oakland Tribune *et al.:* Oakland Tribune, San Francisco Examiner, San Francisco Chronicle, San Jose Mercury News; and interview of confidential journalist source who spoke on FBI and Oakland Police off-the-record briefings.

170   *"Reasonable cause" for arrest and search warrants:* Interview of Tom Orloff, Alameda County district attorney.

170   *Bureau agent Phil Sena on "secret" tipster:* Court papers for the Bari/Cherney civil trial.

170–71 *Dennis Cunningham's comments on the secret source:* Interview of Dennis Cunningham.

171   *Mike Geniella as "go to" journalist for timber issues and as conduit for Bari:* Interview of Mike Geniella.

171–74 *"Lord's Avenger letter":* Reproductions in *Flatlands,* February 1999; and in Bari/Cherney civil trial briefs.

174   *"Argus letter":* Ibid.

174   *Bari's accusations against Irv Sutley as author of Argus letter:* Bartleys' interviews of Bari; interview of Steve Talbot; and Ed Gehrman in *Flatlands,* February 1999.

174–75 *Sutley's denials:* Interview of Irv Sutley; and Ed Gehrman in *Flatlands.*

Chapter 15

177   *Bari's surgeon at Highland on her injuries:* Steve Talbot's documentary, *Who Bombed Judi Bari?*

177   *Evidence from nails:* Newspaper accounts; Bari/Cherney civil trial briefs; Talbot, *Who Bombed Judi Bari?*

178   *Limited immunity request; Bruce Anderson's reaction:* Interview of Bruce Anderson.

178–79 *"The Lord's Avenger very skillfully used...":* Bari interview in *New Settler,* 1995.

179 *Mike Koepf's charge that Bruce Anderson had written Argus letter:* Interview of Mike Koepf.

179 *Stenberg's charges against Mike Koepf:* Interview of Anna Marie Stenberg.

179 *Anderson on Koepf..."Where's his motive?":* Interview of Bruce Anderson.

179 *Bari never considered Staley the bomber:* Bari interview in *New Settler,* 1995.

180 *Sweeney "novel" fragments to Carol O'Neal:* Interviews of Anna Marie Stenberg and Don Foster. (Stenberg turned the Sweeney novel fragments over to the archivists Russell and Sylvia Bartley for safekeeping; she also had copies of the memos, which she forwarded to Don Foster for textual analysis.)

181 *Sweeney's three alibis:* Alexander Cockburn in *North Coast Journal,* May 2000.

181–82 *Discussion of the bomb:* FBI and police reports as reproduced in the Bari/Cherney civil trial brief; and interviews of Josiah Thompson and Mark Shattuck.

182–84 *FBI "bomb school" and Frank Wigginton:* Interview of Frank Wigginton.

183 *Under the auspices of the College of the Redwoods:* Interview of Andrew Black.

183–84 *Bari on the bomb school and Frank Doyle:* Bari interview in *New Settler,* 1995.

184 *Sergeant Myron Hansen...said that he "wasn't about to tell him...":* Deposition in the Bari/Cherney civil trial brief.

184–85 *Memo from the U.S. Justice Department:* Copy of the letter in the Bari/Cherney civil trial brief.

185 *Oakland triple-digit homicide caseload:* Ibid.; also interview of former *Oakland Tribune* reporter Lance Williams.

Chapter 16

187 *Gina Kolata taking Bari's daughters into her home:* Interview of Catherine Bishop.

187 *Rehabilitation hospital and Robin Latham's anxieties about Bari:* Interview of Anna Marie Stenberg.

188 *Bari's complaints about Sweeney demanding that the Redwood Valley property be settled:* Interview of Steve Talbot.

188 *Cherney's accounts of Bari's nighttime pain:* Interview of Steve Talbot.

188–89 *Cazadero safe house, and San Francisco rally before the Federal Build-*

ing: Interviews of Anna Marie Stenberg and Mary Moore. (According to Stenberg, Bari said Stenberg was the only one she trusted to deliver her to and from the rally, a sentiment she repeated verbatim later to Bruce Anderson regarding the trip to the String Creek picnic.)

189 *The mock bomb at Susan Crane's home: Santa Rosa Press Democrat,* July 24, 1990.

189 *Bari's comments on the "camos" et al.:* Interview in *New Settler,* May 1990; and Bari, *Timber Wars* (Common Courage Press, 1994).

189 *Bari's visit to String Creek:* Interview of Bruce Anderson.

190 *Landlord John Phillips working on the cabin:* Interview of John Phillips.

191 *Lisa Bari's tale to her parents about Aunt Gina's personal shopper:* Interview of Mark Dowie, who heard it directly from Mike Sweeney.

191 *Bari's lobbying the county for a double-wide trailer classroom on String Creek:* Interview of Bruce Anderson.

191 *Caretakers and visitors to help the injured Bari:* Interviews of Zack Stentz and Bruce Anderson.

191–95 *Redwood Summer activities:* Interviews of Pam Davis, Kelpie Wilson, Steve Talbot and Catherine Bishop; various newspaper accounts, and Bari's own accounts in *Timber Wars.* Also various Earth First publications from summer 1990.

196 *Donation of $5,000 for Bari:* Interview of Bruce Anderson.

196 *Bari and Lisa Henry:* Interviews of Bruce Anderson, Steve Talbot and Zack Stentz.

197 *Breakup of friendship between Bari and Stenberg:* Interview of Zack Stentz.

197 *Return to Highlander Center:* Interview of Anna Marie Stenberg.

197–98 *Carl Hammarskjold on Bari and IWW chapter:* Interview of Carl Hammarskjold.

199 *Bari, Mary Moore and Kwazi Nkrumeh:* Interview of Mary Moore.

199 *Bari and Steve Talbot rift:* Interview of Steve Talbot; and Bari, *Timber Wars.*

199–201 *Bari and Dave Foreman:* Bari, *Timber Wars.*

201 *Bari attends Dave Foreman reading:* Interview of Bruce Anderson.

201–3 *Bari's "Showdown at the Earth First! Corral":* Bari, *Timber Wars.*

Chapter 17

205 *Investigators for Bari:* Interview of Josiah Thompson.

205 *Susan Jordan visit to Ukiah Police to discuss Bari case:* Interview of

confidential source close to Bari investigation; and phone interview of Susan Jordan, who did believe that police agencies were
no longer interested in the Bari car-bombing case once Bari was
eliminated as a suspect, but who could recall virtually nothing
about a visit to the Ukiah Police or about telling the Bari crowd
after her bombing and arrest to refuse to answer questions by
the Oakland Police or the FBI.

207 *Bari as paralegal:* Interview of Dennis Cunningham. Bari "not a
big reader of literature…": Interview of Bruce Anderson.

207 *Dialogue with Bari, Joseph Sher and the FBI's Phil Sena:* Transcript of
deposition, Bari/Cherney civil trial brief.

208 *Enchanted Meadows demonstration:* Interviews of Bruce Anderson,
Frank Wigginton and Roanne Withers; Bari, *Timber Wars.*

208 *"They were killing us…I didn't want her to get hurt":* Interview of
Frank Wigginton.

209 *"She walked purposely…":* Interview of Bruce Anderson.

209–10 *SLAPP suit, Bari and Enchanted Meadows:* Interview of Roanne
Withers.

209 *Bari's $5,000 victory against Mendocino County:* Interview of Bruce
Anderson.

210 *Bari on KZYX and her home:* Maryanne Vollers in *Bazaar,* August
1990.

210–11 *Bari's visits around the county:* Interviews of Kathleen Stewart of
Downtown Bakery and Lanny Colter.

211–13 *Bari describing after-effects of bombing:* Bari interview in *New Settler,* 1995.

213 *Bari's nonviolence appealing to county feminists:* Interview of Bruce
Anderson.

214 *Bari's breast cancer discovery and treatment:* Interview of a confidential source familiar with her medical treatment and history;
and interview of Lisa Bari.

214 *Bari's admission to trying alternative treatments:* Mike Geniella
writing in the *Santa Rosa Press Democrat;* and Geniella in an interview.

215 *Bari's fundraising and charts in cabin:* Interviews of Mark
Scarmella and Bruce Anderson.

215–16 *Description of Alicia Littletree during Bari's last days:* Interviews of
Lisa Bari and Bruce Anderson.

216 *Walt Penny helping set up Bari's estate:* Interview of David Katz.

216 *Reported deathbed visit by Mike Sweeney and Bari's ousting him:*

Bruce Anderson reported this after a discussion with the wife of one of Sweeney's closest associates in Mendocino County.

217 *Bari's parents and sister Martha arriving to say goodbye:* Interview of Lisa Bari.

217 *Banning her sister Gina Kolata, and Lisa Bari's refusal to comply:* Interview of Lisa Bari.

217 *Bari's deathbed instructions forbidding "ohm-ing":* Confidential source.

217 *Gina Kolata at Bari's memorial and description of the event:* Interview of Lanny Colter.

217 *"That was Judi at her best...":* Interview of Steve Talbot.

Epilogue

219 *Cherney buying fork with Sutley's DNA:* Interview of Irv Sutley.

219–23 *Ed Gehrman's investigation into Irv Sutley as possible snitch or FBI agent, and analysis of letters:* For the most part recounted in *Flatlands*, February 1999; but also part of my discussions with Irv Sutley, Ed Gehrman, Jim Martin (publisher of *Flatlands*) and Don Foster, as well as unpublished writings that Foster shared with me.

224–27 *The civil suit trial:* Reported almost daily by the *Oakland Tribune*. The other local papers—the *San Jose Mercury News*, the *San Francisco Examiner* and the *San Francisco Chronicle*—had more intermittent coverage. The *Anderson Valley Advertiser* offered weekly roundups. I attended several sessions, including when Earth First rallied in the Federal Building plaza outside and held aloft giant puppets of Bari and ex-FBI local chief, Richard Held.

229–30 *Julia "Butterfly" Hill:* From Internet articles and citations, and from newspaper accounts when Luna was attacked. Criticisms of Butterfly: from interviews of Pam Davis and Lisa Bari; and *Earth First! Journal*.

231 *"If Judi Bari had looked like...":* Interview of Bruce Anderson.

231 *Siphoning money from competing organizations:* Interview of Roanne Withers.

231 *La Tigresa:* Associated Press, "My Forest, My Breasts," November 13, 2000.

232 *Roanne Withers' reassessment as of spring 2004:* Phone interview of Roanne Withers.

INDEX

INDEX